# DOING IT ALL

# DOING IT ALL

## THE SOCIAL POWER OF SINGLE MOTHERHOOD

## RUBY RUSSELL

SEAL PRESS

New York

Seal Press
Hachette Book Group
1290 Avenue of the Americas, New York, NY 10104
www.sealpress.com
@sealpress

Printed in the United States of America

Originally published in 2024 by Dialogue Books in Great Britain
First US Edition: May 2024

Published by Seal Press, an imprint of Hachette Book Group, Inc. The Seal
Press name and logo is a registered trademark of the Hachette Book Group.

The Hachette Speakers Bureau provides a wide range of authors for speaking
events. To find out more, go to hachettespeakersbureau.com or email
HachetteSpeakers@hbgusa.com

Seal books may be purchased in bulk for business, educational, or promotional
use. For more information, please contact your local bookseller or the Hachette
Book Group Special Markets Department at special.markets@hbgusa.com.

The publisher is not responsible for websites (or their content) that are not
owned by the publisher.

Typeset in Berling by M Rules

Library of Congress Control Number: 2023949162

ISBNs: 9781541602199 (hardcover), 9781541602205 (ebook)

LSC-C

Printing 1, 2024

Dedicated to all the vagabond mamas in my life.

This book is full of anecdotes about things that happened to me or to women I know. I've changed names, and some biographical details of women who were generous enough to share their stories but do not want to be identified. Some events (and some men) have been simplified or amalgamated for narrative ease. I have endeavoured to remain true to the essence of these experiences – as I remember them or as they were recounted to me – and to faithfully represent the power dynamics they illustrate.

# Contents

# Chapter 1

# Conception

When I was younger, I used to feel a sudden, sharp grief after sex. A sadness in the wake of orgasm that was accompanied by an equally abrupt thirst. Or rather, they didn't just coincide, they were the same distinct feeling: a melancholy so deep it wants flooding, a pang of pathos to be quenched.

Private, entirely unconnected from whoever I happened to be with, it passed as quickly as it came on. And I felt it less as I got older. Until one day it hit me again – inverted somehow, profoundly amplified, yet distinctly familiar – when my baby latched onto my breast for the first time.

Oxytocin.

All those times I'd heaved my head from some sweaty chest to reach for the glass of water by the bed: a chemical rush carrying a scrambled message about bonding and hydration.

Motherhood was something I wanted very much. But it's hard to say why exactly. It can be impossible to know how desires central to who we are have taken root. How can we know if our hormones are driving us to do what's expected of women – or if what we've been led to expect of ourselves defines how we understand our bodily drives?

And how might we interpret them differently, if we had different ideas about what it means to be a woman? Or a mother?

I remember thinking, from not long after puberty, how extraordinary it was to have a body that could grow a whole new person inside it. It seemed so unlikely, so extreme, I should really try it.

One day.

When that day came, I hadn't made a conscious decision to conceive – not then, there, with that particular man. And yet, it happened right on time. I was thirty-two, the perfect age for a middle-class, northern European woman to make the transition from person to mother.

In just about every other sense, the circumstances of my motherhood weren't what society, or I myself, might have demanded. There was certainly no white wedding. But tracing back how I came to be where I am now, I have my own conception fairytale.

When I was in my mid-twenties, a doctor put me on the Pill to suppress my body's androgens and enforce the monthly cycle it had given up on. On a sonogram, my ovaries appeared as clusters of black grapes and she told me I was unlikely ever to become pregnant without medical help.

I recoiled at the thought of fertility treatment. Making the huge decision to have a child – to open up so much space in my life, to commit to motherhood and to go through such interventions with no guarantee of success – wasn't something

I could imagine ever being ready for. So I worked on being happy not to have children. I took the daily Pills, observed the monthly break to bleed. I used contraception.

But not diligently.

A few years later, I logged onto the Aeroflot website, not thinking about family but work. And, at the same time, arguing with my boyfriend. 'It's a *work* trip,' I said again. But he won. I booked two tickets to Bishkek. And, as expected, we kept arguing when we got there. The work was stressful and consuming, and he had nothing to do but sample the local vodka and simmer at me being too busy to join him.

And then I had a few days' break.

We hitched a dramatic twelve-hour ride from Kyrgyzstan's capital in the north to Arslanbob, a Garden of Eden near the Uzbek border. It was well after dark when we tumbled out into the cold mountain air. But the guy in charge of the community-based tourism scheme had waited up for us, all welcoming smiles as he led us up stony tracks, past low wooden cottages and plots of pasture picked out in sharp monochrome by a full moon.

We reached a family compound with a shuttered shop at the front and entered through a courtyard where animals skittered in the darkness. Behind the shop was a storeroom crammed with plastic-packed clothes imported from China, blankets and household goods. Along one wall, four narrow wooden beds stood end-to-end.

A woman bundled in woollens and a bright headscarf showed us through to a parlour with steaming bowls of manti and soup. But before I could eat, she took me aside. I don't remember how she posed her woman-to-woman question.

We had no language in common, but perhaps she did know the English word *husband* or perhaps she didn't need it. I answered that he was, because, in the context, this seemed more true than not.

After our meal, our host summoned us back into the storeroom and beamed. She'd cleared a space in the middle of the floor big enough to lay all four mattresses side-by-side and arranged a deep nest of blankets on top. Left alone, we burrowed into our marital bed and opened layers of clothing to share each other's warmth.

In the morning, the courtyard was brilliantly alive. Snot-smeared children ran with goats and chickens, women who might be mothers or sisters or aunties busily attending to their needs. Above us, the green-gold slopes of the Tian Shan mountains rose to snow-capped peaks that were too bright to look at against a violently blue October sky. We were in the midst of hundreds of square miles of walnut forest interspersed with pistachios, plums and ancient varieties of wild apple.

Blinking it all in, I felt a warm trickle in my crotch and cursed my period – absent since I'd run out of the Pill months earlier – choosing this moment to return. Closing myself into the wooden latrine clutching a wad of tissues, my immediate concern was the availability of tampons. So it was with relief that I found not blood in my knickers but a milky trail of semen.

The following days were among the best the boyfriend and I ever spent together. We hiked to waterfalls, snacking from the trees. We spent afternoons on the wooden veranda of a teahouse over a rushing mountain stream, playing chess and making plans for the future. Not domestic plans, but shared adventures and creative projects.

I never saw another woman in that teahouse, but the men nodded at us in what seemed friendly approval.

Two months later, Arslanbob was a faintly luminous memory. The boyfriend and I were fighting again and no amount of sleep banished my exhaustion. I installed carbon monoxide sensors in the office where I worked. I suspected clinical depression.

But I had reasons to be down.

An old friend was in cancer's final chokehold. So I dragged myself to London to sit by his bed. And while I was there, stalking hospital corridors and streets mysteriously untouched by my friend's horrific, impending absence, I took the chance to pick up free contraceptives on the NHS.

Waiting at the pharmacist's counter, idly scanning racks of condoms and supplements for expectant mothers and thinking about death, it occurred to me: I'd better check there wasn't anything *already in there* first. I picked up a pregnancy test, slid its smooth box into my bag alongside those containing the Pill, and then quickly forgot it as I hurried to meet my friend Emily at a gastropub in King's Cross.

Emily was immersed in the final months of her PhD. I was busy with a labyrinth of distracting little story arcs centred around my unstable career and this latest of my unsuitable relationships. But as we picked at our over-order of patatas bravas and crispy squid, conversation honed in on a topic that had begun to displace all others.

Not the magazine the two of us had started, or Berlin,

where we'd moved together but which she'd left by then. Because these things, being the kind of people who moved to Berlin at the close of our twenties and started dubious creative projects, were not, precisely, the cause of the predicament we both found ourselves in. Of a group of women who'd been friends since school, only Emily and I were yet to achieve, if not actual children, then at least the relationships that should bear them.

The others were starting to imply Emily only had herself to blame. I felt defensive of my brilliant, steady, focused friend. Of her high standards in work and men. But also, perhaps, guiltily, that maybe they were right. And sad too, that maybe Emily might feel the same. That at our age even the most brilliant of us – especially the most brilliant of us – had to compromise.

We'd hit our thirties doing what liberal society loudly demanded of us – making work, exploring our sexualities, forging individual identities – only to find we'd neglected the whispered imperative that we *complete* these projects in our twenties, and at the same time line up suitable fathers for our children.

It's almost unseemly to talk about settling and starting a family before you're thirty, and close to failure if you're not cradling an infant by the time you're thirty-five.

In a few months, Emily's PhD would be done and she would join the legions of women of similar age and ambition attempting to seduce men into cooperating with our reproductive schedules.

Men we had once walked with side-by-side.

Our generation, on the cusp between X and millennials,

didn't notice ourselves at much disadvantage in our youth. In student bars, a girl who chose a different guy to go home with each night had better do it with style, but she could drink hard with the boys, she could get better grades than them and imagine her future to look much like theirs.

But by thirty-two, a fissure that had been quietly running between us and them was beginning to yawn open. The question of children had become unavoidable, and if we did want them we needed men. We needed to build partnerships across the divide between an identity central to notions of what it means to be woman, and the logistics of careers designed for men. To ask them to fall into step with the rhythms of our wombs.

Quietly though. Because modern love isn't supposed to be a pragmatic contract for raising children.

We were into our second bottle of red when Emily suggested another way. Maybe we didn't need men to become mothers. Or just one between us, and only briefly. From there, we could manage things together, the two of us. I suggested Luis, a geneticist I'd been seeing briefly when Emily was still in Berlin, but who'd always seemed more interested in her than me.

Returning thoughtfully from a cigarette – Emily noted approvingly that I was managing on far fewer than usual – I questioned whether actually, Luis, pretty as he was, was really good-looking enough to father Emily's baby? But she liked Luis, she liked the Luis idea, and I felt pleased as a congratulated child.

Last to leave the pub, we hugged tight and went our ways, leaving big questions unbroached. What would raising a child with another woman be like? How might platonic co-parenting work? And who could possibly have made a better partner in something so important, than this brilliant, sane, kind woman I'd loved for two decades?

There was a forerunner to the pregnancies I conjured with Emily that night. When I was nineteen, before my ovaries went polycystic, I had an abortion. I knew I didn't want a baby then so it didn't feel like a much of decision. But afterwards, hormones, or perhaps the ghostly idea of a child, left me feeling vaguely bereft.

And it was then that I consciously decided to have children. One day. But that day was innumerable years, experiences and life-changes away.

Now, I'm not so sure this biological switch was as decisive as it felt. My own mother took to the role with some reluctance, under pressure from my father who's ten years older than her. She was just beginning to be rewarded for doing creative work she loved and aborted her first planned pregnancy. But she got pregnant again quickly, carried me into the world and conceived my sister as soon as I was weaned.

In her telling, motherhood was such a joy she'd have happily stayed home expanding the family indefinitely if my father hadn't insisted two was plenty. Instead, guiltily, she went back to work when my sister was six months old. Freelancing at Soho animation studios, she rarely let slip to colleagues that she had two young children at home, and garnered a reputation as aloof and asocial because she sped home every evening instead of heading to the pub with the boys.

Dinner was on the table when she got back. My dad cooked

and did the school runs, packed lunch boxes and was up first to bring my mum coffee in bed before he walked the dog. Coffee cups were chipped and the milk sometimes curdled. The house was never very clean. But she earned the bread and he stepped up to the other side of the bargain. My mother couldn't have told you when bills were due, how her taxes were calculated or when parents' evening was coming up.

Balanced (if not perfectly), loving (if not always harmonious) and self-sufficient (at least from my childhood perspective), the family model to which I was raised didn't nurture a strong desire for me to become a *wife*, exactly. But finding my partner in life seemed, if not inevitable, then perhaps the greatest imperative.

Motherhood wasn't just contingent on the right man; I imagined it only as a development, or expression, of this core relationship.

There was a soulmate, Jack, who fathered the pregnancy I aborted.

Moving out of home at eighteen, I discovered I didn't have to be the shy little person I'd been at school anymore. Nor was I one of the girls who could hold her own at the bar and take a succession of lovers. But to my surprise, I paired up with the tall, funny guy at the centre of my exciting new group of friends.

We were inseparable for nearly five years, discovering the world together, our expanding perspectives focusing into shared visions. He was gregarious and charming, compensating for my social awkwardness. But we kept such good company together we hardly needed anyone else.

Later, I sometimes wondered if I was too young and stupid to realise how lucky I was with Jack. But our relationship was never very sexual. We broke up as firm friends, and I needed what came next.

With Lyam it was heat and scents and the delicious tackiness of skin on skin. We were both busy. He was making art and I was trying to manage the chaotic office of a tiny independent publisher. But when we weren't doing these things, we were usually in bed. And then we took a few weeks off to drive around the French countryside. If I was quiet – sleepy or pensive – he got irritated at doing all the driving alone. I dozed off and woke with his hand between my thighs on the hot car seat. He made me come as we sped along the motorway. When we pitched out tent in the evening, silence swelled: an emptiness between us that we could only fill with sex.

When we got back to London, I broke up with him.

So it went on. I loved men, whatever that meant, but none offered the perfect combination of lust and companionship, intellectual and erotic connection. And always, guiltily, I moved on.

On some level, I think I believed the perfect union would magically overcome my infertility. In hindsight, this might explain the chaos of rage and despair I remember as the only time I had my heart broken – by a consultant obstetrician who dumped me after we'd been together a few months. Later, Emily said she'd never seen me like that, losing my mind over a man who was unlike any of my other boyfriends, who'd all been so nice. This one, it's true, wasn't kind like Jack or Lyam. But he did know a lot about bringing babies into the world.

Looking back, what stands out about that brief relationship

are the things I wasn't part of and the friends I let down while holed up, claustrophobic and insecure, in the doctor's expensive little Shoreditch flat.

But I didn't need true love, or a man with a dozen years' medical training, to make a baby. With a sore head from the red wine (we should at least have finished the tapas) I found the pregnancy test in my bag. Over the following days, I stared incredulously at two more before binning them.

Eventually, a GP told me that the only explanation for three tests indicating I was pregnant, was that I was pregnant. But I'd need a scan to tell me how far along I was. And on the NHS, that meant a few weeks' wait. Unless, he suggested, there was a problem – bleeding, for example – and I went to A & E.

So my sister drove me to the Whittington Hospital where I sobbed real tears for a pretend miscarriage, when a ten-week foetus, a little white bean with shoots for limbs, appeared on the screen.

There is an old idea that female orgasm is essential to conception.

In the thirteenth century, this constituted a legal defence against accusations of rape. If the law conceded that a woman wasn't necessarily to blame for being violated, pregnancy was always her own fault. Her body wanted it.

Apart from a few extreme pro-lifers who still cling to archaic notions of 'legitimate rape', we know better now. Science confirms that it is quite possible for human life to begin in violent violation of the woman's will. And yet science doesn't seem entirely comfortable with this fact – given its odd obsession with pinning down an evolutionary explanation for female orgasm.

Male orgasm, they imagine, is a perfectly uncomplicated example of anatomy driving behaviour that follows evolutionary function – compelling men to procreate regardless of whether they have any conscious desire to be fathers.

You could argue female orgasm and reproduction are just more complexly linked. More social, contextual – more intellectual, even. But biologists prefer neatly physical explanations. Some imagine the clitoris as an evolutionary remnant like male nipples: an aborted attempt at a penis, diminished and half-formed. Others describe the vagina actively imbibing semen, pumping it up towards the uterus – a fairly dubious theory, but one that at least resonates with how orgasm feels: a vigorous, muscular action that becomes more complex and more powerful with practice and maturity.

And this image has merit in itself. Because mostly, male-dominated culture – from religious iconography to romantic fiction to porn – pictures both female ecstatic climax and conception as moments of swooning, disintegrating surrender.

It may be a woman's ruin or it may be divine, but it is always a moment of vanquish.

It is also, ostensibly, a private moment.

For a long time, when a woman married – the first step to becoming a mother, if she did things right – she didn't just surrender physically, she also surrendered her legal personhood. The man who took her as his wife, took her as his property and took her property as his: in the eyes of the law, she was no longer an individual in her own right.

But the union was only consummated later, when her husband took her beneath the sheets. Her public surrender sanctified her private surrender, and her private surrender confirmed what had already played out publicly, before the congregation or the law. And if her conquest happened within this stronghold, the moment when a woman was shattered and remade a mother was secluded, her modesty preserved.

These days, society doesn't demand we get married before we become mothers. But there are other standards the relationships that bear children must meet. A good eighteen months, say, of monogamy, love, companionship and intellectual connection. Sex that is consistent and exciting. Consistently exciting, in fact. Someone who you can have wild fun with – and depend on as a sturdy partner through the drudgery and joys of work that carries round the clock, week after week, year after year.

And whatever the prevailing convention, when women become mothers outside its stronghold, conception ceases to be a private matter. The mothers of children without fathers, with the wrong fathers, have always had questions to answer. Moral and legal questions and, still, questions to satisfy society's demand we be made an example of.

Did she surrender willingly, or was she taken by force? Was it an act of wile on her part? Of slovenly irresponsibility? What right has she to bring a child into the world all by herself?

To whom does her child belong?

And to whom does she herself belong?

\*

These were not, exactly, the questions going through my mind as I left the Whittington, my life at a crossroads. Mainly, I was turning over signs of a transformation that I had ignored or misinterpreted. But already what it meant to call my body my own was getting complicated.

One Saturday a few weeks earlier, I'd arranged to meet a friend at a gallery at three in the afternoon. At one, I was still in bed, utterly, wretchedly mortified at the prospect of getting up. If I'd known I was pregnant, I might have understood my despair as a consequence of physical exhaustion: my body prioritising the new person it was growing over *me*. Instead, I'd assumed the exhaustion was a symptom of depression.

Until pregnancy, my body had a self-perpetuating integrity. I've been lucky with my physical health, and so the biggest threats to my body had come from *me*. My mind – anxiety, depression – or my *self*: overwork, unprotected sex, smoking, cycling home drunk.

But this dragging misery wasn't just *me*. *I* wasn't just me. And once I realised this, my body was both more alien and mechanical – following a bizarre programme beyond my control – and a more powerful aspect of my *self* than I'd known. Physical processes were changing my mind, reshaping my thoughts and identity more profoundly than my conscious will could ever remake my body.

And yet, the one autonomous, thinking person in this conjoined metabolic system still had the final say. My metabolism was committed to keeping this foetus alive – even fighting its own addiction to nicotine with feelings of disgust – but was I?

I was pregnant in a society that recognises a woman's reproductive rights. I just had to decide whether to exercise them. And maybe this is another reason I drifted through the first weeks of pregnancy so out of touch with what was happening inside me. Maybe I didn't want to confront this choice.

Legally, I still had time. But knowing it had quietly hung on in there through most of the precarious first trimester made me feel we were, this would-be person and I, already in some way committed to one another. And if I was going to veto its becoming, I didn't want us getting any more attached.

So I booked in for an abortion, which in the UK means counselling first.

When I terminated my first pregnancy, counselling was a brisk, friendly formality in an office next door to the room where I would undergo the suction aspiration procedure immediately afterwards. Not a moment for soul-searching, but professional reassurance that I was absolutely doing the right thing.

This time though, I actually wanted to talk through my dilemma with someone who didn't have skin in the game.

In the back room of a women's centre, a kindly woman in her fifties swivelled an office chair around for me to face her and pushed a stack of paperwork aside to place a box of tissues within my reach. Blades of fluorescent lighting reflected in the winter-black windows. Her colleagues had all left for the evening. But she listened as if she had all the time in world, while I weighed the sensible path of abortion against my aching desire for motherhood.

When I stopped talking, she asked me a question I hadn't been ready for: 'It sounds like you want this baby, but you don't want to be with the father. Do you think you could manage alone?'

Her question made no sense to me.

Had anyone asked before I conceived, the responsibility of raising a whole human alone would have been too daunting to contemplate. But now, it wasn't fear of loneliness, inadequacy or unmanageable logistics that made single motherhood impossible, so much as the unavoidable fact of the father's existence.

The boyfriend wasn't the first person I told I was pregnant, but once I'd managed to get him on the phone he had rushed to London – to support me in whatever decision I made, but also to make it clear he wanted me to have this child.

His child.

He saw it as his child, and so, equally, did I. As much his as mine. As long as it was only a *potential* child, whom only my body could realise, the choice was clearly mine and mine alone. But I saw it as a choice between abortion and the whole package, father included. Motherhood meant the boyfriend. For life. Or the next eighteen years.

The question was not *do I want this baby?* (I did), or *could I raise it alone?* (unthinkable) so much as *can this man be an adequate partner and a good father?*

Faced with perhaps the biggest decision of my life, I made the decisive factor something beyond my control: the potential of fatherhood to change a man. Any man. Even this one.

Now, I imagine the counsellor thinking, *this child will change you, in ways you can't yet imagine. But him? Don't count on it . . .*

I wonder, if it hadn't been so late in the day, if I wasn't as obstinate as I am, might she have tried to explain – a bit of realism now might save a lot of future hassle and heartbreak. But she probably knew: some people have some notions ingrained so deep they won't see the obvious until they're living it.

I brought my indecision all the way to the abortion clinic and away with me again when I left, still pregnant. If a woman's transition to motherhood is supposed to be passive, I was making it as passive as possible.

Told I was functionally infertile, I didn't have the nerve for assisted reproduction's deliberate, overwrought steps to motherhood. But now, I think it wasn't just disappointment I feared. I think *unplanned* was the only kind of pregnancy I could imagine. Even just saying, *yes*, consciously seizing the power to bring a whole human life into being, seemed outrageous.

Who was I to do something so bold and reckless?

How could anyone carry a responsibility so big?

And I'd seen the narrative played out so often in fiction. The faint blue line, shock, tears and the irrational decision met with joy and approval.

Conception had to be something I surrendered to. And so, happily, I surrendered to my failure to go through with termination. My failure to *not* be a mother. I let my body keep doing what I was compelled to.

Week after week, I googled unexpected symptoms – Braxton Hicks contractions, jumpy legs that kept me up at night, bright yellow colostrum that stained the sheets in the morning – and was assured that everything was progressing as it should. But these were all just quirky side-effects to the main event: the growth of a creature that was no longer quiet but pushing for space, treading on my bladder, tossing and turning at night.

In the final weeks, I lolled on the sofa, huge and hot and immobile, watching Cronenberg movies. The boyfriend had always been a fan, but the body horror never did much for me until now: I enjoyed a kind of superiority over men who fantasise the gruesome contortions and inversions we mothers take in our stride.

But while my child's becoming was viscerally real, intellectually, I couldn't fathom the idea of an actual, distinct person nestled within me. In fact, as my due date loomed, the reality of my baby – of my motherhood – didn't feel more definite but ever-more elusive.

It took three pregnancy tests and a sonogram before I could say, *I'm pregnant*. And then, after all that agonising, it felt strange and exciting to say, *I'm going to be a mum*.

But, *in six weeks I will be holding my baby in my arms?*

This was impossible to picture.

The closer the miracle of birth came – the more it had anything to do with me, the me I was now, not some future self, transformed into an actual *mother* – the further it retreated into realms of the miraculous.

And the foetus didn't seem any more convinced by the big day marked in my antenatal notes than I did. With a few weeks to go, it should have turned, its head pointed at my cervix like bullet. Instead, I winced at the terrible grating of a human skull against my ribs.

In a softly lit birthing centre, a wispy midwife who insisted on referring to my not-yet baby by a name we hadn't settled on, laid me on a patchwork quilt and gently skimmed my distended abdomen with the light on her iPhone.

To my great surprise, the creature responded. Several times, it made a quarter-turn, but always righted itself again. I left with the foetus still resolutely upright. But I was lifted in wonder at this quiet demonstration of consciousness and curiosity, at contact made between my own world and the dark, mysterious one inside me.

I don't know if there's a technical term for the torch trick, but the next method we tried was called external cephalic version (ECV). This time I lay under fluorescent lamps surrounded by medical professionals. A doctor with big hands grasped the foetus through my flesh and tried to shove it into a flip. It wasn't painful, exactly – or not for me. But the pulsing monitor, and the professionals reading it, said the foetus was in distress. Its heart rate plummeted with each attempt, recovering briefly only to come under assault again.

Finally, the doctor shrugged that ECV had a low success rate. Then he saw my face, screwed up against tears. The professionals frowned in over me and asked what was wrong. But I couldn't articulate why this encounter between worlds was distressing for me, the bodily connection between them.

At our next appointment, one of those big hands balled into a fist, pressed against my vulva and wiggled to feel out the space between the bones either side. The owner of the fist checked notes on the foetus's estimated weight and said there should be enough room for a vaginal breech birth.

There were no breaking waters, no midnight scrambles to

the labour ward. I was booked in for an induction ten days after my due date. And when the contractions started, the foetus reacted much as it had to ECV.

There was an atmosphere of controlled emergency and forms to be signed, quickly. And then the monitor went silent. I was nothing but raw, yowling terror. Two women handled me onto the bed, one injecting a drug to halt the contractions, the other waving Rescue Remedy under my nose.

With my body shut down and the professionals in charge, the foetal heartbeat returned. Calm was restored. The last thing I saw before I lay back on the operating table was a junior doctor giving me a big, smiling thumbs up through a glass panel in the door opposite.

Birth happened elsewhere. Behind a green curtain. I didn't do it. I wasn't even allowed to see it. All I felt was the strange sensation of someone else in there – the surgeon's hands rummaging around the private space that belonged to my baby – and the awkwardness of lying with my head too low, the alien bulk of my paralysed body splayed above, as if it might slide and crush me.

But then, there she was.

A sudden, shocking human.

Held aloft in latex-gloved hands: a whole, new, complete, tiny, astounding – person. Blinking at her unexpected world.

We called her F, after a feminist hero who had died weeks before. A name spoken in creative resistance, reverberating on the air, waiting to announce the start of a new story.

I don't know why her heart stopped, or even if that is

exactly what happened. Once she was here, alive – so very, brilliantly alive – I didn't think to ask.

F had arrived. Nothing else mattered.

Two years later, in another King's Cross pub, I gave a terrible speech, infant on my breast and one eye on whether the boyfriend, rolling drunk, was about to become more embarrassing than my public declarations of love – for the woman who (I did not say) might have been my co-mother, on the occasion of her marriage to the extraordinary man she'd found right after her PhD.

The wedding was a low-key gathering of friends and family. And my speech didn't much matter, because right after it came Emily's announcement that she was pregnant.

Emily didn't have to compromise after all. She didn't need a platonic co-mother and she didn't have to bet on fatherhood changing some Tinder guy into the perfect spouse. Weeks after she finished her PhD, she met Ben on a post-doc library fellowship in the States.

What are the chances? Had the Fates destined this extraordinary woman to be matched to an extraordinary man? Who knows? Who even asks?

Emily's motherhood didn't raise questions. But Mariam's did.

Mariam was humbly excited. Almost bashful, like someone awarded an unexpected prize. We met at a cafe with our friend Cara, hugging warmly, toasting her news over alcohol-free beers while F bounced on my lap. We put aside questions about *how* and *whether* and *are you sure*. All three of knew this wasn't going to be easy but Mariam knew this best.

And she was so pleased.

Mariam is the same age as me and Emily. But in Syria, where most women marry in their mid-twenties, she'd been consigned to the shelf. For me, children had been secondary to the soulmate. But Mariam was coming at motherhood from the opposite direction. She'd always known she wanted kids but never met a man she wanted to spend her life with – and had never been convinced any such man might exist. Now, in Berlin, where she'd arrived a few months earlier, she was preparing to become something unthinkable back home: a single mum.

But as the baby grew, so did her anxiety.

During my own pregnancy, I had worked for a journalism start-up and followed the early stages of the Syrian war closely, talking to activists in Homs and Idlib over Skype, matching their information against wire reports, tracking fronts on the ground and shifting internal and geopolitical alliances. But it was all abstract.

Until F arrived.

And then, I shut out all news from Syria. I closed any lines of communication that might confront me with the image of a broken little body, or the total anguish of a mother unable to protect her children. I leaped up to switch off the radio, banishing the incomprehensible knowledge that there were *children* there.

Mariam, watching reports of airstrikes and chemical weapons, didn't have this luxury. Her home town of Damascus was still relatively safe and her family were sitting tight, for now. But she couldn't be alone in her flat. Friends slept on her sofa to ward off the terror that seeped up at night. She was diagnosed with OCD.

Once her first trimester was through, she told her family she was pregnant and they began making arrangements for her mother to come to Germany for the birth. But by the time Mariam was heaving full-term weight, it was clear no return air ticket or family ties would convince immigration officials that Mariam's mother wouldn't claim asylum the minute she touched down on German soil.

And nor were they sanguine about Mariam's baby: an *Ausländer* she would be bringing into Germany whether they liked it or not.

Mariam's parents held to a respectful silence over the question of paternity, which her mother broke only once: she just needed to know nothing awful had happened. When Mariam assured her mother that conception had been consensual, the matter was closed. The immigration authorities had no such tact. They didn't care about Mariam's wellbeing. They wanted to know to whom the child belonged.

It belonged to the person in whose body it was coming into being: a single Syrian woman living in Germany on a limited work visa. But for the officials who repeatedly brought her in for questioning, this wasn't a complete answer.

But Mariam dug her heels in: there was no father.

And this left the German state with a duty it has never acknowledged. Because a child can only inherit Syrian citizenship from a father. And under international law, a child who would otherwise be stateless must be granted citizenship of the country where they are born.

Syria is one of twenty-four countries where mothers don't have the same rights as fathers to pass nationality on to their child. These laws of national belonging are patriarchal in the most literal sense: not just the dominance of men over women, but the rule of the father over a rigid family hierarchy.

Patriarchy, in this original sense, defines identities by paternity. A father gives you the name, the kinship, the genealogical line, the status, the wealth – or absence of it – to which you belong.

When European marriages were defined by coverture – the laws that prepared a woman for motherhood by subsuming her independent identity under that of her husband – taking a wife was how a man claimed ownership of his children. The whole family were his property. And a child who belonged to no man – whose mother belonged to no man – was illegitimate.

Laws of coverture were gradually phased out from the late nineteenth century, beginning a process by which women have become full citizens in our own right. We have gained rights to own property, to work, to vote, to participate in political life. And having the same autonomous social standing as men, we've come to expect marriage to be a partnership of equals.

Yet for many of us, realising our fertility is still a moment of surrender. Because if rights to public life are no longer defined by gender, the responsibilities of private life still are. We take time out from our careers just when they might be getting interesting. Men who lagged behind us gallop ahead. The wage gap opens up. The more time we spend home with the kids, the more the domestic life becomes our domain and the weaker our claim on lives beyond it.

We fought for space for careers and independent identities

loudly, collectively, publicly. We relinquish these gains privately: in rows over bills, or quiet resignation that what's best for family is more important than who we were before we became mothers.

And the fundamental patriarchal principle that *mother* is a channel through which a man's progeny is brought into the world and nurtured into an heir, still hangs over even the most 'gender-progressive' societies.

One of the most important fundamental demands of Western feminism is the reproductive right not to be a mother. But if we have the right *not* to bear children, then saying *yes* is itself a choice. And what happens then?

What becomes of our rights and responsibilities when we choose against abortion? When we leave the family planning clinic still pregnant? Do we still get to be individuals in our own right? Have we *chosen* to surrender our autonomous selves?

And if so, to whom?

What does it mean when – in the absence of a father – some other patriarchal authority defines the identity and belonging of a child from whom you are inseparable?

Past and present, women who have had children with the wrong man, or at the wrong time, have been punished by families, communities, state institutions – whoever stands in for a husband that isn't. My own predicament pales in comparison. I just had a crappy relationship.

When I kept my pregnancy, I didn't think I was surrendering my identity or my autonomous self. What I sacrificed for motherhood was the soulmate. I gave up on the dream of a relationship that would complete me for one that, even before our child arrived, was fatally imbalanced.

Fatherhood did change the boyfriend – in a careful-what-you-wish-for way.

When, in the first days and weeks, he criticised how I held F or how I fed her, I was too loved-up to mind – in fact, I welcomed him taking an assertive interest. Before we became parents, he'd been more committed to me than I was to him. Now, each committed to F in a way that exceeded our feelings for each other, I hoped our shared focus would bring new balance.

But when she was a few weeks old and we took her to visit his home city, he strutted and showed off his new family in a way that didn't suggest a partnership at all. He was even quicker to scold me in front of his old friends and rolled his eyes ostentatiously when he told them he had to take the missus out for dinner but would meet them later for a proper night out.

While I was on maternity leave, he worked in gallery bar and was usually gone all day. But he quit when I went back to work and grew resentful of any time I was away from him and F. I rarely saw friends because his anger would simmer on for days afterwards. Going out to work to pay our bills was unavoidable, but still treated with suspicion.

And over time, his aggression became intolerable.

Before F arrived – and particularly while I was pregnant – our rows had usually begun with my exasperation at something he'd done or hadn't done. But by the time F was eighteen months old – and we wed at a London registry office to cut a sorely needed couple of hundred euros off our monthly health-insurance bill – I'd got used to doing something I'd never done in a relationship, with this man or any other: quietly working around the things he'd done or hadn't done, just to keep the peace.

Holding the family together meant trying not to ignite his fuse. But I couldn't hold on for ever. F was three when I finally blew up his life.

He raged and begged and pleaded. How could I *do* this to him?

But really, my transition to single motherhood was as passive as my transition to motherhood. I'd weathered the cycles of his rages and apologies until the fights were so frequent and his drinking so disruptive, it wasn't much of a decision at all.

He pushed until I broke – or until breaking our nuclear family was the only way to hold myself together. The only way I could protect the family I was utterly committed to: F and me, in a safe and harmonious home.

In Margaret Drabble's 1965 novel *The Millstone*, a young academic conceives by a one-night stand. She drifts through pregnancy, falling short of decisive action either to abort or to notify the father. As a new mother, she fantasises about running into him by chance, admitting that the baby is his and reuniting as family.

Yet when the moment eventually comes, she senses the gulf that has opened between the brute certainty of her motherly love and the unwitting father's world of 'half-knowledge' and 'indifference' and realises it is too late:

It was no longer in me to feel for anyone what I felt for my child . . . A bad investment, I knew, this affection, and one that would leave me in the dark and cold in years to come; but then what warmer passion ever lasted longer than six months?

I felt a pang of recognition reading this passage, written half a century ago. Like Drabble's protagonist, I let the transition to motherhood happen to me. For her, as for me, the realisation that motherhood could be so consuming as to stand entirely independent of romantic love, came late.

But now, for the first time, I was ready to be enough without an other half.

I had to be.

This wasn't what family life was supposed to look like: this three-year-old and me, two people amid shared chaos, picking together through the fridge for something to eat or the mess on the bedroom floor for clean clothes.

Intimately bound, but each with much to do in her own life.

Early childhood is a strenuous time, with its constant learning; desires and perspectives reinventing month to month. And my perspectives were changing too. No longer anyone's girlfriend or wife, no longer responsible for an irresponsible man, I was my own person again. And if the logistics could be exhausting, the relief was euphoric.

Knowing that F, this perfectly innocent and wonderful person, had only me to depend on could be terrifying. But by the time her father left, becoming a single mother didn't mean stepping up to overwhelming responsibilities – these responsibilities were already all mine.

And I couldn't wallow in self-doubt, because to believe I

was not enough would be to consign her to a wanting child-hood – and whatever consequences such deprivation might have for her future. My child needed me to be the steady centre of her expanding world, and so I became more assur-edly myself.

Growing into this new sufficiency, I sought new reliances. As isolated as I'd become in our family of three, this often meant turning not to old friends whose support might have been based on years of solidarity, but making new ones with whom solidarity sprang from leaps of generosity. And the most generous were often women like me.

Women who live lightly or heavily with our poor choices or misfortune – and women for whom single motherhood is not an unexpected current they've been swept into after a wreck, but a deliberately navigated course.

When we meet, we ask each other questions always asked of single mothers – about how we got here, how we keep going. But between ourselves, these questions quickly move on, to: why didn't we think of this sooner? What were we thinking? Why *should* mothering without a man be so hard?

And how might we all do family better?

# Chapter 2

# I Love Men; I Just Don't Want One of My Own

An idea at least as old as orgasmic conception is virgin conception. I don't mean Mary. Mary's conception doesn't seem all that virginal – she was married after all, and there was a moment to which she surrendered, even if it was spiritual rather than carnal.

I'm thinking of Amazonian conception.

There was a time when anthropologists theorised a primordial, female-dominated, goddess-worshipping age. It was a creation myth that recognised the power of female fertility and supposed there must have been a time before patriarchy when the potency of life reigned supreme.

The men who imagined these prehistoric societies categorised them as either matriarchal – ordered and nurturing – or Amazonian – wanton and warlike.

The Amazons of Greek mythology worshipped Artemis, the goddess of wilderness and hunting, of nature and the moon. Yet Artemis is a complex figure, both virgin and mother goddess, goddess of chastity but also of childbirth.

Which isn't contradictory if you trace the original meaning of *virgin* as *one-in-herself*, or *she who is one unto and of herself*. Not an untouched maiden, so much as a woman who has never married, who belongs to no man – or even an androgynous figure who stood before and above gender, sexually free and autonomous.

The crux of virginity, then, is not whether a woman has had sex, unless male penetration has the power to fundamentally alter a woman's essential being, to shatter her into fragmented identities – lover, bride, wife, mother – defined by her duties to men.

Amazons were neither sexless nor childless. An Amazon was one, unto and of herself. She galloped in to take what she needed from men – by force if necessary – and returned only to offload any male offspring. Amazons weren't considered maternal because their mothering wasn't something they did for men. They were virgins in the sense that sex didn't rupture their distinct selves.

Once I'd finally told my husband we were done I left for a week-long ecological economics conference in Budapest. Between lectures I nipped out for cigarettes. Among the smokers convening on flagstones overlooking the Danube was a beautiful young PhD student. After a party on the last night, he and I left together because we were walking the same way. When he shyly invited me back, I was surprised.

'With you? To your hotel? For sex? Yes please.'

We emerged in the late afternoon sunshine, kissed goodbye and promised to meet again when the conference reconvened in two years' time. A lie – but a romantic lie. Brevity intensified pleasure in the moment. But romance tugs into the future, turning desire into something more. Something momentous.

We didn't use condoms. I told him I was on the Pill – which I was – but only after he'd come inside me. If I got pregnant, the decision to keep the baby or not, the power to change his life, would be mine.

Afterwards, I wondered why he hadn't been more careful.

But his instincts, if that's what they were, were right. I didn't want another baby, or another man. The one I'd just got rid of bitterly predicted a new boyfriend would quickly take his place. But he'd left a void in my life like a festering splinter leaves a void.

That night in Budapest didn't herald a future with a beautiful boy, but a new, freer phase of my sexuality. Single, my reproductive urges satiated, I could fuck as freely as a young man starting out on his academic career.

Some of the men I had sex with wanted to take care of me and F. There were men who came round to help when I was overwhelmed. Or took us away for a weekend by the seaside. Men who gave unsolicited advice on my parenting. Who came round to cook for us, and left my sink full of dirty pans.

One attentive lover with child-rearing experience behind him was particularly keen. His daughters had grown up and left his marriage to fall apart. He was great with F. And he even offered to keep the relationship open. Stella, the mutual friend who'd introduced us, thought this should have sealed the deal.

I told her I'd promised myself at least ten years of singledom. She looked at me like she couldn't decide whether I was fooling myself or fooling myself that I was fooling anyone else.

But my home was full of love, only as messy as two people

could make it, a space where tantrums and rages were all age-appropriate. My family was complete and my life didn't need any more complications.

Google dating and single motherhood and you get two kinds of article. There are tirades by pick-up gurus on the dangers of dating single moms: we're all gold-digging whores with loose pussies and no capacity to serve a man. Advice for single mums comes in sympathetically toned listicles: we must protect ourselves and our children. Don't jump into bed too soon – *you'll only get hurt! again!* – and sort your life out before you pull a man into its broken chaos.

We're either soiled goods or the walking wounded, one rejection away from annihilation. Either way, we're after what all dating women are after: a nice man to settle down and make a family with.

Or now, someone to fix our broken families.

But what if we like being single?

What if our families don't need fixing?

My love for F is so big. And so *easy*.

I mean – it's hard. Emotions that big can be gruelling. But there is never any question. Even when a child is behaving horribly, or mothering takes more of you than you believe you've got, you just keep doing it. Total commitment. And that kind of faith feels transcendent.

How could any relationship with a man compete?

Life-long monogamy used to be pretty much compulsory for women. But now, we can always leave if we want to. And now, maybe, I always would.

When we were younger, and I complained of some horribly stressful task I didn't want to do, Emily would say, 'At
least you don't have to go and break up with your boyfriend.'
(Whether I had one at the time or not.) And we'd laugh and
agree that telling your boyfriend he's dumped is the worst. It
isn't though. Ending it with the father of your child is much
more stressful. And I've got the T-shirt.

On a date with a man who calls himself a single father, we
talk about the joys of parenting, that transcendent love, the
wonder of seeing a child become ever-more themselves. And
I know he knows the pleasures I have shaped my life around.

'Yes,' he says, and he sees his kid every weekend, since he
moved out because 'the lifestyle didn't suit me'.

All that joy for so little effort. I suddenly feel exhausted
and make my excuses.

A different man strides into a different bar. Tall, well-built,
older than his profile pic, but commanding the room. Later,
he says that when his then-girlfriend got pregnant he wanted
her to have an abortion. She declined, and he told her the child
would be hers to raise. He refused to give up his freedom or
change nappies. But he would support them financially.

That's the other thing about this man – he's rich. Very rich
and very tall and very white. With a big cock.

She had her baby, he set up a direct debit and visited when
he wasn't travelling or partying. And he suggested she have
another one. It was up to her, but the offer was there, if she
wanted more semen and more money to go with it. She took
him up on it.

Now the kids are older – more fun – their big, fun, rich dad regularly takes them out on weekends.

'Being an absent father is the best,' he laughs.

And I laugh with him. It's funny because it's true.

He knows the responsibilities of raising children are huge and never pretended he was up to them. Or that the money he's lucky enough to be able to provide is equal or equivalent to the work of mothering. He doesn't know what it's like to shape your life around a child. But he does know that he doesn't know.

In *Of Woman Born*, Adrienne Rich says that whatever external forces might threaten our children, their wellbeing is a responsibility a mother carries alone: 'in the eyes of society the mother *is* the child's environment.'

Marguerite Duras describes a mother's body as a landscape: her children are 'on her as they might be on a hill, in a garden ... and sometimes she sleeps because they are on her body.'

'The woman is the home,' Duras writes in *Practicalities*.

When you've become accustomed to being lived in, and lived on, allowing your body to articulate active desires, to act on another body for your own pleasure, can make you feel a little closer to one unto yourself.

Or a different self altogether.

Flirting with the naked bar staff at the KitKatClub, sipping whisky sours with another newly single mum. She tells me that when she was young she had sex for attention. Or affirmation. To hear the words *you're beautiful*. In marriage, sex became a way of saying *please* and *thank you*. She was reduced to fucking her husband so he would take the bins out or let her have an evening off.

As she slides from the bar in the arms of a young man in lingerie, her laughter sounds like, *I'm free!*

We launch into single motherhood – me, my friend at the bar and many more of us – with a kind of second sexual youth. But wiser this time. More confident, knowing our bodies and what we want. And freer than ever before, now that sex doesn't have to be momentous.

Because where would the momentum lead?

Shaped around my child, there's no flexibility to entwine the trajectory of my life with a man's. I can lose myself in the present with lovers who want different things, or whose domestic habits aren't compatible with mine. Enjoying the space we have for one another in our lives, without trying to force open space that isn't there.

Sex doesn't have to be a story that defines me, but a bubble of suspended reality.

With Sol, an art historian I meet on Tinder, a delicious night of sex and other intimacies carries on into morning. While he dozes, I make coffee and scrape pancake mix left over from F's breakfast the day before into the pan. We have breakfast in the tangle of damp sheets and pick up conversation we'd distracted each other from earlier.

I ask him if he's single.

He chews pensively, sets down his plate and tells me a story that's probably, mostly, true.

His girlfriend is on the other side of the world while he's in Berlin for a half-year fellowship. They moved in together just before the pandemic, and settled into the hyper-domesticity in warm, comfortable companionship. But they stopped having sex. And now there are thousands of miles between them.

I don't judge. Not really. I know how much – will? conditioning? – it takes to resist. All the same, I don't want any part of this dishonesty. So I won't see Sol again. But I don't say so. Instead, I agree that six months is a long time to be celibate and ask if she's sleeping with other people too. 'No, I don't think so,' he says. 'No.'

That their sex life has died seems a problem for my Sunday morning lover mainly because they've decided to have children. He was never sure. Or didn't feel ready. Until now. He's forty-five. She's twelve years younger, 'the biggest age gap I've ever had in a relationship,' he says defensively.

But he loves her. Enough to plan a life, a family together.

*One built on lies* – I don't say it, but maybe he hears my thoughts because he says he envies my freedom to have different lovers without the duplicity. 'It's much harder for men,' I sympathise. 'There just aren't so many ways to do fatherhood.'

'What do you mean?' He's genuinely puzzled. 'Surely men have the advantage – we're not limited by our biological clocks.'

I picture Sol's future, his girlfriend's, with the hindsight of many single motherhoods: stories intricately unique and, often, depressingly alike. Is she really faithful to him? It's not unlikely. Does she believe he's faithful to her? Less likely. Deep down, I'm guessing, she knows, though perhaps she won't admit it even to herself.

He's right, the arrogant sod. It'll probably take a few dismal years of playing happy families before she realises her biological clock wasn't the real issue. That her fertility was always more powerful than his virility.

Studies say men are almost twice as likely as women to cheat on their partners. But also, that women find monogamy harder. One explanation, both for why women are more likely to want more, and for why we are less likely to take it, is that female sexuality is conditioned to be about more than just sex.

We find it harder to get excited about sex that isn't coming from or going anywhere new. But we're also more prone to picture the worst places it could lead.

If male libido is resolved in the moment, climaxing and done, women have always risked reaping the consequences. Male virility, the power to impregnate, is imagined as a power of creation – to seed new life – but also of destruction – to ruin the woman who carries that life. Female fertility, with its longer narrative, isn't imagined as an active force at all. More a field of dangerous potential.

And so, for a long time, a woman could only surrender to her desire for a man, or his desire for her, if she first secured a lifelong commitment.

The moment always had context.

Contraception was supposed to change all this, freeing female sexuality from its life-shaping consequences. But notions of female sexuality as a delicate thing coddled behind our defences against the driving force of male libido haven't been written out of heterosexuality just because, in physical terms, sex is less risky.

And stories of men as predators and women as prey continue

to shape our desires. Talking about how depictions of sexual violence absorbed in childhood shape adult desires, Maggie Nelson writes, 'I don't want to talk about "female sexuality" until there is a control group. And there never will be.'

Stella's partner, Max, says, 'BDSM isn't a kind of sex, sex is a kind of BDSM.' And maybe sex is always about power: the thrill of exerting it, or of being overcome, submitting to your own desires, allowing someone else to take you completely – and take complete responsibility.

In the sex-positive spaces that abound in Berlin, where bodies and desires of all shapes are out, loud and proud, so too are these gendered dynamics of conquer and surrender. Detached from social consequences, exaggerated for erotic effect, dominance and submission are confined to sex itself. They can be the grammar of conversations that can say new things about how we feel and what we want.

But if kink brings spectres out from shadowy recesses of the psyche to be declawed, in dating, power-play all too often happens *around* sex: who texts first, who makes room in their lives, who chases, who evades.

Women might be liberated now to assert our sexual power, to play the predator – or to submit, if that's what we have an appetite for. Our bodies might be free to give in to the moment. But in the dynamics that happen around sex – the rules of commitment, responsibility, give and take – in the long game of heterosexual dating, relationships and family, women still have more to lose.

Because having the power to suppress our fertility is quite different from asserting it as a power in its own right.

*

Women were already claiming lives and identities beyond motherhood when societal conversations about economics and overpopulation – as well changing gender roles – spurred the invention of hormonal contraceptives.

'The Pill did not so much change women's lives as enable them to make changes they longed for. Their sex was more free, their educational plans more achievable, their wage-earning more stable, their domestic labour reduced,' historian Linda Gordon writes.

But female fertility wasn't any more free. Women could better protect themselves – their defences redoubled – but if their reproductive potential was realised, they were still fucked.

And not everyone who moved to the quickening tempo of free love had access to the Pill. As cameras rolled on long-haired men and bare-breasted women declaring the power of love, Mother and Baby Homes were busier than ever. Mostly Church-run institutions, they addressed the problem of female fertility by erasing thousands of single motherhoods and silencing their trauma.

Later, some of these mothers did tell their stories.

Under some pretext of distant work, study or illness, a young woman is shut away before her sin becomes too big to hide. She toils through mountains of laundry. Hard labour against bodily filth. If she goes out to work in other institutions, she's given a gold-coloured band to polish the night before, to twist around nervous fingers on the morning bus.

As her body swells, the work gets harder. A proportional penance. When her body opens, she is laid on her back for her darkest hours. She's not dying, they tell her, she's being reborn.

For a few weeks she might swear she was a mother. New rhythms, of two bodies, feeding, the touch of skin on skin. A gaze beginning to focus. Two new identities, two selves that are also one. But in the language of the Home, she's not a mother and still a girl.

Each time someone leaves, the others shift seats around the breakfast table. When a girl reaches the head of the table, she knows she's next. Gently, a matron says the baby will go to a good home. One of the other girls saw them arrive in a motor car. They looked very well-to-do.

The baby leaves first, in the motor car. No longer a shameful secret, but the joy at the heart of a real family. The priest performs a ceremony to complete the girl's cleansing. And then her own mother takes her home on the bus, telling her, 'We'll never speak of this again.'

For many of these women, the secret was kept throughout their lives. Not just in long years of unspoken grief that came after, but before their sins manifested in flesh.

They might have heard about wicked girls who didn't have husbands and probably never would after what they're done. But often, they didn't know exactly *what* they'd done. They knew boys were dangerous, that there were parts of their bodies that were dirty no matter much they washed. They knew the pleasures and pains of new womanhood were unspeakable. Their first menstrual cycle came as a shock, never explained, just more stains to be concealed and scrubbed at.

These erased mothers weren't punished for making bad

choices – they didn't know any better. Female fertility was beyond rational thought or moral choice. Their sin had always been latent in their bodies, waiting to be articulated.

As women claimed the same freedoms as men, so they demanded the right to make active choices over their repro-duction, and female sexuality became more virile – sex didn't have to break a woman.

Reliable contraception meant women could control how many children they had, and when. It meant they could say *enough* – and it meant they could wait. Fewer children meant more time for other things, like work and education, other kinds of creativity. For pursuits that used to be almost exclu-sively male. For free love, even.

But as women's lives outside the home expanded, the space for motherhood contracted. You can spend your twenties living, working and fucking just like a man. But then wash up in your thirties not like a man at all.

Women who have access to contraception tend to have children later. But men can see our *later* and raise us *later still*.

The difference between Sol and his girlfriend is a dozen years he took to dither over whether he wanted family. A decade of fucking, not committing, advancing his career. Now, she's waiting at home, committed to making this rela-tionship work because ending it will mean the horrors of heterosexual dating as a childless woman in her thirties.

Sol, meanwhile, knows there are plenty more women out there running out of time.

And this is what puts women at a disadvantage in hetero-sexual relationships. Ostensibly, our biological clocks. More, the competing demands of motherhood and everything else. But really, that even as taboos on female sexuality have been smashed, single motherhood is, if not an unspeakable shame, still an anomaly, failure or misfortune.

Sol's girlfriend may not have much longer to conceive a child, but Sol can't conceive one at all. On their own, each single, she could still become a mother. She could replace her boyfriend with a sperm bank, a one-night stand or a sympathetic friend with five minutes to spare.

But if Sol wants to be a father, he needs a woman to carry his child for nine months. Unless he's ready to pay vast sums to a surrogate and take on the even more anomalous role of single father, he needs this woman, one way or another, to make him a big part of her life.

Patriarchy has so successfully contained female fertility, men like Sol have forgotten it has any autonomous power at all. But worse, so have women like Sol's girlfriend.

At the height of the sexual revolution, Shulamith Firestone recognised that the Pill's severing of female sexuality from fertility would only get us so far and anticipated true emancipation through more advanced technological developments.

In 1970, she published *The Dialectic of Sex*, arguing that gender inequality was rooted in 'biological reality': that because women suffer menstruation, childbirth, breastfeeding and menopause, because we are naturally burdened with the care of infants, we have always been naturally dependent on men for our physical survival.

Real gender equality, she famously argued, would come

by only by eliminating the bodily aspects of motherhood altogether and gestating new humans in artificial wombs. But
my own sexual revolution came not from evading my fertility
but realising it. Not from rejecting motherhood, but from
doing it a little differently.

I only wish I'd realised this power sooner.

Over lunch, a colleague shows me the profile of the Tinder
date she has lined up for the evening. I show her mine. We
laugh and groan at the pitfalls of online dating.

I have a lot riding on the evening because of the trouble
I've taken to organise for F to spend the night with her father.
But Amber, this younger woman, in her early thirties and
childless, is more anxious. I'm hoping for good sex. She's
hoping to meet a man with whom she can spend her life and
have a family.

Neither of us will announce our intentions over the first
drink. We'll play the game, conversation circling around what
we're after. If all goes well, by the second drink my cards will
be on the table. If all goes well, by her third date Amber still
won't say what she really wants. Because to be forward about
sex isn't really shameful anymore, but a woman desperate to
secure a mate in time is still supposed to send men running.

A man lies between my semen-damp thighs and tells me
about women who steal men's seed. They have one-night
stands and nine months later they file child maintenance
orders. It happened to a mate of his.

So maybe some men are afraid of the power of our fertility?
But he doesn't look scared. He seems scandalised that there

are women out there who fail in their duty to protect men from their virility.

Something women aren't supposed to say: I don't like condoms any more than men do. And I don't like the kind of sex condoms dictate. Sex that comes after foreplay. As if female pleasure isn't sex at all but just an appetiser. *Foreplay* – I would banish the word.

I know, I know. And I tell myself I won't do it next time. But why do I always have to be the one to put the breaks on?

And sometimes, stopping them isn't enough.

Once, I wriggled free and asked a man to put on a condom but he managed to lose it again before he came. He called it an accident and apologised.

I asked when he'd last been tested, and he told me not to worry because he never had unprotected sex, this was a one-off. Which seemed unlikely, given how ready he'd been to barge in moments before.

'That was different,' he said, 'I knew I was safe with you because you're a mother.'

'I'm not *your* fucking mother,' I muttered as I made for the door.

Before his #MeToo shaming, Louis C.K. did a bit about abortion where he says, 'Women have to decide who lives and dies . . . We give them this responsibility when we fuck them, we go, *here, you decide what to do with this shit, see ya later!* . . . Women have judgement . . . Men have intent . . . *More of me! More of me!* It's her job to go, *that's enough of you, I think.*'

The audience cheers. You can hear women whooping in agreement.

There are men who see abortion as a threat to their virility. If a woman can always say *no* to a life they started, every mother's *yes* is an assertive act of creation.

A power we have that men do not.

But that's not why it's funny. It's funny because C.K. is getting at a profound inequality in heterosexual relationships that isn't about female vulnerability, so much as female responsibility. Women have to take responsibility for babies, or abortions, when men say *see ya later.* But we're also responsible for making sense of what sex means. For the damage it might do, to us, or to the people we have sex with.

We're responsible for all that comes after.

Watching this routine is uncomfortable now we know it wasn't just a joke. Offloading his pathetic intent onto unconsenting women was something C.K. got off on. Abasing himself and leaving women to figure out *what to do with this shit* fetishised these feminised responsibilities.

Like a 'stealther', who puts himself at risk to inflict risk on unsuspecting women, for Louis C.K., getting off and offloading were one and the same.

#MeToo was important because it reframed private consequences as public questions. But there are no easy answers. And so far, what we've agreed on, mostly, is to kick the conversation back behind bedroom doors.

Long silenced, articulating female desire can be empowering. But as Katherine Angel argues in *Tomorrow Sex Will Be Good Again*, in the post-#MeToo era age of enthusiastic consent, 'women's speech bears a heavy burden: that of ensuring pleasure; of improving sexual relations, and of resolving violence.'

If kink plays on limits within which anything is possible, between people who actively claim vulnerabilities, powers and responsibilities, then affirmative consent assumes female vulnerability and demands we assert unmistakable boundaries between what we want and don't want, for men who are assumed incapable of responding sensitively to a lover's pleasures and pains.

This makes sex less an open conversation between equals – articulating things with our bodies that words cannot say, feeling out the places where power and surrender synthesise, discovering what we want by doing – than a choreographed routine within which men can unleash their virility knowing their female partners are keeping everyone safe.

Carrying the sexual mental load.

And we're supposed to do all this – be responsible, decisive and articulate – in language that describes female sexuality in the passive tense. Why is being consumed an active process, but engulfing, swallowing up – the forceful action of a muscular vagina working herself around him – passive?

Silencing active female pleasure in the moment leaves women with narratives that cast us as victims or manipulators. Guarding against male virility or allowing things to be done to us. The subtext is that there is always a price to be paid, a score to be settled in longer narrative: if she doesn't pay the price for letting him have his way, she's probably extracting a price from him, in coupledom, affirmation, motherhood or money.

And it would be nice to move on and talk about other things. But some topics are even harder to talk about than female sexuality. Like that these days, men have power in heterosexual relationships not so much because women risk having children, but because we risk not having them. Female fertility can still be a bigger taboo than female sexuality. 'I want kids' can be harder to say than 'I want sex'.

'I don't need a man,' might be OK, but 'I don't need a man to have a baby,' less so.

'Don't make this a battle of the sexes,' an editor tells me. But it feels like a battle sometimes. Dating does. Dating is awful for women like Amber. The fight is fixed in favour of those who can leave carrying and caring for children to others, those who can wait.

And it's rigged in favour of masculine virility because we're not having conversations about female fertility as a power we can exercise outside long-term monogamous relationships.

Firestone said reproduction makes women dependent on men. But I think the problem is not so much that we're dependent, but that so much depends on us. That from the responsibility we carry for bringing new people into the world, other responsibilities flow and multiply, affirmed and reaffirmed. But our power isn't being articulated.

And responsibility without power is a horrible bind.

We don't want a battle of the sexes. We don't want to wield our power tyrannically. Just as Sol doesn't tell his girlfriend, 'I can fuck around because you don't have time to find someone better,' we don't say to men like Sol, 'Dude, I can get all the sperm I need to make a baby by three o'clock this afternoon.'

But on a societal level, we do need to be saying, 'women

don't need husbands to be mothers' as easily as we might say, 'women don't need boyfriends to have orgasms'.

Solid evidence for a pre-patriarchal age when men and women alike worshipped at the altar of female fertility is scarce. When feminists seized on this story first told by Victorian men, it was dismissed as fantasy. Now, some archaeologists argue that traces of women's central role in the birth of European agriculture and female political power in Neolithic societies have been dismissed in the hurry to disassociate from embarrassing fairytales about fertility goddesses.

But whatever the truth behind matriarchal myths, that primal female supremacy based on reproductive power has been theorised at all, and particularly by men, points to patriarchy's deep unease with female fertility. To the fear that in some natural state, women would rule.

That male supremacy is something that had to be won and could always be lost.

Maybe this is why we don't talk about single mothering as a viable way to do family. If we say it out loud – that female fertility is an autonomous power – we might conjure out of the shadows a terrible truth that would precipitate the ultimate battle of the sexes. Feminists would no longer be able to hide behind the pretence that all we want is equality; we would be claiming dominance.

And that can't end well for anyone.

But conversations about virility, fertility, bodies and babies don't go anywhere useful unless we talk about gender. It's gender – the expectations and conventions that are wildly extrapolated from biological difference – that makes women the needy ones in relationships, that teaches us to see power as dependence and makes us responsible for the emotional and social consequences of fucking, whether those consequences are new life or just complicated feelings.

In Torrey Peters's novel *Detransition, Baby*, Reese says, 'The only people who have anything worthwhile to say about gender are divorced cis women who have given up on heterosexuality but are still attracted to men.'

The divorced cis woman in the story is Katrina, who is pregnant with a child whom Reese, a trans woman, wants to co-parent. If they can find the right conversation, the right language to talk about the future, perhaps they can make a family together. And so Reese draws parallels between her own gender transition and the experiences of cis-het women who find 'narratives given to them since girlhood have failed them'.

If they want children, women like Reese are at a physical disadvantage compared to women like Katrina. But Reese has something Katrina needs just as keenly: in her experience of queerness she offers different narratives of gender, a future beyond the heterosexuality Katrina has given up on.

The power Katrina has that Reese doesn't is biological. But the very real power men have – that neither Reese nor Katrina has – isn't. Which is why the baby-making equipment we're born with isn't the real issue, so much as the stories we tell about it.

The biological reality is that to make a baby, you need a person with a womb to be heavily involved for at least nine months. The story that she must lose her autonomy in the process is just one we've heard so often we rarely stop to question it.

The conversations Reese has with Katrina – and Ames, the third parent in their potential family – are the kind of conversations people of all bodies and identities ought to be having before they decide to parent together. These conversations aren't about, *I love you* or *you're beautiful* but, *how do we negotiate power, dependence and responsibility, social as well as biological, in ways that aren't exploitative?*

In Firestone's utopia, the technology to erase biological difference leads to the dissolution of gender. If this happened, Reese wouldn't need Katrina. She could be a single mother, or she might have had a child with Ames, her gender-queer ex-lover.

Who knows if it will ever be possible to gestate a child in an artificial womb. And if it were possible, would it lead also to the 'disappearance of motherhood' as Firestone intended? Might, then, the question of Reese's motherhood be moot?

I don't think so. Mothering is a power and a responsibility I for one wouldn't want to give up. But if we ever get to find out, it won't be because cis women don't want to be mothers, or because women who are trans do. Just as the Pill was only made available once women had begun to centre their lives around more than home and family, artificial wombs won't be invented so long as the stories we tell about motherhood mean that we don't just take responsibility for children, but for their fathers too.

If women seized our reproductive power and fathers were just one, optional, piece of many socially viable constellations that might form around a child – well, then, maybe, technology might be developed so men could have families without wooing women into relationships we could easily do without.

But until then, women who want to be mothers, and women who have sex with men, should remember that men who want families need us more than we need them. Not just because female reproductive anatomy isn't as disposable as male gametes, but because families need parents who take responsibility.

And as long as responsibility itself is feminised, gambling your long game on a man can be riskier than anything your body might set in motion.

# Chapter 3

# Half-lives of the Nuclear Family

If I had taken the abortion counsellor's advice and ended it with F's father before she was born, we might have found a way for her to have a relationship with him commensurate with the responsibilities he could manage. Instead, my conviction that she needed both parents, together, in the same home, wore down slowly.

And F didn't know any better than a home where aggression was never far beneath the surface.

Though she was too young to articulate her desires, I knew that if she had a say in things, she would have had him stay. Wanting him to leave, I feared putting my own desires above her needs. But what she really needed was a home that wasn't filled with anger and bitterness. And she needed the one person in her life who was taking responsibility for her wellbeing to be happy, healthy and autonomous – even if that meant a less stable father.

When I kicked him out it wasn't pay-off between her needs and mine, it was the point where it became clear to me that they were one and the same. When that moment came, only

I could sense. And only I could – *can* – take responsibility for getting it wrong.

F was two and my every working day began in certainty that I couldn't make it through to the end. On the train, I tried to imagine arriving at work, doing my job, coming home again, but these things were inconceivable. I vaguely expected everything to just stop. I imagined waking up in some institution. But I would arrive at the office. I would come home.

Impossible days kept stacking up.

So did two things: I started taking citalopram and I booked us in for couples' therapy.

Actually, we'd been seeing Frau Voigt for a while before I started on the antidepressants. Each session began with me curling up in one of the twin armchairs facing our therapist and recounting our latest rows. Frau Voigt would spend the rest of our ninety minutes trying to unearth the roots of my partner's aggression and irresponsibility, while I snivelled my way through the box of tissues provided, wondering if there was much point my even being there.

It happened that the day I started on citalopram, she tried a different approach.

The doctor had said it would take weeks for the drug to have any effect. But within a couple of hours of swallowing my first half-tablet, a cage of crackling anxiety descended between me and world: F's chatter, the cheery chaos of kindergarten drop-off hour, the commuter-packed train, the street of imposing villas where Frau Voigt had her basement office, the boyfriend – who didn't believe in antidepressants despite self-medicating with an array of narcotics – walking beside me.

I projected my voice through the buzz to tell him I wasn't sure I could be responsible for F in this state. 'Why, what do you think's gonna happen?' he muttered, his words snapping against the cage. I didn't know, but thought perhaps I might be able to answer when we got there.

But this time Frau Voigt led us into a different room, with a whiteboard. She drew a line down its centre: on one side she would write down everything my partner said I brought to our relationship and family life. The other was to be filled by me with all the qualities and labours he contributed.

The static dropped to a low, numbing hum as he went first, listing off things I did for him and F. Practical stuff like earning our keep, motherly care like bedtimes, personal attributes like patience. I might have welcomed this rare acknowledgement. But I was too busy ransacking my mind for something to go on the other side of the whiteboard.

My turn came. I said he was a good cook. Then I excused myself from the task, explaining that I couldn't think straight under the sudden influence of the citalopram, and silently vowed to come up with a list before our next session.

The following week we were off on what turned out to be the most depressing holiday of my life. I was supposed to email Frau Voigt to schedule our next session when we got back. Each time I reached this item on my to-do list, I thought of the whiteboard. After the holiday, I'd given up the citalopram because I couldn't work on it.

But still.

I never sent that email, and we never went back.

And yet, when I ended the relationship a few months later,

I believed something would fill that half-page. If I couldn't come up with anything, he'd have to do it himself.

The archetypal single mother used to be the girl who didn't hold out for a ring on her finger, or the deserted wife who couldn't hold on to her man. But these days, most of us are women who detonated nuclear families we couldn't tolerate. And so the struggle isn't just to manage alone, but to manage family life shaped by the fallout.

Family is meant to be a private realm of love and care. But when parents split, its inner workings are painfully exposed. Personal matters can become the business of public institutions. Yet public perceptions of what happens in the courtrooms where parents fight gendered battles over family life are often wrong.

Eight or nine times out of ten, when heterogendered parents split, children live exclusively or primarily with their mothers. But this doesn't mean family courts favour women. Most of these arrangements are negotiated between parents with no intervention from judges or lawyers. Only a tiny percentage of custody battles make it to court, and when they do, most dads do get a share of their children's home life.

This hasn't always been the case. The 'tender years doctrine' – first introduced in the UK in 1839 – assumed children were best off with mothers. This was the triumph of a campaign by Caroline Norton, a writer and socialite whose husband barred her from seeing their three young sons after she left him.

The tender years doctrine has been called the first piece of feminist legislation, because until then divorced women had no right to custody, giving every married father the legal power to take his wife's children from her. But it was a victory for a kind of feminism that assumed men and women to be innately different, with distinct roles and responsibilities.

In the second half of the twentieth century, with mothers working and fathers increasingly active in their children's lives, tender years – which had been adopted across the Western world – gave way to more nuanced interpretations of the 'best interests of the child'.

Yet while legal frameworks adopted gender-neutral language, courts continued to understand children's interests in starkly gendered terms.

A 1997 study of gender bias in US family courts found that judges – mostly men – were taking custody from women because of their sex lives, because they worked outside the home, because they relied on benefits to put food on the table – or on friends and family to help them look after their kids.

Courts ruling on 'parental fitness' held men to the standard of a *good father*, while mothers had to live up to the far loftier ideal of a *good mother*. Fathers were rewarded for making kids' dinner or taking them to the doctor – things that would only have a bearing on a mother's fitness had she *not* done them.

And children's interests were often defined in economic terms. Judges were giving preference to the parent with the biggest house, in the nicest area, with the most disposable income for family holidays. Mothers who'd been out of the workplace caring for children were being penalised for poverty, while fathers who'd been busy at work were assumed easily able to step into their wives' caring roles.

Or better still, find another woman to do so.

Judges' preference for 'traditional' family norms, the study found, treated motherly care as 'fungible'. If a man had remarried (divorced men remarry at a higher rate than divorced women, and are more likely to fight for custody if they do), children were often assumed better off in a patch-work nuclear family than with a lone mother.

The right to custody freed mothers to leave men they might otherwise have been stuck with. But even in the tender-years era, divorce often left single-mother families destitute.

A woman could, in theory, claim maintenance from an absent father – even if actually enforcing this right often proved impossible. But if she'd left him, committed adultery, or was guilty of some other behaviour a court deemed good enough reason for a husband to ditch his wife, she and the kids got nothing.

These days, we might have our names on rental leases. We might be able to kick our men out and keep the family home. But divorce is still a financial disaster for many mothers. A study by the Women's Budget Group found that across England, a single man on median earnings can afford to rent or buy an 'averagely priced house' but a single woman – whose median earnings are thirty-four per cent lower – cannot.

And these figures are for single women generally, not just those with children. Around a third of single-parent families in the world's wealthiest countries live in poverty. In the UK, *half* do. And single mothers are about twice as likely to live below the poverty line as single fathers.

The world is, no doubt, full of women in unhappy

relationships they can't afford to leave. But what's striking, given the dire economic impact of divorce on women, is that so many of us do it anyway. More than sixty per cent of UK divorces are initiated by women; in the United States, nearly seventy per cent.

And despite men doing much better economically – seeing a rise in their material standard of living, according to some studies – divorce hits men's mental health harder. Maybe that's because labour divisions in marriage are a win for men. A US study found that single mums actually do less housework and get more sleep than married ones. But women also tend to have more social ties. A divorced man can be a very lonely man.

And worse, his fatherhood may come unstuck.

For a long time, motherhood depended on men for legitimacy. If unwed motherhood was a disgrace, the stigma of divorce wasn't much better. A woman whose marriage failed had failed at family, and so wasn't much of a mother. But now, often, it's men who find their fatherhood contingent on the women in their lives.

Fatherhood is changing. Men's roles are changing. But not as fast as women's have. We've claimed lives outside the home, but men haven't kept up the pace of change inside it. They've lost their status as sole providers and protectors but they haven't stepped up as carers.

All this can be easy to fudge in the privacy of the hetero-gendered home. A man who is both husband and father may not need to examine these roles closely, or put much work into either. But if he's left the burdens of parenting to his wife, divorce means reinventing his fatherhood.

*

Before my family split, I was the breadwinner – but cuddles, bedtimes, tears and tantrums were my job too. And I was trying to help F's father be a happier, more stable person. For all our sakes. He didn't look depressed exactly. But I was pretty sure I wasn't the only one whose mental health left something to be desired. Agonising over breaking up, I feared the chaos he'd be lost in without me and F to tether him.

And he didn't prove me wrong.

While I luxuriated in the peace of a home without him in it, he was in no state to fill up his side of the whiteboard. He was no better able to hold down a job, certainly no more reliable. Often drunk. And angry. Furiously angry.

And soon, we found ourselves accounting to a different expert, on less comfortable chairs. This time, we hadn't volunteered, or paid, to share our problems with a stranger. The police ordered us to see a social worker at the *Jugendamt*, the branch of German social services concerned with child welfare, after my scorned *Kindesvater* smashed down my front door in a violent rage.

Herr Hahn began by explaining that he wasn't there to take sides with either of us, but to represent the best interests of – he checked a file – F. He was her voice in the room, he said, beaming and clasping his hands on the table between us. And I looked back and tried to imagine that this man was, of the three of us, best positioned to represent F's interests or articulate her desires.

This man who'd never hurtled across town to pick her up because her father forgot, or spent the small hours sitting on the kitchen windowsill smoking and weighing the trauma of splitting against the trauma we were already living though.

This man who'd never been consumed with guilt for every cigarette that might leave her motherless, and then lit another and another as indecision circled.

But Herr Hahn didn't need to grasp the texture of our family life. He was more interested in balance. Six of one and half-a-dozen of the other. If the Kindesvater was reprimanded for breaking down my door, Herr Hahn duly acknowledged that I'd broken this raging man's heart. If he scolded the Kindesvater for calling me a cunt, he scolded me for being too focused on my own agenda for the meeting.

My agenda, since the police had made a social worker part of our lives, was to fix some sort of schedule so I knew which days F would be with her father and could plan accordingly. Or, failing that, for him to at least have a functioning phone on him while he was with her so I knew where they were and when she was coming home. His phone – always off, broken or lost – had been a point of contention for some time. Scheduling on an ad-hoc, week-by-week basis was strenuous enough, but not being able to reach him to make or confirm arrangements was pure chaos.

Herr Hahn conceded that for most people, my demand would not be unreasonable. But my Kindesvater, he forced me to admit, was not most people. Managing a phone was clearly more responsibility than he could handle. So Herr Hahn changed the subject by producing a document for us to sign, agreeing that F would stay one night each week with the Kindesvater.

I pointed out that the Kindesvater was homeless, sleeping on friends' couches or in the cellar of a bar where he worked occasional shifts. Herr Hahn scribbled amendments, to the effect that this agreement would commence as soon as the Kindesvater had found himself suitable accommodation. But I wasn't signing anything. A home first, then we can talk about overnight stays in it.

'Don't you think,' the social worker implored me, 'that signing this agreement would help motivate him to set his life in order?'

And that was when I lost my rag, and any sympathy our social worker might have had for me. Because I'd spent years trying to motivate this man to sort his life out. I'd begged, pleaded, cajoled. I'd written job applications for him. Agreed to cut my working hours if he found work – any kind of work – that meant he wouldn't be around to pick F up from kindergarten. I had tried. I had hoped, prayed, forgiven, and tried some more.

When I ended the relationship, I made the decision to stop trying.

I wasn't stopping F seeing her father. She'd already stayed with him when he'd had a room in a flat share – time off I treasured. I wasn't whisking her off to London where I'd have the steady support of my own mother. But I wasn't taking responsibility for him anymore – and I sure as fuck wasn't going to use F as a reward to coax a grown man into looking after himself.

I didn't know many other single mums then, but there was Liza. I'd worked with Liza in various Berlin newsrooms. She'd kicked her Kindesvater out not long before I kicked out mine. But by the time I had my first meeting with the *Jugendamt*, she was an old hand. She'd warned me not to expect much sympathy. And when her prediction was realised and I marched furiously out of social services' grey lino corridors, I called her to vent.

Liza commiserated, but had been through too much herself to muster the outrage I felt my experience warranted. So she added me to a Facebook group for single mums in Berlin where my howls of frustration found company.

The thing was, the Kindesvater hadn't asked for more time with F. And I hadn't refused any overnight stays. The phone was a source of conflict. And scheduling. His drinking and his aggression. The times he kept F waiting and I didn't know if he'd turn up or not. But the Kindesvater's access to his child was not an issue.

Lena, a founding member of the single mothers' rights group *Mütterinitiative für Alleinerziehende* (Mothers' Initiative for Single Parents), replied to my post with a little context. The *Jugendamt*, she said, had an unofficial policy of pursuing fifty-fifty shared parenting arrangements. And if they can work you up to a forty-sixty split of a child's time, fifty-fifty is pretty much a done deal if the case goes to court.

In the UK, Fathers4Justice's overt misogyny and tone-deaf pranks have undermined their demands. But some legal regimes around the world – including states like Kentucky in the US – have adopted one of them: default fifty-fifty shared parenting when a couple separates. In other countries, like Australia, shared custody isn't automatic but courts are encouraged to consider splitting children's home close to equally. And even where there's no legal imperative to do so, judges often view an even split as preferable to choosing one parent over the other or ruling for more complex scheduling.

In Germany, the fathers' rights movement has main-stream political backing. And while they haven't managed to write automatic fifty-fifty parenting into German law, their determined – and well-funded – campaigns have influenced the practices of social services and family courts in some German states.

Advocates of an even split of children's time present it as a victory for gender equality: just because a father hasn't done much childcare in marriage, doesn't mean he can't step up in divorce. A win for dads – but also a win for mums who finally get to share the domestic load. And for some families, it really is a win.

Author Amy Shearn writes, 'before my divorce, I hadn't had more than a few hours alone for over a decade' but since settling on fifty-fifty custody:

I've worked full time with focus and satisfaction. I've parented calmly while managing some tricky stages for my tweens. I wrote an entire novel during my evenings and weekends. I learned to play the ukulele. I've fallen in love at least once. On many weekends, I sleep in, take long walks, read books, see friends. My home is tidy.

Reams of research have been produced on the impact of shared residency on children. The good news is that plenty of data suggests kids can adapt to living in two homes just fine. But few experts think sending a child back and forth between warring parties does them any good.

The problem with family courts perusing fifty-fifty residency is they're *only* dealing with warring parties – if parents could agree on what was best for their children, they wouldn't be in court. And according to an Oxford University study, promoting shared parenting actually drives more couples to court. The Australian experience suggested that 'even subtle legislative encouragement toward shared time arrangements . . . gives litigating parents something new and concrete to fight about.'

Ultimately, the result was 'increased focus on fathers' rights over children's best interests', the study found.

And they were looking at data drawn largely from nuclear families who split. Meanwhile, some courts are imposing shared residency arrangements on families who have never lived together at all.

Beth had been travelling the world for years when she arrived in Germany. She'd left a teaching job in Asia wanting to come to Berlin but ended up with a work visa for a job in a small east German city a couple of hours from the capital. She saw it as a way in. Another stop on her journey.

But she struggled with the language and struggled to make friends. And so she joined a dating app – and met a wildly engaging, charismatic man who spoke English. He was married with kids, but Beth didn't see this as a problem. His marriage was open, she met his wife briefly, and she wasn't looking for someone to settle down with.

And then Beth got pregnant.

Like me, Beth was thirty-two. Unlike me, she knew from the start she'd be a single mum, and was very comfortable with the idea. She'd wanted kids, but not to be confined to a monogamous marriage. That her lover was experienced in fatherhood, and in a non-traditional family set-up, seemed to bode well.

And he was thrilled she was having his child.

But as her pregnancy progressed, Beth's Kindesvater became controlling. He visited unannounced and became enraged if she wasn't home. Or if she was seen out with another man – and then even with female friends. She ended their sexual relationship. But the more she drew away, the more he closed in.

Once their son was born, he forbade her from taking him home to the States to visit her family. He wanted to know where Beth and the baby were at all times, texting incessantly, demanding she reply immediately with photos to prove their location. He hung around outside her apartment, demanding to come in if she was home, waiting for her to return and account for where she'd been if she wasn't. Once inside, he trashed her flat. She shielded her baby with her body while he threw plates and demolished the TV.

To Beth, this man never actually seemed very interested in his child, so much as asserting his power over them both:

> The harassment was constant and the pretext was always about our son. But he wasn't over the relationship. He knew the romantic part was over, but he thought he could control me anyway. Really, that was always what it was about – he wanted full control over me.

He turned up at her office to make demands. He called her boss and told him she was a bad mother and a dangerous person to employ. Suddenly, immigration authorities were digging into possible irregularities in her employment status.

Beth was doing new mothering alone, under constant pursuit, lost in labyrinthine bureaucratic processes in a language and culture that felt impenetrable and stacked against her. But when her Kindesvater said he'd sue for shared residency, she thought it was an empty threat.

His name was on the child's birth certificate, but they'd never lived together. And there were police records of her complaints of harassment, property damage and physical threats. The idea that a court might put her baby in this man's care seemed ludicrous.

But that's exactly what they did, ruling the child should have regular overnight stays with his father and up to two weeks without seeing her during the holidays. Beth reeled out of the courthouse and came home to an email from the Kindesvater: 'You'll have to answer my calls now, bitch.'

Beth was still breastfeeding and her lawyer requested the new arrangement be postponed until the child was weaned. The *Jugendamt*, which had thrown itself enthusiastically behind the father's case, submitted a statement arguing that the father's capacity to care for his child should not be found wanting because of something he was unable to do for 'purely physical' reasons.

The court accepted this argument but gave Beth three months to resolve what it termed 'the breastfeeding problem'. It framed this grace period as an indulgence to help the mother adjust and acknowledged no benefit to the child.

'I was suddenly engulfed in a nightmare situation that I never would have imagined could happen,' Beth says. Twice a week, every week, she handed her child over, and twice a week, every week, she did her best to pick up the pieces when he returned:

> *He came home crying. He'd throw himself on the ground and slam his head against furniture or whatever was around and just cry. He'd cry for fifteen, twenty minutes, crying himself to sleep on the floor – and then he'd wake up a few minutes later screaming again. He'd be screaming, 'Mama! Mama!' And I was there, but he would push me away. This would go on and on, crying until he exhausted himself, sleeping, waking up screaming. He couldn't be comforted. This happened after every overnight visit. For months.*

In cases like Beth's, pursuit of the equality embodied in the fifty-fifty principle means more than assessing capacity to care in gender-neutral terms. It means ignoring any evidence of parental fitness that might be rooted in gender – and ending up in a place where breastfeeding is forbidden and domestic violence ignored so as to preserve the illusion that male parents and female parents are just the same.

Beth's breastfeeding was an affront to notions of gender-neutral parenting. And so it had to stop.

For Beth, there is no question that the court elevated the rights of the father over the interests of her child. But *best interests of the child* is a problematic principle in itself.

In her paper 'The Perils of Innocence, or What's Wrong with Putting Children First', Linda Gordon points out that even the tender years doctrine didn't shift power from fathers to mothers, so much as from fathers to courts. Rather than asserting 'a right vested in women' it 'strengthened state power over children, through granting courts rather than fathers the power to decide on custody.'

And with the rise of the best-interests principle, judges placed still greater scrutiny on the fitness of mothers, whose interests were now explicitly distinct from – and therefore in potential opposition to – those of their children.

Policies that separate children's interests from mothers' – whether in family law, welfare, domestic violence or immigration – result in mothers being penalised and children suffering as a result, Gordon writes. And more, if we understand children to have independent interests that always come first, you end up without any real grounds for keeping a newborn with their mother if a more 'suitable' family wants to take them.

For a long time, mothers who left husbands for other women lost their children if their lesbian relationships were revealed. Across the United States, Canada, Australia and New Zealand, children were taken from Indigenous families to be raised by whites. All these horrors happened in the name of giving children the best possible start in life.

These separations, like the removal of babies from unwed mothers at Mother and Baby Homes, were still going on in the late twentieth century. It's no longer acceptable to tell single mothers – at least those of us with some economic and social stability – that if we really cared for our children we'd have them adopted for their own good. But when courts insist a child is better off with a violent father – or even an unreliable one who will let them down – than without one, the base assumption remains that a single-mother family isn't a proper family at all.

To believe a custody ruling like Beth's upholds the interests of the child rather than the rights of the father, you have to believe children derive such benefit from the influence of a male parent that it's worth whatever disruption he inflicts on the single-mother family unit.

And that doesn't sound very gender neutral.

You have to assume that if a father cannot breastfeed, there are also things men offer our children that we cannot. If only Beth knew what they were, perhaps she could have had the court forbid them.

Of the dozens of custody horror stories I've heard, Beth's is among the worst. But even the most harmonious-looking co-parenting arrangements can conceal feelings of bitter injustice.

Most of us whose exes are involved in our children's lives moan about them cancelling or turning up late, leaving us to deal with our children's life admin while claiming the right to sign off on everything. Or the sinking feeling when his number comes up on your phone just as you're leaving for an evening out – shared parenting evaporating with the first shimmer of fever.

But my friend Chloe doesn't complain about any of these things. Her ex, Stefan, is a reliable and loving father to their son E, who spends every other week with him.

One evening, when both our kids were with their dads, Chloe and I sat down for a glass of wine and a gossip about other men in our lives – a lover I had no time to see, and one she'd thought she would be spending that night with until he cancelled at the last minute. We were laughing at how chaotic this younger man's life seemed for someone with so few responsibilities, and I threw out a comment about how I'd met her ex and he seemed nice.

He is nice. I've met Stefan a few times now. He's charming, in a soft-spoken, self-effacing way.

But I realised Chloe wasn't laughing, she was sobbing. 'I miss E so much,' she said, drawing breath. She didn't know how she would spend the coming week. The cancelled date wasn't such a laughing matter after all. Her married friends were busy with their families, her single mum friends even busier.

If there's a day or two of catching up on housework and sleep, the rest of the week looms hollowly: the house quiet, her motherhood on hold. Chloe doesn't complain much, but this isn't how she imagined family life.

For Stefan, E's conception was an unwelcome shock. He was in his early thirties and not sure he wanted kids. For Chloe, already in her forties, the realisation she was carrying a child came in a flood of euphoric relief. She was too excited to let his dismay tarnish her joy. She was having this baby, no question – and if he didn't want to be involved, she'd go back to Canada, where she had family who'd be as pleased as she was.

She would absolve him of all responsibility.

But Stefan didn't want to be an absent father. So they stayed together and tried to resolve her elation with his ambivalence. She painted the nursery, he skulked into his recording studio. She unpacked shopping bags of baby grows and mobiles, he grumbled about their finances. She talked names and birth plans and read aloud from parenting books. He was silent or changed the subject.

When E arrived, Stefan carried on. With work, his social life, his band. Chloe was happy to put her career on hold. But living parallel lives in the same house – hers utterly transformed and consumed by motherhood, his plodding along much as before – was sad and frustrating. Stefan wasn't even interested in sex.

As the bright shock and blur of the first months of motherhood muted, Chloe decided it was time to go. And she thought Stefan would be relieved. She was looking for a flat in the same neighbourhood and he could see his son as often as he wished – though she suspected this wouldn't be very often, given how little time he spent with him while they were all living together.

But after a couple of days of stunned silence, Stefan told her that if she moved out, he wanted fifty-fifty custody.

E was barely a year old and Chloe's life revolved around his needs. Giving him up for half the week was unthinkable. So she stayed with Stefan for another five years. Under the same roof, looking to all the world like a functional couple but living separate lives.

When Chloe did finally move out, she persuaded Stefan to accept a seventy-thirty split of their child's time, gradually working towards alternate weeks by the time he was seven. Unconsciously echoing the tender years doctrine, Chloe felt this would be a point from which she and her son could both manage living apart.

And they have managed. E is ten now and has a good relationship with his dad. He seems happy splitting his life between two homes. But Chloe still mourns the lonely, sex-less years she felt blackmailed into living with a man who no one has ever said isn't a good father.

I assume that must be important to him – being *a good father.*

Important enough that he was prepared to live with a baby he hadn't wanted. To maintain a loveless pseudo-relationship for six years. Important enough that – now that his father-hood depends on it – he does almost everything Chloe does for their son. But his idea of what it meant be *a good dad* only extended to taking responsibility for his child's day-to-day care when the alternative was the shame of being an *absent father* or *weekend dad.*

Our identities as parents are defined by our active rela-tionships with our children, but they're also defined by social expectations of motherhood and fatherhood. Very often, these align: fathers aren't expected to do much, so they don't.

But just because the role of *father* is ill-defined, amor-phous – no longer head of the household, but yet to roll up its sleeves for the dirty work of mothering – doesn't mean it isn't a powerful identity. In Stefan's case, the identity – *I am a good father* – seems to have transcended any active relation-ship with his child.

The social identity of motherhood is powerful too. Chloe's relationship with her son has always been active and close. But for Stefan to fulfil his idea of fatherhood, she has had to shrink back her mothering to make room.

A father who does half the work is an exceptionally good father. But what does it mean to be a mother who only mothers part time when society expects this to be an all-consuming role?

Chloe doesn't complain much because she knows mothers who have it worse. Like Ginevra, who conceived by a married man who wanted to nothing to do with their daughter, T – until she was three, at which point he confessed to his wife and the couple apparently decided to make embracing his shunned daughter part of their healing process.

Ginevra never had any objection to T having a relationship with her father. But now he's launching a claim on his right to equal standing as T's legal guardian, which will mean Ginevra cannot choose a school for her daughter, approve medical treatment, move house or leave the country without his permission.

She's just praying that shared custody isn't the first step towards shared residency.

T's father has begun visiting her for two hours each week. So far his older children, reeling from the news of a sister they didn't know about, have refused to have her in the house. But if they end up in court, Ginevra fears it is the Kindesvater's household – fractured and volatile as it is, after revelations of his infidelities – that fits the picture of a proper family, not hers.

Ginevra knows – we all know – single mothers are supposed to accept – do accept – impositions and intrusions nuclear families would find unconscionable. And we're expected to do so gracefully, bowing to authorities who know more about what's best for our children than we do.

We know women whose Kindesvaters turned up after years

of absence and claimed custody. Or who whirl in and out of their lives, lavishing attention of their children and then vanishing. And then there are 'stuck mums' like Laura.

Laura grew up in a big extended family and wanted to bring her own kids up among aunties and uncles, cousins and second cousins. And so she had an agreement with her Australian husband that they would return to her native New Zealand before their child started school. But when they split, her Kindesvater decided to stay in Germany, and so, a judge has ruled, that's where Laura and her son must stay too – even though he has moved to a different city and rarely visits.

Taking a child from the country where their father lives without his consent is one of the most dangerous things a single mother can do, because under the Hague Convention on the Civil Aspects of International Child Abduction, it constitutes kidnapping.

The convention was established in 1980 in response to fathers running off with their children and 'the traumatic loss of contact with the parent who has been in charge of [their] upbringing'. But these days, three quarters of Hague cases are against mothers, most of whom have taken their children back to their own home countries, and campaigners say many of these women are fleeing domestic violence.

Hague cases don't consider where a child would be best off – the convention's remit is not to rule on custody arrangements, but to expedite children's return to the countries where custody disputes are fought. But once a mother has been 'Hagued' – branded a kidnapper under international

law – her chances of retaining custody have been dealt an
often-fatal blow.

In theory, if mother and child have good reason to relocate
and the father has little contact anyway, she can apply to the
courts to decide whether the move would be in her child's
best interests. But particularly in countries that favour shared
custody – anecdotally, these include Germany and Sweden –
such requests aren't just routinely dismissed: wanting to put
distance between her child and their father can be enough to
condemn a mother as unfit.

Beth's lawyer advised her that applying to move to Berlin,
let alone back to the States, would almost certainly prompt
her Kindesvater's lawyers to counter by suing for sole custody,
which he would have a very good chance of winning.

The principle at work here is the 'friendly parent test'. If
co-parenting is assumed in children's best interests, then a
parent who shows any resistance to it is on dangerous ground.
And the most devastating way this plays out is in charges of
'parental alienation'.

Parental alienation was first described in 1985 by psychiatrist Richard Gardner, who appeared as an expert witness in
more than four hundred custody cases involving accusations
of child sex abuse.

Gardner wrote much on the subject of child sex abuse,
which he described as an 'ancient tradition' and problematic
only in societies that get 'hysterical' about it. In proven cases
of abuse, Gardner thought the best approach was to keep
families together – which involved dealing with whatever
lack in the mother–child bond that might have contributed

to a child's sexual 'pseudomaturity'. The mother of an abused child was also likely to have 'sexual problems' of her own, he speculated, which she must address and so 'lessen the need for her husband to return to their daughter for sexual gratification.'

But at the same time, Gardner insisted most accusations of child sex abuse were false – and often part of a pattern of abusive behaviour on the part of mothers, resulting in 'parental alienation syndrome'.

Gardner's syndrome – defined as a collection of symptoms exhibited by children 'brainwashed' by one parent to reject the other – has never been accepted by mainstream psychiatry. But that hasn't stopped parental alienation becoming a go-to defence for fathers whose children don't want to live with them, and particularly those accused of domestic violence or child abuse.

And courts take parental alienation accusations very seriously.

A 2019 study of more than two thousand US custody cases found that when a mother accused a father of sexually abusing their child, and he countered with an accusation of parental alienation, she had a two-per-cent chance of being believed. In more than half of such cases, she lost custody of her children altogether.

'When you go to court and you report child sexual abuse by the father, you're done. You're cooked,' the study's author, clinical law professor Joan Meier, told the *Washington Post*.

Until I saw the recent HBO documentary about the custody battle between Mia Farrow and Woody Allen, I had the notion Allen had been tried for abusing his daughter Dylan and found innocent. In fact, the high-profile trial I was aware of but hadn't followed was not a criminal case against Allen but a custody case brought by Allen against Farrow, whom he accused of parental alienation.

Accused of child sex abuse, Allen sued for sole custody of three children with whom he'd never previously lived. Farrow was on the back foot, the onus on her to prove herself a fit mother, under threat of losing her kids to the man she insisted had molested one of them.

The court decided Farrow wasn't guilty of parental alien-ation. But though it called Allen's behaviour towards his daughter 'grossly inappropriate', it rejected allegations of abuse. At which point, further investigation of Allen's alleged crime was dropped to spare Dylan any more trauma.

But mothers aren't only accused of parental alienation in cases involving allegations of abuse. A case study by a psy-chiatrist and founding member of the Parental Alienation Study Group describes how a mother's campaign to alienate her children from their father began long before divorce. This is not a story of a mother or her children telling lies, but of a man who finds his fatherhood untethered when a nuclear family splits.

A young doctor, he 'found work–life balance challenging' and when his wife took responsibility for their home and children he 'assumed this unspoken arrangement was natu-ral'. When they split, he 'was ready to be the parent he knew he was without the overbearing presence of his ex'. But the children 'became distant. After a while, they simply refused to go with him.'

Purporting to illustrate the dynamics of parental alienation, this account fails to pinpoint any malicious behaviour on the mother's part. Her more active parenting becomes sinister only in retrospect. The father 'didn't notice' how small a role he played in his children's lives, until it stopped being a vicarious one contingent on his wife – only then does her 'insidious' power become apparent.

Family courts can be a kind of through-the-looking glass world where gender roles are flipped, twisted and dis-sembled. Mothers keeping house and looking after kids are deviously campaigning to undermine the bonds of the nuclear family. Unpaid drudgery that was resented or avoided is suddenly fought over. Women are banned from breastfeeding and abusers given custody of vulnera-ble children.

Courts like parents to show flexibility. But for fathers, this usually means more time with their children; for mothers it means relinquishing it. And a father claiming his right to a role he's yet to perform can only be judged on his best inten-tions, while a mother's track record, always imperfect, can always be criticised.

Mothers are more likely to say their kids want to stay with them, because children are more likely to be used to their mothers being their primary source of comfort and care. Mothers who do more care are more likely want to move closer to family who can help out. And if accusing the other parent of abuse is an act of aggression, it's a feminised form of aggression because men are more likely to be guilty of these accusations.

Tropes about crazy ex-wives also get plenty of play in

family courts. A Canadian study found that in the language of fathers, judges and expert witnesses, mothers don't just tell lies, they are 'pathological liars'; they don't exaggerate, they become 'hysterical'.

And Lena has an observation she says is common enough to be joked about by divorce lawyers:

> *When mothers appear in court, they take a day off to go to the hairdresser, borrow designer clothes and spend hours on their make-up. They have to look put-together – sane. But the dads grow a two-day beard and make every effort to show they're really suffering.*

Three years on from the shared parenting ruling, Beth says her son still resists going to stay with his father. But neither is her family free of public intrusion, because his father has repeatedly dragged Beth back to court – to try and increase his time with their child, but also for a multitude of minor infractions.

The latest, she says, is an action to sue her for forgetting to pack her son's health insurance card in his overnight bag. 'It was in there,' she says wearily, 'but an hour later I got an email saying he didn't have it and he would be filing a complaint with the court.'

The sheer volume of these proceedings has, Beth says, stolen time she should be spending focused on her son – and forced her to give up a job she loved for a lower-paid, part-time position:

> *I deal with this stuff every single day. I work on it while I'm on the toilet. I go through paperwork in bed because I can't*

*sleep anyway, and I'm on it as soon as I get up in the morning. I have to get advice about everything, so I don't say or do anything that could be used against me. I see a psychologist for this issue, which also takes time. But the courts can never know about the psychologist because that could be used against me too.*

Advocates for victims of domestic abuse call campaigns to crush women under the financial, emotional and logistical weight of relentless legal action 'procedural stalking' or 'paper abuse'. And very often, a mother's mental health is the target – in every sense – of these attacks.

Forced deeper and deeper into debt, trying to maintain a sense of stability in a household she knows may not survive her next looming court date in one piece, a mother suffering this kind of coercive control has to keep it together for the kids – but also to defend against accusations that she's not mentally fit to care for them.

And more, to pass the friendly parent test, she not only has to pretend the abuse isn't getting to her – she must maintain the illusion it isn't abuse at all.

The courts began to look more favourably on Beth – allowing her to take her son to the States for two weeks to visit family – after she hired a coach who specialises in preparing women to present themselves as the kind of mother family courts find sympathetic.

Following her coach's advice, Beth stopped submitting expert opinions from medical professionals testifying to the harm the co-parenting arrangement was doing her child – which the court had anyway dismissed – and instead extolled the importance of her son's bond with his father and how committed she was to nurturing it.

And she told the court she'd got engaged to her boyfriend: whatever you do, the coach had told her, try not to look like a single mum.

Beth tells her story with the detached precision of someone who has had to make her case countless times, in terms that reduce years of tolerating the intolerable to a logbook of evidence. And I listen wondering how she's resisted running away. Going into hiding. Or *something*.

But really, I know: this is her son's life, this is her life. This is how they must live. In some scenario where Beth was suffering alone, perhaps she might risk everything and flee. But the worst consequences for her child are too much to gamble on.

If she recounts these injustices coolly, I don't imagine she feels them less acutely than the first night she left her son with his father – only the shock has dulled. And yet, when she describes how interested the court was in her boyfriend – his background, job, whether he might have family ties abroad – her voice takes on a new crackle of rage: 'I mean, my boyfriend – he has *nothing* to do with what kind of mother I am.'

If officials judge Beth's fitness as a mother on her relationships with the men in her life – her willingness to accommodate her Kindesvater, the stable home they imagine depends on her boyfriend – the same cannot be said of the father's fitness.

Through years of institutional interference in her family life, Beth says the *Jugendamt* has made only one oblique reference to the harassment she's suffered – in a statement that didn't criticise her Kindesvater's conduct directly but asserted that a social worker had advised him that violence isn't good for children.

And in this sense, Beth's case is not exceptional.

Family courts frequently dismiss domestic abuse as a problem within the couple dynamic that should not impact a father's right to access his child. As if you can terrorise the person your child has yet to unfurl from as an independent self, and still be called a *good father*.

My own Kindesvater shouted and punched holes in walls but I never felt in physical danger until he broke into my apartment. His rage that night was fuelled by drink and jealousy, and it was unleashed on the door I had closed between him and what had been his home.

As the wood splintered, my fear wasn't rational, in that I didn't think through what he'd do once he got in and consciously conclude that this time he'd hurt me. It was a primal fear, a high panic in my chest, a cold rush across my skin as every muscle readied to fight or flee. As soon as his boot appeared, his contorted face, hands tearing out panels, I called the police.

But the difference between my Kindesvater attacking my home and Beth's attacking hers, is that in my case it was a one-off. For Beth, the assaults on her home, on her car, her boyfriend's car, were part of a sustained campaign of intimidation that kept her in a constant state of anxiety.

For other women, many women, there is no front door between them and their aggressor. The muscle-tingling readiness for the worst is alive in their intimate space. But the moment that door closes is when the danger peaks. As anyone who works with victims of domestic violence will tell you, men who are violent to women are at their most violent when women leave them.

When Greece passed automatic shared custody legislation in 2021, a piece on the progressive, left-leaning openDemocracy website gave 'three cheers' to the right-wing government that pushed it through, for bringing an end to 'sexist' court decisions that allowed vengeful women to 'weaponise' their children – even as Human Rights Watch warned that the new law was a disaster for vulnerable women and children.

Where shared custody is automatic from the moment a couple splits, women fleeing violence are legally obliged to have contact with their abusers precisely when the danger is most acute. They cannot hide. They cannot take their children to a secret location because custodial parents have a right to know where their children live.

Until they have endured a months-long legal process to prove abuse – which is often impossibly difficult – these women must hand their children over to the men they're trying to escape, or risk losing them altogether.

When the frustrations and injustices contained with a nuclear family detonate, it must reconfigure across different homes, bonds must be reshaped across different axes, into a new constellation that works for everyone, and most of all for the children. And often, parents must cooperate to achieve this elusive goal in a climate of searing hurt and anger.

The problem family courts face is that for all broad trends

and likelihoods – women are more likely to be primary parents than men, men are more likely to be violent than women, and so on – there are always exceptions. Every family is its own private ecosystem, nothing can be assumed and no default – shared custody, favouring primary parents – is ideal in every case.

Pretending male parenting and female parenting are interchangeable isn't fair, and nor is perpetuating the inequalities of the nuclear family in its afterlife. You cannot achieve fairness by splitting a child down the middle as if they were property, or by assuming their interests occupy some dynamic midpoint between those of two warring parents.

Shifts from paternal supremacy to the tender years doctrine to shared custody are a series of flawed responses to changing ideas about mothering, fatherhood and bigger questions about gender. In this sense, the current pretence of family courts to gender-neutrality is a measure of prevailing norms in the twenty-first century. It says we broadly respect women's right to leave marriages they are unhappy in, and it reflects the notion that we live in a post-feminist world where gender equality is a given.

But, as a UN paper puts it, in assuming 'a level playing field' family courts 'do not generally take into account the unequal power dynamics in gendered relations, particularly in the family'. And in what realm of the post-feminist world are female and male roles still so dimorphic as family?

What aspect of life remains as heavily gendered as parenting?

If fathers are not, as is often assumed, routinely discriminated against in family courts, the fathers' rights movement can be seen instead as an embodiment of threatened masculinity: men livid at losing the privileges of 'traditional' family norms.

Their campaigns are a collective howl of the of violent rage some men inflict on women who leave them, articulated as a generalised misogynist attack on all single mothers, would-be single mothers and the institutions these men claim act in our privileged interest – all cloaked in the language of gender-progressive equal rights. But like woolly notions of fairness, the discourse of rights is of limited use in this context.

Because mothers don't have rights, we have responsibilities.

When men fight for the right to be active parents, and particularly when they do so in organised political campaigns, what they don't acknowledge is that this is a choice. Fathers' rights flow from actively choosing to take responsibility for their children. How much responsibility a mother takes isn't a choice – or not one she can make herself. It's a choice made by a father, to claim a degree of responsibility, or none at all.

And a mother's responsibilities are not just to her child, but for fatherhood itself. A father's role in making a woman a mother is over in seconds, but she is responsible for his fatherhood while she carries his child through pregnancy, while she cares for his child in a shared home – and then she is responsible for nurturing his fatherhood into a different, more active relationship after they split.

For helping him fill up his side of the whiteboard.

Mothers are responsible for soothing and cajoling children who don't want to spend time with their fathers. For making space for fathers who choose to be in our children's lives, and filling that space again if they choose differently in future.

And that last-ditch responsibility, knowing the buck always stops with you, is very different from a role you opt into at will.

A Swedish study on the impacts of fifty-fifty custody said the model had advanced the 'gender revolution' women launched when we started working outside the home.

For all the achievements of Nordic women's liberation, Swedish women still do more unpaid domestic labour than Swedish men and fathers still only take thirty per cent of parental leave. But more than half of separating parents now adopt a fifty-fifty shared parenting model and the gap between the number of days separated mothers and fathers take off work to look after sick kids is closing.

And so, the authors conclude, 'we believe that what we are in fact observing is that these fathers are taking on the final, most stubborn, stage of the gender revolution'.

I can relate to the experience of revolution in the aftermath of nuclear family. Mothering in a dysfunctional partnership, and redefining my motherhood beyond it, made me rethink deeply held assumptions about love, sex, relationships, family, autonomy, dependence, responsibility and care. So much so, I have the revolutionary zeal to write a whole book about it.

But what use is a revolution that mothers and fathers must fight behind the closed doors of family homes and court-rooms, again and again, replicating the same bitter struggles and casualties?

We need a post-nuclear family revolution on a societal

level. A revolution in how we do mothering and fatherhood, in work and care, how we share domestic labour, is long overdue. It's the sphere in which feminism has made the least progress, and the core inequality that's stalled the progress we have made in work, politics, love and sex.

The gender revolution cannot be confined to the private lives of individual families, and it won't come by supposing gender equality already exists. It'll come only when society as a whole – not just individual mothers in miserable relationships – seriously questions the supremacy of the nuclear model and gives single-mother families our due as the most popular alternative around.

# Chapter 4

# Capitalism Hates Mums

*He was a very difficult baby. He had really bad colic and cried for hours every day. It made me feel like a failure. Like, it's my job to make this person happy and I'm just not doing it. I felt my baby hated me. And I felt so guilty because, you know, everybody's like, 'Isn't it so great? You should enjoy this time, he'll never be this small again.' But I needed to get out and do things to feel like a normal person, you know, and not just this twenty-four-seven life support system that you become.*

*My husband slept in the guest room every night and I slept with the baby every night. And I was just constantly on, you know? It was constantly my job because we kind of fell into these very conservative mother/father roles. I felt like I had no identity anymore besides this milk machine.*

*Postnatal depression is just like a sense of disillusionment with everything. Not being able to enjoy anything at all with the baby. Just the thought of getting up would make me really mad at him. I even spanked him a couple of times when he was little because I just lost control and was really upset. I feel so horrible about that – I mean, if I heard of anyone doing that I'd call it child abuse. But I felt so desperate and there was just no relief.*

*And I tried to talk to my husband about it. I said, 'I feel like I'm gonna have a nervous breakdown.' And at some point he got tired of hearing it. He was like, 'You're not allowed to say this anymore, I don't ever want to hear you say that again.'*

*It was kind of horrifying how things went, how somebody I felt I could be so close with became a complete stranger.*

*The whole separation really destabilised me a lot and I ended up having to go into hospital for five weeks. I was admitted because I was hearing voices telling me that I should kill myself. And that's when I was diagnosed with borderline personality disorder. I think the stress and the postnatal depression brought it out.*

— MEGHAN

When women become mothers, we necessarily give parts of ourselves to our children. In pregnancy, we make space for another living being within us, our bodies prioritising the needs of this almost-other. It can be hard to know if you're one person or two.

When F was born, I was startled at how complete she was – a sudden, whole self all of her own. But to her, still feeling out the boundaries of her self, I was still an extension of her. And our metabolisms were still conjoined: my motherly body, the mass I'd gained during her gestation, diminishing as she fattened up at my breast. And as far as we were now physically distinct, emotionally our bond was ever-more intense.

Enmeshing so tightly, this incomparable connection to another can be euphoric. But it can also feel like a destabilising challenge to your autonomous identity.

Or both.

And in an experience so transformative, does the consuming identity of *mother* erase the person you used to be? Are you both? Or – if find you cannot fully inhabit the notions of motherhood you've been raised on – neither?

I was lucky. F was an easy baby. In the hungry early hours, the world was quiet and still and all ours. When she slept I curled round her, dozing or with a book. It didn't matter what time of day it was because there was only one place I was supposed to be and that was with her. Having been at a chronic loose end in life, overworked and unfulfilled, I liked the clear responsibilities of those early days.

I was ripe for motherhood because I wasn't very happy with the self I was.

The pressure of working life had been intense. Not just to produce, but to find meaning in production. As a journalist, I was filing stories I didn't have the time or resources to research deeply. Newspapers want things fast. But churning out reports that skimmed the surface of huge events didn't feel meaningful. And it was all I did. So I didn't really know who I was.

And then, I was F's mum. What a lovely, clear identity. So human. And what a relief that it wasn't all about me anymore. Existential questions were, for the moment, settled.

One day, while F was sleeping and I was doing laundry, Cara called for advice about a story she was working on. Stuffing the washing machine with one hand, I suggested dividing her material into two separate reports, which made her think of an entirely different approach. We bounced ideas back and forth till she told me she really had to get on.

'How are you though?' she asked with a note of concern.

I looked at the laundry strewn across the floor and returned to the question I'd been occupied with when the phone rang. 'I'm well,' I said, 'but can I just ask you one thing – do you think it's OK to put towels with shit on them in the same wash as non-shitty towels?'

Cara was pleased to say she had no expertise in this matter. But I was just as pleased not to have to get dressed, meet a deadline, talk to anyone I didn't want to talk to.

It was a hot summer. I walked along the Landwehrkanal with F strapped to my chest, spread out a rug to cuddle and bounce on. Or, craning over her sleeping body, I studied from a great brick of an economics textbook propped up on a cafe table, careful not to detach her mouth from my nipple as I turned each page.

By the end of that year, I'd started writing for an online publication that paid next to nothing but was relaxed about deadlines and let me write at length. I annoyed some of the people I interviewed for these stories, when I had to cancel calls or cut them short, because the Kindesvater wasn't home that day after all, or F woke up howling. But others kept talking for hours – or as long as a nap lasted – and recommended further reading, ways to delve deeper.

Everyone should get maternity leave, I thought. You shouldn't have to have a baby to get a paid sabbatical, to step out of the rush of life, regroup and take each day as if achieving any more than eating, sleeping and keeping on top of laundry is a bonus.

Like I said, I was lucky.

A few years later, I'm working and Cara calls me from her own maternity leave. She'd been looking forward to slowing down too. But the shock of it is more than she bargained for. Not just the change of pace, but the confinement. It's winter, and when you're not at work, when life revolves around life itself, seasons are important.

'We cannot spend another day shut up in this mess,' she growls. 'I can't even take him to a cafe because people on laptops give us the evils. We can only hang out in freezing bloody playgrounds . . .

'I want to go back to work,' she adds doubtfully.

I was working even as the state paid me to stay at home and focus on my baby because I needed more intellectual stimulation than a baby can provide. Cara felt drawn back to the office because there was no space for her mothering.

A full year of parental leave – on benefits we could actually survive on – was a major factor in my decision to stay in Germany when I realised I was pregnant. I can't imagine how mothers in the States cope without it. But it's a moment of suspended reality. Cut off from the rest of life. And mostly confined to home, which is precisely the place women have fought so hard to escape.

Visiting Lena to talk to her about her work on single-mother rights, she opens the door dressed like the slick professional she is. A lawyer in a silk shirt. She has a pot of tea ready in the front room, where boxes of toys are stacked under the bay windows. We discuss gendered bias in German family courts. She fills me in on legal history and the evolution of the fathers' rights movement. And also, her own custody battle.

Her husband left her for another woman shortly after she gave birth to twins, and he fought for sole custody of all three of their children on the grounds that her postnatal depression made her an unfit mother.

Lena is a data protection lawyer at the top of her field. As well as *Mütterinitiative für Alleinerziehende*, she is a founding member of another non-profit organisation that finds expert witnesses for complex legal cases. She's also the single mother of three primary-school-aged children, one of whom has both Down's syndrome and autism.

And her hair is perfect.

But before I leave, I push open her kitchen door to put our cups away. She hates it when I say this – she'd done a frantic tidy before I arrived and I 'wasn't supposed to see the kitchen' – but for all Lena's insights and openness, just as valuable was the image I committed to memory of that little kitchen. Every surface piled with dirty dishes, sink full, bin overflowing onto grubby laminate flooring.

A kitchen just like mine.

A woman's worth is no longer measured by her domestic prowess. It's hard even to imagine Lena-in-silk scrubbing at stained lino. But if we're not supposed to be house-proud, we can still be house-shamed. If you're a welfare mum being investigated by social services, domestic disorder can be acutely dangerous. And even for a high-powered lawyer, it suggests the rhythms of domestic life have spun dangerously out of your control.

It's more acceptable, these days, for women to be a bit slutty in how we dress or fuck around. But a mother who's a slut in the original sense of the word – having lax domestic rather than sexual standards – is failing in her most basic responsibilities.

It's easy to say, 'Oh I'm so busy, my house is a tip!' but when friends appear at my door unexpectedly, I feel horribly exposed. The disorder is shameful evidence of a particularly maternal crime: not coping.

There was a time, though, when to open the door to a woman's home was not to lay bare her most intimate sins, but to glimpse a bustling locus of real life. A time when work and care weren't so strictly compartmentalised and mothering was just part of what everyone was busy doing.

In the dark old days of feudal Europe, the home wasn't just the heart of family but the heart of industry. Grain was ground, bread baked, meals shared, yarn spun, clothes tailored. Making and mending were done by the same hands, under the same roof. And whole cycles of human life revolved through one another too. Children and grandparents, infants and the dying, young men and women yet to be wed.

The transition from feudalism to capitalism split industry from the domestic, productive work from reproductive labour. Men produced things that could be sold. With households no longer supported by collective labours, home and family were something men paid for with their individual wages.

And something bought is something owned.

Women's role was to nourish, heal and revive. To provide the mulch of care in which everything else was rooted. Labours against the entropy of life – cleaning, setting to order what will unravel, filling bellies soon hungry again, birthing and nourishing mortal bodies – can be invisible precisely because they never end.

But also because they happen behind closed doors.

As boundaries came down between public and private life, between work and care, so communal lands were also enclosed. Meadows, woods and rivers that had been open for anyone to graze, hunt and fish, became private property.

Care was privatised. But so was society's ecological base.

And the texture of time changed. Fallow months were no longer times of rest, but of stagnation and unemployment. Childhood and old-age became the dog-ends of a productive life.

This wasn't a peaceful transition, but marked by what Silvia Federici describes in *Caliban and the Witch*, her account of the European witch hunts, as a genocide against women.

Communal celebrations and rites that celebrated nature came under attack and sexuality was oppressed. Pressure to marry intensified. In England, hosting an unwed mother in your home became a crime, and in Germany it was illegal for women to live alone, or together without a man in the house. In France, all pregnancies had to be registered and if they didn't result in a child being presented for baptism, the mother could be put to death.

It wasn't feudal lords who were targeted in the overthrow

of the old order, so much as impulses – irrational, communal, wild, sexual – that were incompatible with an emerging economic system based on private property and waged labour, the control of time and space by capital.

Men were guilty of these unruly impulses too, and men too were burned as witches. But the divisions being cut through society cast them as essentially female forces.

Capitalism's gendered rupture of society still rules our lives to this day. Still, reproductive work – not just birthing and raising children, but cooking, cleaning, looking after those who cannot work, holding families together, mending, listening, soothing, cleaning up the mess – isn't real work.

The gender pay gap isn't so much a gap between men's wages and women's. It's between waged labour and work that isn't paid at all. And these days, the pay gap between mothers and women without children is bigger than the pay gap between women and men.

Now, Cara's gone back to work. And she went for a promotion. The interview was supposed to be a formality so she went in confidently, talking about projects she was excited to manage, skills she could bring from her years of experience.

But also, at the end, she mentioned that as a mother she wanted the security of a full-time role. She'd applied for a managerial position as an ambitious journalist, as an accomplished and respected employee, as a mother and as a breadwinner. And she said as much.

Afterwards, she got two phone calls. A human resources

officer advised her, for future reference, never to mention her motherhood in a job interview. And her boss ticked her off for citing security as a motivation.

We know mothers are discriminated against in the workplace. We know we're not supposed to talk about our children in job interviews. But Cara's boss knew Cara had a young child, and we know she knows the responsibilities of being a working mother, because she has a young child too.

As a mother, you're supposed to put your child first, always. Professional life is a privilege that mustn't impinge on mothering. And at work, you must prove you've earned the privilege of working by quietly accommodating mothering around it in your 'free' time.

At work, you must pretend your only motivation to work is work itself. Waged work, that is. Because the work you do at home isn't work. It isn't work, so it doesn't need pay. As in, it isn't paid, but also, you're not supposed to admit you're working to support your family.

Mothering is a huge amount of work, which you should keep quiet about because everyone knows it's probably not going to leave you space to do your job properly. But also, it isn't work at all. It's nothing. Or nothing your employers should have to know about. Because responsibility for people, families, children – life – was severed from work a long time ago. It's a private matter. It's care.

And work doesn't care.

That's what mothers are for.

We know Cara's boss knows what managing this charade is like. She must do. In fact, she must be managing it so well, cutting herself so cleanly in two, she hasn't just left her mothering at home, she's left whatever part of her might articulate her own struggle to do it all – that might recognise that struggle as more than a private matter – shut up somewhere too.

In the Hoover closet, perhaps. A cupboard you slam the door on quickly so the mess doesn't disgorge.

Now that women's identities are defined at least as much by our professional status as domestic roles, a year out of the workplace, having to go part-time or juggle the double shift, can threaten things central to your sense of who you are.

But at the same time, the messy, connected experience of birthing and caring for children – mothering itself – can undermine deep-rooted ideas of what it means to be fully *one, in and of her self.*

When Western culture erected barriers between the domestic and industry, female lives and male ones, a new kind of self began to emerge. A free individual no longer defined by his relationships to others.

The Enlightenment reimagined man as a lone hero. Master of his own destiny. A detached observer of the world. Man became distinct from nature, mind distinct from body. His rational, thinking will was what elevated him above the rest of creation.

These new ideas upended the social order. No longer defined by his God-given place in a hierarchal social order, man's relationships to others became something he entered into of his own free will, and in his own self-interest.

This was called the social contract.

A citizen submits to the powers of the state in exchange for peace, security and prosperity. A worker exchanges muscle and time for cash. And – in theory at least – if the relationship isn't working for both parties, the contract becomes void. A new government elected. A new job sought.

But women didn't really meet the Enlightenment definition of what it meant to be a proper person. Women's lives were shaped by forces of nature that ran right through their being. In their wild multiplication, the boundaries of the female self blurred.

The mother–child bond isn't rational or self-interested. There's no social contract between a mother and her baby: once you've given birth to a child, you kinda have to look after it. And if a woman's bond to her child was formed in the flesh, her relationship to their father – should he choose to acknowledge it – was bonded into her body too. And just as immutable.

So women didn't get a social contract. They just had marriage: a contract that explicitly erased a woman's autonomous identity. Hereditary rule of society was going out of style. But families were stuck with feudal relations of power.

The kind of men who overturned Roe v. Wade still see women as bits of nature they claim as their own when they impregnate us with boundary-shattering life. But they're not the only ones.

A new mother posts in a women's Facebook group about a dilemma she's in knots over. Night feeds mean she's hardly getting any sleep. A cup of warm, milky coffee in the morning sharpens her senses enough to connect with a new day. But her partner says she shouldn't be consuming caffeine while she's breastfeeding.

He's vetoed this precious treat.

Much of her post covers her research into the effects of caffeine in breast milk, and insisting the coffee in question is a very weak one. She's convinced it isn't doing the baby any harm. But she doesn't feel she has the right to unilaterally decide what 'our' child ingests.

'I really want us to be equal as parents,' she writes.

We want to be equal as parents – women who have children with men. You even see couples announce, 'We're pregnant!' Pictures of beaming women, with their beaming men's hands on their bulging bellies.

Like the post about coffee – 'When he grows a pair (of tits) he can decide what to put in his own body!' – these announcements elicit howls of indignation. 'Do you have to squeeze a watermelon-sized person out of your lady-hole?' as Mila Kunis put it on *Jimmy Kimmel Live*.

What it reminds me of is how my mother describes preparing me for my sister's birth. Worried I'd be jealous when her attention was divided, she told me the baby in her tummy was my baby. When my sister arrived, I doted on her, calling Mummy to feed my baby when she cried.

But I was two. We shouldn't have to make-believe equality with grown men.

It might seem harmless. After a long history of fathers treating the physical aspects of mothering as ungodly witchcraft that might wither their manhood if they got too close, it's nice they want to be involved. But it's not just our wombs that make room for new life, not just our breasts that nourish it.

These couples who become a single entity in pregnancy – when they say, 'we're going to share night feeds' or 'we're both going to take time off work' do they mean these things in the same way they mean 'we're pregnant'?

I've heard newly single mums say it wasn't the unequal division of labour they couldn't live with, so much as going through the seismic transformations of new motherhood while their men just pootled along as they'd always done.

This in itself, this imperviousness, can make us despise them.

But if, in pregnancy, birth, in the dyadic bonding of early motherhood and confinement of maternity leave, we change in ways they that they do not and aspirations of equality slide out of view, we'd at least like them to bear witness. To help us weave who we used to be with who we are now. To affirm that we do still exist as individuals in our own right.

Instead, too often, these men take still more of us than our children do.

I began this project because I wanted to read a history of mothers who'd avoided this entanglement with men, but the book I was looking for didn't seem to exist. And I shushed the voice that said there was perhaps an obvious reason it hadn't been written.

Until, one dark February morning a few months before my deadline, I found a creditor's demand for three thousand euros in my mailbox. And the whole precarious balance of my life came crashing down.

A single mum *has* to earn a living. She *has* to mother her child. She doesn't *have* to write a book.

It took a few days for the reality of this to sink in. And then I got a message from an old friend who's also a writer. A self-professed feminist. And the father of a young child. And, he'd recently published a book of his own.

He asked how mine was going. I said it was on the back burner. That I'd have to push the deadline. I didn't know how far. I was feeling sorry for myself. He cheered me on. 'Don't give up! Keep burning that midnight oil!'

He'd had to get his book done in eight months, around a teaching job. I asked him how he'd managed, and he talked about whisky-fuelled all-nighters in a 'man cave'.

Under closer questioning, he admitted his marriage was finished. 'If you had to choose between me and the book, what would you choose?' his wife would ask him. The writer was incensed at this 'false choice'.

'She never forgave me for devoting myself single-mindedly to the book,' he told me.

As a writer, he expected me to relate. But I'm writer second and a mother first. Always a mother first: I think that's what his wife was getting at. I don't think she was asking him to give up the book. I think she was asking: is there something that comes before the book? Before the creative drive? Before *I am a writer*? If you *had* to choose, would you make the only choice a mother can make?

*Single-minded* is precisely what mothers don't get to be. Our attention split, our identities kaleidoscoping. To achieve focus is always to neglect something. To steal back the parts of ourselves incorporated into others. The child still yet to gather a distinct self of her own. The partner whose independent identity depends on your time and labours.

I imagine the writer's wife wanted to know that in enmeshing into family, she'd become part of something greater than herself. That there were parts of her husband that equally belonged to her.

A lot of us, women as much as men, believe that with the right person, compromises won't feel like sacrifices. But mothering dispels the myth that love does the work so you don't have to.

Love itself, it turns out, engenders work.

And the kind of love that compels us to couple up, and the kind of love that sustains us through that work can be quite different.

In the old days, love was considered a far too fickle and frivolous basis for the life-long partnership of marriage. The point was to pick a reliable partner for the joint enterprise of family life. Someone honest, hard-working, well-resourced and pleasant to get on with. And, through familiarity, patience and common cause, affection would, hopefully, grow.

It takes a much more individualistic mindset to come up the idea of a soulmate. Someone you stay faithful to for life not because *them's the rules*, but because they are *The One*. Someone so special they stand out from all others and who, in turn, sees your unique and immutable self with perfect clarity.

Someone spiritually committed to the project of you doing you.

My hard-drinking writer friend said a woman who framed their domestic struggles in terms of a choice between his driving ambition and family was 'not the woman for me'. The choice then, was one she made, by not being able to love him in the way he needed to be loved.

Modern romance – love as a transcendent force, to which we dedicate the kind of verse once reserved for religious worship and imbue with similar powers of transformation and salvation – owes much to medieval tales of courtly love. But these stories of star-crossed lovers were all about adulterous affairs, unrequited passions, unrealised potential.

Europeans began to wed for love in the eighteenth century. But it was the Victorians who really got carried away with marriage as both the spiritual union of two fated souls and the sturdy, nurturing family unit at the heart of a healthy, prosperous society.

And the Victorians thought a lot of things – about families, mothering, gender – that were pretty problematic. But then they had a lot going on, what with the fallout from the Enlightenment still reshaping the entire social and economic order.

The Age of Reason precipitated the French Revolution, which tore down monarchy and declared the Rights of Man, on the basis of the social contract.

It didn't say anything about the rights of women. But women did.

Mary Wollstonecraft insisted that women were rational, thinking beings too. A social order built on reason, she argued, could no longer call half the population inferior and deny them full citizenship rights.

Less well-remembered is Olympe de Gouges, a single mum

who arrived in Paris as revolution was fomenting and has been called the first European thinker to assert a universal concept of human rights. Insisting that people of colour, women – and even children – had rights too, de Gouges called for the abolition of both slavery and marriage.

Most Enlightened men were having none of it, of course. They insisted such women weren't proper women at all, but mannish abominations or uppity, weak-minded whores. The First French Republic sent de Gouges to the guillotine, and Wollstonecraft's affairs and mothering of an illegitimate child obscured her reasoned arguments in scandal. But they voiced things a lot of people were thinking: questions that could only be answered – or shushed – with new ideas about gender.

Under the old feudal order, women hadn't been thought of as very different from men: they just occupied a lower rung of the hierarchy. But as essentialist hierarchies lost legitimacy, so women were increasingly defined not as inferior, so much as ostensibly equal but fundamentally different.

Qualities of selflessness, compassion and dependence coagulated as essentially female; independence, rationality and assertiveness as male. Women weren't subjugated but protected. They weren't demeaned, they were celebrated for their gentle pity.

The Age of Reason also brought the Industrial Revolution. And these new ideas about gender played a vital role in the new economic order too.

With industry turbo-charged by fossil fuels, there were ever-more opportunities for male striving and greed. And feminising the human empathy that might have kept these impulses in check allowed capitalism to fully exploit these opportunities. Women still belonged in the home. Care was still a private matter. And so compassion, generosity and self-sacrifice could also be shut away from industry and public life.

If capitalism arrived on the scene in a whirlwind of violent misogyny, the Victorian era was one of those moments when the abuser has a moment of clarity. Capitalism hates women. But it needs us. And so femininity was love-bombed with praise for its higher moral values.

As cotton mills whirred, amassing wealth for a new capitalist class, fed by slavery in far-off lands and tortuous labour in British factories, notions of femininity reached ludicrous extremes. The Victorian True Woman, pious, pure and selfless in her perfect dedication to home and family, was a kind of spiritual counterweight to all this aggressive, masculinised expansion and accumulation.

In *Marriage, a History: How Love Conquered Marriage*, historian Stephanie Coontz writes:

> Writers on domesticity across Europe and the United States held that women could exert a unique and sorely needed role in the public world through their influence at home. Only a wife could combat the businessman's tendency to close his ears to 'the voices of conscience' as he competed in the struggle for 'worldly aggrandisement.' But a wife could do this only if she herself stood apart from the pressures of competitive capitalism. Keeping a woman in the home guaranteed that someone in the family would uphold the higher ideals of life ...

... Even some of the most sincere admirers of women, including many women themselves, believed that although they were exceptionally virtuous in personal matters, they did not have sufficient reasoning powers to deal with issues of public morality, such as political and economic reform.

Human nature was rent apart and marriage was where two broken parts were made whole. A wife was the sentimental heart of the home, her husband its head. But the head must always rule the heart and so irrational whims of feminised compassion could be indulged or ignored according to cool masculine reason.

And more, by making morality women's business, society's ethical failings were, essentially, female failings. As the lower classes underwent mass urbanisation – rural communities pulled in by the demand for bodies to work the factories, crowded into unsanitary slums – infant mortality soared. But blame fell not on factory owners and slumlords so much as mothers.

If caring for children was women's responsibility, women were at fault when they died.

Another female archetype, the lady philanthropist, overflowing with soft-hearted pity, toured tenements, lecturing working-class mothers on cleanliness and childcare. Breastfeeding was central to these campaigns. Long disdained by those wealthy enough to have someone else do it for them, the bond at the breast was now increasingly seen as a spiritual expression of motherly love, which Victorian ladies took great pride in. Then, as now, it was symbolic of an idealised femininity that working-class mothers needed lecturing on.

The Victorian lady could exercise her higher moral character by pleading with her husband for restraint, or she could dedicate herself to charity that tried to ameliorate the damage done when he ignored her pleas. But her most important influence on society was mothering itself. And, since all men were now, supposedly, born equal, this was fantastically important.

Enlightenment thought made childhood a special, protected phase of life. Early experiences inscribed on the blank slate of the newborn mind shaped a person's intellect and moral character. So mothering wasn't just about the physical and emotional care of children; a good mother embodied the gentle, nurturing and humane environment within which innocent babes developed into morally healthy members of society.

Mothers weren't just to blame when their children died, they were to blame when their children grew up to be the kind of men who worked child labourers to death.

Writing as she awaited execution, de Gouges declared that history would vindicate her. I doubt she expected it to take so long. French women didn't get the vote for a century and a half after she was executed.

But we did get full citizenship rights, eventually.

We've won rights to participate in public life. We can be proper people, rather than just proper women. We've gained the right to live like men, instead of like mothers.

But when we do become mothers, those rights can look

pretty flimsy. The awesome responsibilities of mothering remain – and they remain enclosed in a domestic space shut off from *real* life, neutered of productive power and economically dependent on work done elsewhere.

How society resolves the need for both productive and reproductive labour, for work *and* care, is still a private matter. To be resolved behind closed doors. Between exhausted couples.

Or within the psyches and daily workloads of individual women.

We're supposed to have it all these days. Which sounds a lot like capitalism turning up on our doorstep with more flattery and flowers. Because *having* it all sounds great. But *doing* it all is exhausting.

And *being* it all can leave you wondering if you're anyone at all.

The life of a 'working mother' isn't just a double shift of performing two roles at once. It's a kind of split-personality madness. We must be homemakers and breadwinners. Selfless and strident. Gentle and assertive. Carers and careerists. Connected and independent. Rational and emotional. Keep house and make successes of ourselves in the real world.

And still, there's no madder witch than the single mum, who lays these contradictions bare.

The myth that fathers now pull their weight around the house allows partnered mothers to preserve the hush around reproductive work. If they work hard enough, if they cut back on sleep or can pay for help, they can pass in the workplace.

And perhaps if Cara hadn't stressed her triple role as

journalist, mother *and* breadwinner, the interview panel could have assumed her family's economic security was irrelevant because her partner was taking care of it.

But single mothers have nowhere to hide.

If every working mother fears she's not performing either role well enough, single mothers know everyone knows we can't. We feel under constant watch for the inevitable signs of the weakness, the insanity, of breaking society's last refuge of cooperation and care – and not coping.

About a year into my single motherhood, I made a terrible parenting decision that also went against all my political impulses. I sent F to a private preschool.

She was suffering from an anxiety disorder I thought this privileged institution – which espoused individualised, child-focused learning and diversity – would be better able to deal with than the ordinary local school. So I wrenched her away from her family-like local kindergarten to a glossy building in the centre of Berlin whose walls were papered with slogans about respect.

She hated it.

Each morning, I had to tear her weeping body from mine at the classroom door. My own tears, held down in her presence, would overflow as soon as I turned my back. I became intimately familiar with the motivational posters – *If you think my hands are full, you should see my heart!* – in the adult loo, where I dragged toilet paper across smeared mascara before heading to the office.

And far from adapting to her 'special needs', the preschool was failing her on tests she couldn't perform because of them.

As months wore on, my anxiety climbing, F's dulling to a persistent state of withdrawal, it became clear the place at the private school I'd been tacitly assured of wasn't going to materialise, and we wouldn't want it anyway.

So I called a meeting with the preschool's two headteachers. I wanted them to think twice about taking on another child whose needs they couldn't accommodate.

The meeting took two hours and I never got my complaint in. It was my anger they focused on, not the cause of it. My anger, and my tears: those messy mornings had been observed, they told me. And the cause of all this unbound emotion was clear: *I was not coping*.

They said F looked happier on the rare occasions her father picked her up. That I needed to involve him more in her life. That in their professional opinion, my child showed all the signs of not being properly cared for at home.

I met their accusations with measured arguments in my defence – to which they did not respond. Each time I spoke, they silently locked eyes with one another. With weighty stares, wry smiles or raised eyebrows.

That year, the year of the private preschool, still finding my feet as a single mum, trying to mitigate the impact of her father raging in and out of our lives, trying to keep F's spirits up, scrabbling for scheduling solutions, trying to sleep at night, trying not to fall asleep on the train, trying to focus at work, trying not to pour a second glass of wine, were all just *coping*.

Or, *just* coping.

Walking away from the shiny building with its shiny slogans, I was afraid to go home and be swept under by my failure to cope with having picked a fight and lost. And I felt something else tugging at my sanity. As a journalist, why had I not had the presence of mind to switch on my phone's voice recorder and document this attack? Not so much to hold them to account but because I feared I would not believe myself. That I'd fall into the madness of distrusting my own memory.

The next day I called Emily, who sympathised with me going through this alone. If I'd had a partner there, she said, I wouldn't have needed the recording. I would have had a witness to confirm, to validate, my experience. Only then did it occur to me that if I'd had a partner at my side, in the room or even at home, at work, offstage but on the scene, a man to validate my motherhood, to validate F and me as a family, it wouldn't have happened at all.

The hatchet was ruthlessly well-aimed. Failing a child with special needs is a serious matter, and friends urged me to escalate it. But I dropped my complaint. I had been called an unfit mother, and this is also a serious charge. It would have been the word of respected educationalists against a crazy single mum.

Friends assured me I wouldn't have F taken from me. But I'd heard too many horror stories. Rational or not, the worst possible outcome, the threat that has hung over single mothers throughout history, loomed in my imagination.

The personal is political. But also, the psychological is social. And if to be emotional, connected, to give yourself to others is irrational – if a bodily self is never in her right mind – then mothering is always close to madness.

When F was a few weeks old, I got into an argument with a male paediatrician over a scan I'd been told she needed. Her hip joint hadn't settled properly in the womb because she'd been breach. Doctors on the labour ward had told me a decision over whether it needed intervention would be made on the basis of this scan – which I was now trying to have done.

But the paediatrician at our local practice – a big, shaggy man with a Hawaiian shirt under his whites who barked at his female underlings – didn't think it was necessary. Instead, he launched into a lengthy explanation of the cause of the problem, in my body, which I was already quite familiar with, thank you very much.

When I began to raise my voice, he turned to address the boyfriend sitting next to me as if I wasn't in the room: 'When a woman has a child, she becomes soft. A woman must be soft to bring a child into the world, but mothers are easily upset when the child is new and they are still soft.'

But the disintegration of a mother's mind into a woolly mess begins before birth. With 'baby brain'. And even before we conceive, men fear our moods, swept on lunar tides, threatening to toss them in our frothing rage.

Madness rises from our most female parts. Hysteria is named for the uterus and used to describe a very female disorder. In the days of the witch hunts, hysteria was associated with devilry, but over the centuries it took on an increasingly scientific aura, making a bodily disorder of errant women's politics, art and nonconformity. But it could also be the cause of a woman's refusal to wed, inability to conceive – or of her conceiving without being wed.

The flip side of the Victorian Angel in the House was the

fallen woman. Bringing a child into the world adrift from the anchoring of the complete, bigendered home made her a sinner against sexual morality and a betrayer of true femininity. But the fallen women was also degenerate, mentally unfit.

Well into the twentieth century, unwed mothers who avoided the workhouse might instead end up in the madhouse. And if getting pregnant didn't condemn you as a 'moral imbecile' what came after – the trauma of separation from your child or going to terrible extremes to hide your motherhood – must have driven many mother out of their minds.

There were many incarnations of the male maverick or outsider, the eccentric or hero. But for a woman, a mother, her entire identity defined in relation to others, the social death of single motherhood might be worse than actual death – or murder.

In 1840s Ireland, infanticide was the most common cause of violent death. But in tacit recognition that lone mothers had desperately few other options, many were convicted not of murder but the far lesser crime of 'concealment'.

In the early decades of the twentieth century, the medical profession still described unwed motherhood as a symptom of 'feeble-mindedness'. In the 1940s, single mothers were diagnosed as neurotics.

Pathologies change with social mores.

No one's called me insane for having a child out of wedlock, or for deserting my husband. But various doctors have tried to treat the results.

When the milky bliss and maternity payments of the first

year dried up, I saw a psychotherapist who set himself to uncovering what childhood trauma, or lack in my relationship with my own father, was at the root of the rage I felt towards my partner. But my childhood was fine – if my parents did anything to mess me up, it was to give me an idea of what it means to be a woman, and what to expect from men, that is off kilter with reality.

When I became a single mother, days began at six and ended when F finally fell asleep at nine or ten – or later if I was making an effort to keep on top of housekeeping or admin – with eight-hour office days in between. Commuting, meetings, cooking, school pick-ups and drop-offs, checking homework, arguing about screen-time and reading bedtime stories were complicated by repeatedly losing my keys and forgetting things I was supposed to do at work. I was diagnosed with ADHD and given amphetamines.

The more you deviate from the normative idea of a proper person – white, straight, male, coupled, and so on – the more likely you are to be called crazy. Not only because nonconformity itself is pathologised, but because constantly battling systems that weren't designed for you can feel like madness.

Around a quarter of families are single-parent families. Yet tax regimes, benefits, the welfare state, schools, working hours, conferences, dinner parties, parents' evenings, mortgages, family discounts, package holidays – and anyone who asks you to do anything outside school hours – operate on the assumption of a two-parent norm that scarcely exists even in two-parent families.

What doctors call an attention deficit disorder, I experience as a frantic struggle to switch between modes of thinking, back and forth, day in, day out.

Trying to write, remember to buy cat food, do a mental inventory of the fridge, pursue an idea, check F's sports kit, remind her father he said he'd pick her up today, empty the washing machine, call the doctor, fill in forms for schools, welfare offices, health insurance, answer important questions – *Why do grown-ups have to work? Why don't we give homeless people somewhere to live? What are chemicals?* – keep the whole show on the road, keep hold of the reins, keep all the balls in the air. Take out the trash. Preserve the sanctity of our nurturing domestic space.

The companies making the stimulants used to treat ADHD must be making a killing off single mothers. I got mine from a psychiatrist after filling in a questionnaire – forgetting things? can't focus? taxes filed late? – and having my blood pressure taken. Soon, I had friends, friends of friends, single mums I've never met, contacting me for their details.

We welcome the diagnoses and the pills. Because if it turns out that actually, really, we *can't* cope, we'd rather it was a physiological disability than a moral failing. We'd rather be unwell than admit we've bitten off more than a sane person can chew.

A few weeks after the meeting with F's headteachers, my GP sent me to a psychiatric clinic clutching a slip of paper with her signature under the words *depressive breakdown*.

It was a featureless building set back from the road behind a lawn scattered with daffodils. Inside, it was very quiet. A receptionist directed me to a plastic chair in a deserted corridor, where I waited in the stillness until a young male doctor ushered me into his office.

I tried to answer his questions. To explain why I was there. I knew I wasn't making much sense. But he grasped a few details of my life. Then he looked at the clock on the wall, asked what time my kid needed picking up and said I'd better get going.

I tried, vaguely, to protest. But he was right. And if I had broken, it didn't stop me picking F up on time. It didn't stop me from coping. Whatever that means.

My friend Imogen, though, was able to get into a clinic; she sent her daughter to stay with friends for three weeks. Imogen's diagnosis was the same as mine. And I hoped a rest, being looked after, would help. But when she got out, she said she didn't feel much better.

'I can barely get up. I don't want to do anything. The thing is though – they say I'm depressed. But I don't actually *feel* depressed. It's just . . . *intolerable*.'

'What exactly?'

'Not having any money.'

Clinical psychologist Sanah Ahsan says the current proliferation of mental health diagnoses 'depoliticises our distress'. Three quarters of people diagnosed with borderline personality disorder (BPD) are women, who Ahsan says, 'are often survivors of extreme sexual abuse, oppression and violence, which could surely explain the "emptiness, inappropriate and intense anger, mood swings and distrust" that are so-called "symptoms" of the disorder.'

Studies say single parents are twice as likely as coupled

parents to suffer with their mental health and are at heightened risk of depression and chronic stress. But we're also twice as likely to be living in poverty. And when money's tight, it's not just the material things you have to forgo; having no room for error is chronically stressful. The acute attention to scheduling, meals, bills, the vigilance against having to reach into empty pockets or pay a late-fee. Never being able to fall back on a taxi or a takeaway because your day unravelled.

Individually, we might be diagnosed with BPD, burnout, ADHD or generalised anxiety disorder. But in their epidemic proportions, these ailments might better be described as symptoms of masculinised society disorder.

Calling a woman's choices, reasoning, politics or identity a matter of physiological imbalance – or the hypersensitivity of too many hormones, too much emotion, too fierce a love – means you don't have to address her arguments or her outrage.

You don't debate with crazy.

But more, insisting that connectedness – opening yourself to others, encompassing others' needs – is irrational feminises and pathologises essential aspects of human experience. Things we all need, individually and collectively.

Calling motherly care *self-sacrifice* – the defining virtue of Victorian motherhood, and still central to how we think of it today – tells women we must sacrifice our actual *selves* in motherhood. But also, it implies that compassion and flexibility are a kind of madness that can only be expected of mothers.

Isolation, inequality, overwork, can grind down anyone's

mental health. But only a society that sees itself as a collection of distinct, self-contained selves operating in their own individual interest could atomise its structural disorders into a multitude of personal pathologies.

Mariam is the only woman I know to have been refused antidepressants. Her anxiety didn't ease once she had a baby to care for and the war had engulfed Damascus. But her doctor said that these were not things that could be medicated. As if the stresses that drive the rest of us to pills are all in our heads – or as if our anxieties are a problem to be fixed, but the suffering of an immigrant single mother whose family are stuck in a war zone is natural and proper.

But whatever contorted (and possibly racist) logic behind his prescriptions, Mariam's doctor was also right. She got meds elsewhere, and they did help – but not as much as her family finally making it to Berlin.

Helping her mum and dad settle into a new life they never wanted, to integrate into a city that is often unwelcoming, Mariam's responsibilities are greater than ever. But now that her daughter has two devoted grandparents in her life, at least they're shared.

The madness of single motherhood is a microcosm of societal madness. We're forced to internalise capitalism's crazed compartmentalising of different kinds of labour and different ways of being. But between unhinged superstructures and what they do to our heads, there are realms we have a little more control over.

The best way to hold it together is social.

When her daughter was christened at a squat brick church in the Grünewald forest, Mariam was the heart of the gathering she'd drawn in around her and her child. Proud grandparents. Friends who'd kipped on her couch while she was pregnant. Mums, dads and kids speaking Arabic, German, English. People who know who she used to be, and people who are part of the life she's made as a mother.

You cannot be *one, in and of yourself* if you are a mother only – or only a daughter, a writer, a journalist, a homemaker, a lawyer, a Syrian or a Berliner. We need space to flex the different aspects of who we are. But equally, we need relationships that affirm them.

If madness is a state of social dissonance, butting against oppressive norms, then the best way to stay sane is to find your people. A community in which you're not the crazy one – or not the only one.

I connected with Meghan wanting to share experiences of single motherhood and trying to find the right treatment to alleviate its symptoms. We'd met only a couple of times before, while we were both on maternity leave. I remembered her as a thin, delicate young woman, skin leached sallow-and-mauve, stoically trying to handle her rigidly restless baby into a state of calm like a person persisting with a deckchair she knows is broken.

This time, we got together without the kids at her local Italian, where staff called her by name. Diners sneaked glances as she strode in, full-fleshed, luminous marble-and-rose against lustrous black hair.

She filled me in on the intervening years, her time on

hospital wards and in a women's shelter, her struggle to piece herself back together, redefining her motherhood beyond a family unit that had reduced her to a milk machine.

In the space opened up by a functional co-parenting relationship with her ex, Meghan established a new career she loves, as a dominatrix. And she has a particular speciality in playing a sadistic occult priestess. An imperious, punishing witch.

# Chapter 5

# Choice and Circumstance

*I know exactly when he was conceived, to the minute. I took a picture of myself in the elevator when I was going out of the clinic, within ten minutes of conception. It's the most – sometimes I look at it – that's it, when it all changed.*

*And again, when I think about it, I still don't know if I had thought more – I almost had to trick myself into it. Like a component of me being slightly irrational but very pragmatic. Because if I'd really thought about it more and tried to make plans, thought through – how is the first year going to be – and so on, I would not have done it.*

*In a way, it's the craziest thing that I've done: to go ahead and make L. To decide, I'm going to use reproductive technology and I'm going to go through all these motions and all the steps to make a child and I'm going to do it alone. It's the most natural thing, of course, because reproduction is so abundant – there are like, eight billion people in the world. But it seems crazy to take control of this super-fundamental aspect of my life and really determine how it's going to be.*

*It's not the most pleasant thing, I must say that it ranks high on the scale of icky – intrauterine insemination – that's basically what they do to cows to impregnate them. But then, I guess it's the kind of experience that's so profound, I almost mythologised it. It became this reflection of my own power that I really did not need a guy to do this; I didn't need to fall in love.*

*I felt so much like an Amazon when I did it, like, you know the mother of Wonder Woman? Especially doing it in the lab, it felt totally cyborgy.*

*The part that I'm still kind of astounded happened was the decoupling of romantic love and family. Because that was like tearing something apart that has always meant to be together. This is where I had to sit myself down and give myself a big talk, like, OK, you have all these preconceptions and pre-baked notions of what happiness is supposed to look like, what is self-realisation. And the package that you were fed involves self-realisation through romantic love. Maybe there is some truth in that, but families come together in many different ways, so let's separate that. I can make the family that I want.*

— CARMEN

The single mums' Facebook group Liza introduced me to became a lifeline. Women post with childcare emergencies and others rally to make sure they don't miss court hearings, college exams, medical appointments. We share tips for navigating bureaucracy, family courts and fertility clinics, pass on children's clothes and freezer bags of breast milk, turn to one another with parenting dilemmas and exchange recommendations for vibrators and dating apps.

We excoriate the men in our lives. We pull together in emergencies. It's an imperfect, chaotic – and sometimes bitchy – kind of mutual aid network, buzzing with solidarity in a society that says mothering is something we are each responsible for alone.

We also organise offline get-togethers.

The first I attended was a Mother's Day brunch at Carmen's beautiful Charlottenburg apartment – a huge expanse of old-wood floorboards, lofty stuccoed ceilings and bookshelves packed with art volumes. The kitchen was busy with women opening Tupperware and popping bottles of Sekt. I'd never met any of them before, but recognised a few from profile pics.

I got chatting with a fellow Brit and writer, and when she introduced herself as Kate I realised we'd been on opposing sides of a debate over who has the right to call themselves a single mother.

Kate's Kindesvater had never been around and had only met their daughter, P, a handful of times. She and P moved from London to Berlin with a German boyfriend who promptly ghosted her. Now, she was working all hours with no support and tired of hearing complaints about unreliable men, who, nonetheless, took the kids for whole weekends.

Kate didn't think women with fifty-fifty co-parenting arrangements, time for themselves, social lives that were out of her reach when she couldn't afford a babysitter, had the right to call themselves single mothers. Someone else questioned whether you're still a single mum if you have a boyfriend. Mums with boyfriends argued they still carried sole responsibility for their children, and major topics of conversation in the group – strife with Kindesvaters and social services – were as relevant to them as anyone else.

Is being a *mum who is single* the same as being a *single mum*? How, precisely, do you translate *Alleinerziehend* into English? Maybe Kate meant she was a *lone mother* or *solo mum* – but do they mean the same thing? And if so, why does *lone* sound desolate, and *solo* kinda girl-bossy?

Mums at the mercy of abusive men, or who dreaded the lonely weeks their children were with their fathers, told Kate she didn't know lucky she was.

And some of us argued that, raising children outside the nuclear family, we all share more than divides us – and anyway, why should single motherhood be defined by hardship? One way or another, most of us escaped shitty relationships, so shouldn't we all celebrate the possibility that single motherhood might be a kind of freedom?

That morning, avatars defined by allegiance to one camp or another stepped into three dimensions. Through windows on to a quiet Sunday street, a wan spring sun illuminated tired faces, lined brows, pregnant-plump cheeks, scarlet lips, saggy leggings. Topping up each other's glasses, exchanging phone numbers, planning playdates.

Carmen padded from room to room, bare feet, long tan legs under a muslin tunic, while her son, L, with her thick curls and dimpled cheeks, danced delightedly through the throng. And as the party wound down, over washing up, she told the half-strangers at her sink how she'd joined another subset of our motley demographic: Single Mothers by Choice.

\*

There's a moment in the story of every single mum I've heard – a moment of resignation, clarity or liberation – when the kind of family she expected moves out of view and new possibilities open up. Mariam's moment came on discovering she was pregnant in a foreign land where the conventions of her Syrian home didn't apply. For Meghan, it was amid the unexpected solidarity of a women's shelter.

Having told the Kindesvater to leave, I'd relented to give things one last go. The condition I set was that we get our finances in order. A few weeks later, I was filing an online police report, genuinely believing my bank card had been cloned, when he admitted he'd sneaked it out of my wallet to go on midnight spending sprees.

I closed my laptop, bundled F out of the flat and had my moment in a shopping mall cafe, sharing a plate of chicken nuggets and looking out over a rainswept car park. When I texted him and told him it was over, I knew I meant it this time. And I felt space opening up ahead of me, light flooding in.

But where I had to fall into motherhood, letting it happen to me, and then fall again into single motherhood, Carmen wilfully directed this moment in the abstract before her fatherless child began to come into being.

And she's not alone.

More and more women aren't letting feckless, indecisive men stand between them and motherhood. They're refusing to settle for good-enough, hope-it-works, he'll-get-his-shit-together-when-the-baby-comes relationships. Cryos International, the world's largest sperm bank, says more than half its private customers are single – women who call themselves Single Mothers by Choice (SMCs) or Choice Mothers to assert mothering without a man as an empowered choice.

From early in her pregnancy, Carmen was open about her decision to have a child alone. A successful artist, she didn't want the art world whispering and wondering, 'What do you think happened to her?' The last thing she wanted anyone thinking was 'poor Carmen'. And she wanted to prove she was 'still fully herself'.

If most women feel a degree of societal pressure to have children, for a successful artist more complex expectations are at play. Mothering and making art are each supposed to consume a person entirely and the assumption that you cannot fully commit to both means, Carmen says, 'you're expected not to be a mother – if you're a mother you're an imperfect artist'.

She knew artists who hid their motherhood, or were 'forced into the horrible situation of having to choose between a career or a family'.

Carmen, though, had a solo show six weeks after she gave birth: 'I planned it like that because it was very important to me to show that I could be there, making all this new work. To show myself, and to make the stand of being able to be a mother and an artist.'

Achieving this as a *single* mother feels like even more of a statement. Carmen didn't have a partner to share night feeds or hold the baby while she worked. But for the first few weeks of L's life, she employed a former neonatal nurse to help out for five hours each day. Over the years, au pairs have allowed

Carmen to travel abroad and from an early age L got used to her being away for days at a time.

Carmen's motherhood seems to encompass breathing space I only achieved as F gradually became comfortable with someone else putting her to bed. And I don't know what blows the furious rows of her first three years have dealt F's psyche: she herself may spend a lifetime finding out. But L 'has never witnessed a fight,' Carmen says. 'I've never argued with anybody about my travel schedule, about what I feed him, is he going to get baptised, is he going to spend time with your family or my family?'

Carmen is, in many ways, the archetypal SMC. Successful, strong-willed – and she began the process as her fertile years were waning, conceiving at a private fertility clinic.

If the unwed mother used to be a young woman who hadn't held out long enough to make it down the aisle, these days our demographic is shifting towards the woman who held out 'too long'.

For women who have dedicated most of their fertile years to their careers and accumulated enough resources along the way, single motherhood can be not just a viable option, but one very much in keeping with the identity of the independent, empowered woman who charts her own path.

Women like Carmen have always had to compete against men, always on unequal terms. No one ever thought a male artist shouldn't have children – if anything, leaving a trail of babies in his wake only enhances his virile mystique.

Another single mum in our circle, Dominique, who works in elite spheres with high-powered businessmen and politicians, says she keeps quiet when these men talk about their children. Guys who tell stories about the funny things their kids do come off as reliable, down-to-earth family men. But if she were to let slip she was a mother – let alone a *single* one – her competence and commitment would suddenly be up for question.

Dominique is silent about her motherhood, Carmen outspoken. Both stay on top of their game by working very hard – and they buy in help from cleaners and childminders to keep on top of the domestic work their male peers have wives to do.

And Single Mothers by Choice aren't just paying for wifely labours, they can also order in the one thing we do need dads for – swiping through sperm bank websites that have all the trappings of dating apps: selecting for physical attributes, race, IQ and educational achievement. Alternatively, there's an unregulated market where men offer their services privately and women can choose to have a vial of semen delivered, or to pay a man for sex.

As downtrodden as single mums have been, there's something thrilling in this turning of tables. I was exhilarated to meet women who hadn't had to go through what I did before realising that single motherhood could be a positive choice. Amazons challenging patriarchy at its core, reclaiming the power of their fertility and refusing to compromise for any man.

But if autonomous mothering that relies on passing reproductive labour down the ladder to other carers doesn't sound very radical, the origin of the term *Single Mother by Choice* is positively reactionary.

The first woman to assert her identity as an SMC was psychotherapist Jane Mattes, who was thirty-six when she made her choice to have a child alone. 'I was the director of a psychotherapy clinic and I was teaching and supervising at a training institute. I had accomplished just about all of my professional goals. However, I had not been able to find a suitable life partner and I realised I did not have much time left to start a family,' she explains in her handbook for SMCs, published in 1994.

When Mattes's son was a baby, she looked for community with other mums, much as we do in our Berlin Facebook group – except Mattes specifically wanted to connect with women who'd made the same unconventional choice she had. And, finding them scattered across the States, she founded a non-profit called Single Mothers by Choice, in 1982.

The group started small but it garnered a disproportionate amount of attention. Decades before *lean in*, glass ceilings were shattering, power-suited women shouldering their way into boardrooms and men having to answer to female bosses for the first time. And in this climate, women like Mattes became a minor cause célèbre of contemporary culture wars – particularly after the eponymous protagonist of long-running sitcom *Murphy Brown*, a wise-cracking journalist, took the SMC route to motherhood.

In a speech that blamed the Los Angeles Riots – sparked by footage of the LAPD beating Rodney King – on the breakdown of 'traditional' family, Vice President Dan Quayle said, 'It doesn't help matters when prime-time TV has Murphy Brown, a character who supposedly epitomises today's intelligent, highly paid professional woman, mocking the importance of fathers by bearing a child alone and calling it just another lifestyle choice.'

Mattes's organisation was suddenly under the media spotlight. But she didn't use her platform to stick two fingers up at patriarchy. Instead, she hastened to assure conservative America that the Choice Mother posed no threat to the nuclear family.

In her book, Mattes describes how she strived to correct the assumption the 'choice' part of SMC referred to the choice to be single: rather, these were women who lamented their failure to wed but nonetheless chose to be mothers.

She points to studies indicating that instability and broken homes are what put the children of single mothers at a disadvantage, not the lack of a father *per se* – and even notes some advantages to mothering a child without having to care for a husband too. But she stops short of criticising the dynamics of heterosexual relationships.

Mattes defines SMCs as 'single women who *chose* to become mothers; single mothers who are mature and responsible and who feel empowered rather than victimised' (italics hers). 'We are *all* well educated and financially secure,' she writes of her organisation's membership (italics mine).

Above all, Mattes stresses that Single Mothers by Choice should never be confused with 'divorced or teen-aged single mothers'. And throughout her book, she frames the challenges of mothering solo in contrast to 'perfect' or 'ideal' married motherhood.

'We would all surely agree that having a child in a family with two loving parents is the ideal,' she writes.

*

Mattes's moment came when she felt time to find Mr Right was running out. But it also came at a certain moment in history, when moral panic unlike anything since the Victorian era was being whipped up over single motherhood.

As Mattes's biological clock ticked, inflation rates were soaring. More and more families were depending on benefits to survive, and Ronald Reagan was campaigning for presidential office. Politicians were slashing public spending and blaming the idle poor for sapping the country's wealth.

And single mothers were first in the firing line.

It was the dawn of a neoliberal era in which personal responsibility was everything and dependence shameful. And the welfare queen emerged as poster child for poor personal choices and failure to stand on one's own two feet.

The number of children being born out of wedlock had been rising steadily in the decades before Mattes conceived, and during the 1970s the Supreme Court had overturned most legal discriminations against 'illegitimate' children. But motherhood outside marriage still struggled for legitimacy. Mattes claimed that legitimacy by creating an identity defined not in opposition to the married mother, but in opposition to the welfare queen.

Interestingly, Mattes began her career working at a Mother and Baby Home. Her book doesn't dwell on the experience, mentioning it just briefly as she describes how, many years later, she realised she could 'turn around and do exactly what I had always thought to be unacceptable'. But she could do this only by distancing herself as far as possible from the young, irresponsible motherhood she had witnessed – and perhaps helped to erase – years before.

Mattes's SMC was everything the welfare queen was not: a mature, self-sufficient woman making a rational, responsible choice. And by the time she published her book, assisted reproductive technology was broadly available to single women in the United States and the SMC could rid herself of any last contamination from irresponsible sex.

How much further, after all, can you get from walking away from a one-night stand vaguely wishing you'd used a condom, than the expensive gleam of the fertility clinic?

Carmen was the first Choice Mother I met. But single mums are birds of a feather and I soon met more. Maya intrigued me because she didn't seem to fit the classic – older, wealthy, professionally established – SMC profile. And in fact, though I'd seen Maya call herself a Single Mom by Choice, it turns out this was controversial.

She tried to join a Facebook group for SMCs and had to answer a lot of invasive questions – on the basis of which she wasn't deemed worthy of the title.

Maya grew up in the American Midwest. Her father died when she was twelve and she had a difficult home life with her mother. By the time she was twenty-two, Maya had run away from home, got pregnant by an abusive boyfriend, miscarried, split up, married a different man, qualified as a nurse and then left for Europe after she caught her husband in bed with another woman.

Somewhere in all this, she began to nurture the dream of having a baby all by herself, and to investigate which countries had the most accessible clinics to conceive at. In the meantime, she explored the Hamburg kink scene before moving to Berlin – pregnant. For Maya, the means of conception were incidental and serendipitous, allowing her to accelerate plans that might otherwise have remained on hold for many more years. But she understood it to be sex that set her apart from the SMCs who'd used anonymous donors or signed pre-conception agreements before accepting vials of trusted friends' semen.

'The concept that someone so young could want this and actually follow through – it was insane to them,' Maya says. 'So they were like, no way, you got pregnant by accident, right?'

And yet if keeping an unplanned pregnancy doesn't get you in to the club, the gatekeepers of Choice Motherhood would have had to refuse Mattes herself, whose story is remarkably similar to Maya's.

Mattes says she was looking into adopting a child when she 'accidentally conceived with a lover' who was 'very candid about the fact that he was not interested in marriage or family'. Like Maya, Mattes 'left the door open' for him to be involved in her child's life, and like Maya's source of sperm, he declined.

I can only guess what the SMC admins saw, or thought of, Maya's Facebook profile, with its stream of sex-positive slogans and photos – selfies and studio shots – just shy of social-media censorship, body of a fertility goddess, gaze of a femme fatale. But my guess is the biggest mark against her wasn't her sexuality so much as her age.

Maya had accumulated enough life experience by the time she gave birth at twenty-three to make a choice that didn't occur to me until I was already a middle-aged mum. But *maturity* isn't central to the Choice Mother identity because of the years it takes for the scales to fall from our eyes – but as a mark of responsibility and stability.

For Mattes, age is also important because it makes *single* motherhood a woman's only rational choice: a younger woman should hold out for the right man. In fact, Mattes still hadn't given up on Mr Right when she conceived, but describes her single motherhood as getting her family started in the hope a father would join it later.

In the meantime, she urges SMCs to provide sturdy male role models for her child in uncles, godfathers and adult male friends. But having some guy kick a ball around with your kid isn't the same as living in a heterogendered family unit.

The real struggle of single motherhood isn't the absence of some masculine influence but the waged male's pay cheque. It's balancing work and mothering in a world that assumes these labours are split between a couple.

And the SMC's solution is, in essence, just what any middle-class professional woman is supposed to do: get your professional goals out of the way first, and then focus on family. Mattes has ten questions for any woman considering mothering alone – and right up at number one is: 'Have you accomplished all of the personal and career goals that are, in your mind, essential to your feeling good about yourself and your life?'

A mature, responsible single mother can pay someone else to perform wifely duties, or she can treat career and family as distinct goals to be achieved at different stages of life. First, you're a productive worker and then, having reached a plateau of professional status and economic stability, you step back and transition to True Womanhood.

Maya isn't a true SMC because she's doing everything at once, in the early years of both her motherhood and her career, juggling nursing studies with mothering, supplementing state benefits with sex work, doing it all, all at the same time. Work and family aren't milestones to tick off sequentially, they're all just life, all happening at once and – along with dating, partying, exploring Europe – equally important to what Carmen calls *self-realisation*.

The checklist that Mattes begins by asking mums to relinquish any future professional aspirations is aimed at an SMC demographic she calls 'thinkers'.

The thinking stage of the SMC narrative is a like a pre-pregnancy gestation, through which a woman must measure her desire for motherhood against the rigorous standards of responsible choice. 'You cannot responsibly bring a child into the world unless you have sufficient money to support the two of you,' Mattes writes.

Ideally, an SMC should have a college fund and emergency savings amounting to a year's living expenses. She must also consider how she'll secure a support network, whether her 'coping mechanisms' will get her through the first two years, if she will be 'flexible' enough to accept a child whose 'basic temperament and personality' may not be all she hoped for – and how she will balance mothering this potential problem child with care of her own elderly parents.

But who can really answer these questions in the abstract? Not Carmen, whose motherhood was a matter not just of pragmatic planning, but of *tricking herself into it*, of surrendering to the *irrational*.

You can prepare for motherhood a thousand ways, but what you cannot really grasp until it happens, I think, is how completely bringing a child into the world can upend the logic of good choices and bad ones. On paper, every decision that led to F's birth – where I was living, with whom, the unhappy job that took me to Kyrgyzstan where she was conceived – was a bad one. But if I were to edit my past, I'd be terrified of smoothing out the smallest imperfection lest unintended consequences lead me to different world: one without F in it.

This isn't logical.

If each choice we make creates a parallel universe, there must be infinite alternate worlds in which I mother different children and, no doubt, love those children as passionately as I love F.

But love isn't logical.

I only have to look at F and such thought experiments implode. There is nothing so irreversible as having a child. It's something like fate – not in the sense things could *only* have turned out this way, but rather that she is so real, so fully of *this* world, that I cannot but commit to it, to the here and now.

How we got here is immaterial.

And this is where I would like to introduce Lisa. Lisa doesn't get embroiled in the spats about who gets to call themselves what. But since I asked:

*It's like a rank – that the saints among us are widows because, you know, they're single moms not by their own choice. Fate dealt them a wrong hand. And then it's divorced moms. Like, OK, you tried on a relationship, it didn't work out, you broke up. But you're still respectable because you did things the right way. And then there's, like, somewhere down the line, the unwed moms like me. There's no-father-involvement, and in between there's co-parenting.*

*And then there's the curveball: Single Moms by Choice. Who feel a need all the time to assert themselves as Single Moms by Choice as a way to differentiate themselves from, you know, those* other *single moms.*

*So it kinda grates my gears being one of each. Having one by – I say by circumstance, and then one by choice. So I just say that I'm a single mom. I'm a solo mom, I don't have a partner. Yeah, one I had by circumstance of being in a relationship with a selfish asshole and one I chose to do on my own. But I don't volunteer that information 'less it's asked. You just assume whatever you want and put whatever label you have on me, I don't care.*

Lisa's single motherhood moment came when she was pregnant and her relationship with the father was falling apart. She was living in Berlin but back in the States visiting her mom and stalking her boyfriend on Facebook when she discovered he was seeing someone else:

*Something just clicked. Because up to that point, there was like a cloud over my entire pregnancy because I was mourning this idea of a relationship, or an idea of my child having a father. Then it was like, OK, boom, I'm done. I'm done being upset about it and I'm just gonna have my baby on my own.*

*Then I was looking forward. Because before that point, I was thinking, is he going to be there for the birth? When the baby comes, is he going to be involved? I didn't care about any of that anymore, I just shifted focus. I mean, I needed to build support for me, because he wasn't it. It just shifted the focus from him and the relationship to – I'm going to be a mom.*

That focus, on the here and now, on where she was at, held fast. Because if becoming a mother for the first time is always a leap into the unknown – a choice that's never quite rational – when Lisa decided to have a second child, her vision was crystal clear.

The daughter of a teenage single mom, Lisa was raised in a large and loving family. She talks to her three younger sisters on the phone every week, and they've flown across the Atlantic to help her out in emergencies.

And she wanted her son, C, to have that too.

'In a certain way, I didn't feel like I was enough,' Lisa says. 'I felt like people – kids – deserve as much love as you can give them. And I can't make his dad show up but I can make a baby, easy. He's so loving and he deserves another substantial relationship.'

When Lisa began scrolling though sperm bank profiles she was taking control of circumstances she hadn't chosen and creating a new life as an act of love for the child she had.

*What I was looking for was someone that has the same involvement as C's father. I didn't want a situation where somebody would pick up M and kind of leave C behind. But I can tell C things about his dad, his personality. I wanted to be able to also tell M the same, like, 'Oh, your dad is this way', or 'Your dad makes that face'. So, basically, I was looking for a donor but I wanted a known donor.*

*One guy wanted to co-parent, and I'm just like, 'are you willing to co-parent my oldest as well?' Because nobody is just picking up the child and leaving my oldest to be like, 'Where's my papa?' So I wasn't looking for a co-parent. I didn't really care about height, I didn't care about – like, some people ask, you know, IQ, but did we click?*

*Some people might think this is weird, but I was single and I was like, 'I don't necessarily see myself going to a sperm bank so would you be interested in doing it the old-fashioned way?'*

What Lisa calls 'the old-fashioned way' went like this: she created a free profile on a sperm bank website and reverse-google-image-searched donors she liked the look of to find their social-media accounts, through which she approached them directly, avoiding sperm bank charges. She quizzed them about previous experience and chatted till she felt like she'd found the right man for the job. She tracked her ovulation, with her best friend on standby to take C when the moment came.

And with everything in place, fingers crossed, she flew her donor to Berlin, where they had sex, resulting in her second pregnancy, at just the cost of his travel expenses.

Lisa's two kids each see their biological fathers – occasionally. But they see C's paternal grandparents, his half-siblings from his father's previous relationship and even his father's ex-wife, much more regularly. When C's little sister, M, arrived, they welcomed her as another – equal – grandchild, sister, niece.

Lisa is grateful for how the European side of her family has embraced her and her kids. But for her this has a natural logic. The women and men she grew up calling aunties and uncles weren't necessarily blood kin. She was mothered by her grandmother alongside her own mother, who has been both a mom and a sister to Lisa.

Lisa's choices are shaped by circumstance. Her family is shaped by tendrils of genetic lineage and active bonds of care that reach across continents, and the day-to-day support of her community in Berlin: single-mother families and nuclear ones.

In his essay 'Every Child Needs a Father', Dwayne Avery reflects on how 'the "good" postfeminist single mother is championed as a symbol of the self-rewarding possibilities associated with neoliberalism.'

If the nuclear family is capitalism's last refuge of communal care and freely given labour, SMCs break even these bonds. Hard-working, self-reliant and 'utilising their postfeminist powers of choice, these strong, educated, and well-to-do figures are free to create their own destinies'.

And what could be more neoliberal than a family reduced to just its mother-child core, turning to the free market for intimate reproductive labours?

But if this is how we define Choice Mothering, the most neoliberal thing about the SMC narrative isn't independence so much as the progressive, technocratic gloss it applies to age-old power dynamics. Unwed mums climbing out of the gutter and paying men for sex might look like revolution, but elite mothers have been outsourcing reproductive labour to poorer women for as long as we have had any kind of class or race hierarchy.

Yet like the welfare queen, the hyper-individual SMC is more stereotype than flesh. A 2015 paper titled 'The Single Mother by Choice Myth' asks if the true SMC really exists at all, and concludes that by 'any definition there are few "single mothers by choice", and there are even fewer women who match the age and educational profile proposed by media portrayals and SMC support organisations.'

Women like Carmen, Maya and Lisa certainly have more in common with the rest of us divorcees, knocked-up students and welfare mums than the Choice Mums you see in movies. Like Jennifer Aniston's in *The Switch*, who leaves her Manhattan loft and media career right after her 'insemination party' and returns seven years later, having aged not a day, to ultimately marry the guy she friend-zoned at the start of the movie – who, of course, turns out to be the biological father after all.

The single mums I know aren't holding out for a fairytale ending – especially not with the kind of guy who would secretly impregnate a woman. Whatever our choices and circumstances, we're all caught in tension between autonomy and community, scrambling for solutions, making it work as best we can.

The reason Carmen invited us all to her home that day – the reason she gathers single moms and our kids into her spacious kitchen to fashion misshapen pizzas, and hosts a huge Christmas dinner every year – is that au pairs and cleaners don't replace a village. And like Lisa, Carmen has an embodied understanding of this rooted in her own childhood:

*My mom was single. Things with my father didn't work out, and at some point we were living in this building, like a small building in Mexico City with a lot of families in it. One family had a phone and one family had a car. Somebody knew how to cook, somebody was a doctor and I had a grandmother. And it was a pooling of resources, where my grandmother cared for eight kids and then we would all sleep over with somebody else and somebody else again would cook for us. The doctor would take care of us all, and the person with the car would take us to school.*

*Everybody had their own apartment – it's not that the adults were constantly in each other's business. But I understand now they were taking turns who to dump the kids with. And we formed friendships, and some of those friendships still hold.*

*And that's my image of something that was actually working. My mom was not a happy single let's say, and because of that I was highly averse to the idea of being a single mom. But I also knew how it works. It was a thing I kept in the back of my mind: if worse comes to worst, you know you can do it.*

Carmen says that when she decided to *decouple romantic love and family*, she drew on 'lifelong experience of not doing what is expected of me'. Her single motherhood had become something 'I wanted, very much'. And, she stresses, 'I can afford it – that's a very big thing to understand, that I was able to afford to.'

But also, she grew up poor on the 'wrong side of the tracks'. She knew what it's like to rely on community, not cash. Carmen moves in exclusive art-world circles, but she's also part of the remittance economy, working in the Global North and sending money home to support her mother in Mexico.

She's never had a live-in nanny, but she has used her lovely big flat to host refugee families and mothers and children fleeing domestic violence. And this is particularly important to her, because when Carmen asserted her reproductive power independent of any man, she wasn't actually single at all. She was still in an abusive relationship, with a man who found her career 'emasculating'.

Her success didn't shield her from his attacks – it was a threat he lashed out at. But it was when she told him that she was thinking about having a child alone that this man, whom she loved but could not imagine fathering her child, became a violent assailant who threatened to 'rip out her uterus' and kill her baby before he killed her.

Carmen, Maya and Lisa are each, in their own ways, doing things differently from their own single mothers – to spare their children hardships they experienced themselves, or to avoid the shame, bitterness or discontent their mothers suffered. And to keep their children safe.

But they *knew how it works*.

Women like Mattes might think they can reinvent the wheel, but the Choice Mother came on the scene only after generations of sexually active teens, domestic violence escapees, women who never tried very hard for – or with – husbands, women who quit work to raise kids on benefits, or left them with their own mums to do menial jobs, made single motherhood a thing.

Whatever choices we make now – conceiving without a husband, leaving an abusive partner, decoupling our sexual and domestic lives – these are the women who broke ground and made our choices possible.

There is also a direct lineage between the SMC's choice and queer families who have fought for assisted reproduction. When Mattes set up her organisation, gay parenting was still taboo – whereas single mothers were an inevitability society was used to, if rarely best pleased about.

In just a few decades, same-sex couples have gone from outlawed to married, from having their biological children removed by force, to legally adopting.

At the height of the AIDS crisis, queer rights activists demanded universal health care to replace a marriage-based system that meant gay men dying of AIDS weren't covered by their partners' insurance. But just as Mattes sought to extend the legitimacy of married motherhood to a minority of single women, so the movement for same-sex marriage came to accept the principle of privileging some kinds of love and family over others.

The demand for marriage equality drowned out radical calls to smash the heteronormative status quo and revolutionise family because the establishment amplified them – a small price to pay for keeping marriage and the nuclear family intact.

Yet more than half of European countries still restrict access to assisted reproduction for single women and lesbian couples. Still, this far into the twenty-first century, women are being denied fertility treatment if they don't have a man to sanction their use of their own bodies.

And while same-sex nuclear families have become increasingly respectable, single-mother families are still treated as imperfect, broken, an anomaly that needs engineering out of existence. High rates of single motherhood are still taken as a measure of social malaise, and right and centre-left governments still use benefits and tax regimes to try and get our numbers down.

Four decades after Mattes had her moment, women still feel the need to assert their identity as Choice Mothers, if not to deliberately ostracise the rest of us – though Maya's experience shows this still happens too – then to refute the assumption that single motherhood is always a misfortune or mistake.

Which it really shouldn't be.

I don't think women are giving too little thought to motherhood and how it changes our lives – far from it. But we would do well to think about whether we want men to be involved in our motherhood, and how. Though I waste little time second-guessing the circumstances of my own motherhood, I urge younger women, the childless on the hunt for Kindesvaters, to consider Lisa's clarity of vision, Maya's maverick multitasking and Carmen's articulate redefinition of family.

Because, like Carmen, they might dodge a bullet. But also because the more we question our dependence on men, the more alternatives to the nuclear family we explore, the more we empower our choices to challenge patriarchy at its heart.

Carmen says of the terrifying rage her boyfriend flew into when she suggested she might start a family without him: 'I did not understand the magnitude of that reaction.' But she made a recording of his chilling threats to mutilate her womb. And to me, his disembodied voice – not shouting, but hissing the words *selfish*, *bitch*, *whore* – sounds like pure, distilled misogyny escaping from patriarchy deflated.

Because what could be more threatening to male dominance than a woman seizing her reproductive power for herself?

But to realise the radical potential of single mothering as a positive choice, to join the queer cause of dismantling the gendered oppressions of family, we must turn back to vagabond motherhoods that have never been respectable. To women branded whores not just by individually scorned men, but a whole economic order enraged by female bodily autonomy.

# Chapter 6

# Whores and Welfare Queens

Elevated on so a high a pedestal, Victorian womanhood had a long way to fall. Sex brought her down. The wet, carnal womanliness under her stiff petticoats. The cunt of clay beneath her high ideals.

As a trope of the Victorian morality tale, the fallen woman succumbed to vanity or greed and ended up exiled or dead. More recently, the single mother is an object of pity or a burden on society. At best, a paradigm of endless self-sacrifice, striving against the odds to make good what will always be broken and deficient. At worst, a symbol of pathological dependence.

If the fallen woman was a sinner against sexual morality, the crimes of the welfare queen are explicitly economic. But either way, when people get upset about women escaping their proper place in society, sex and economics are always entangled.

Boris Johnson – father to an undisclosed number of single-mothered children – called it 'outrageous that married couples should [pay for] the single mothers' desire to procreate independently of men'. What, after all, could be more scandalous in a mother than a witchy brew of money, independence and desire?

The *Spectator* published these words in 1995, at the height of a neoliberal era when the single mum was a stock villain of the right-wing media. Tabloids fleshed out the *Spectator*'s image with scandalous stories of working-class single mums with too many children, too many Kindesvaters, in too-small a flat with too-big a telly – and these stories remain a *Daily Mail* staple.

Yet mostly, the stories of single mothers aren't flagged as being about single mothers at all. They're just stories of women at the bottom of the social heap. Mostly, single mums have made headlines and history books when bad things happen to them. Women who fell so far or so hard, they were ruined. Or worse.

Women like Wilma McCann.

On the night of 30 October 1975, Peter Sutcliffe bludgeoned McCann to death on the playing fields a few minutes' walks from her home in Chapeltown, Leeds. A twenty-eight-year-old single mother of four, McCann was (as far as we know) the first woman Sutcliffe killed. By the time he was arrested nearly five years later, he'd left twenty-three children motherless.

Society abhors the murder of a young mother almost as much as the murder of a child. But the lurid media reports that followed Sutcliffe's crimes didn't focus on his victims' motherhood. They speculated that the killer was a crazed zealot on a crusade to rid the world of whores.

Some of his victims sold sex to support their children. It's not clear that McCann did. But in a society that rarely recognised a woman as both, Wilma McCann was more whore than mother.

The investigation that eventually brought Sutcliffe to justice only really got going after he murdered 'respectable' women. When the body of sixteen-year-old shop assistant Jayne MacDonald was found in June 1977, police called her the Yorkshire Ripper's first 'innocent' victim. They supposed he must have mistaken her for a prostitute. Once Sutcliffe began killing middle-class women in less downtrodden neighbourhoods, they issued an unenforced curfew on all women in the towns he stalked.

To avoid being taken for whores, the onus was on all good women to prove their innocence through self-confinement in the home.

McCann raised her children in poverty after her abusive husband left her. She is remembered because she was a minor, tragic, protagonist in the bigger story of one of Britain's most notorious serial killers. But she's also remembered because of the people who have spoken out for her since her death.

Her son, who was five when his mother was murdered, has described the devastation Sutcliffe – as well his father – wrought on his childhood. And there is the English Collective of Prostitutes, formed the same year McCann died. The ECP loudly decried the police's failure to catch Sutcliffe for so long and the assumptions they made about the women he murdered, protesting under banners that read 'all human life is respectable'.

Most sex workers in the UK are mothers, a statistic that

was at the heart of a campaign in 2016 under the hastag #makemumsafer, which tried to humanise sex workers in the public imagination by collapsing the division between mother and whore as two mutually exclusive identities.

At the same time, the campaign protested the Cameron government's austerity politics, which were forcing more and more single mothers into sex work to support their children.

The Madonna–whore complex isn't just a male sexual foible, it's a dichotomy that has ruled women's lives. As long as women have been economically dependent on men, there have been few life paths open to us that didn't entail either a life-long contract to care for one man or selling intimate wifely labours on a freelance basis.

The history of the single mother moves in the shadows between the female archetypes of mother and whore. On a gloomy street corner, or wreathed in candlelight and chiffon, her motherhood vanishes. Pass her pushing a pram, and you'd never guess what she got up to after dark. It's not a trick of the light, but a trick of patriarchy, that we rarely glimpse the whole woman, or confront how closely these roles have always been entwined.

The term *fallen woman* described both streetwalker and unwed mother – and often there was little material difference between the two: single mothering has often meant selling sex to survive. But another, older, term for sex workers was also still in use in the Victorian era: *public woman*.

Where the lives and labours of married women were private matters governed by husbands, the public woman brought shameful sexualities out from behind closed doors.

She was a social problem, and subject to intrusions by public authorities, who rounded up prostitutes and locked them away – to clean up the streets and control the spread of filth and disease, subjecting these women to intimate examinations and dubious medical interventions.

Yet being a public woman could also have its advantages. History is full of fabulous tales of women eschewing respectability to live richly – in every sense of the word – as prostitutes, courtesans or madams.

In Ancient Greece, a female merchant didn't have to sell sex to be branded a whore – married women were so strictly confined to the home that just her presence in a public marketplace was enough to cast aspersions on her respectability. Meanwhile, high-class whores known as hetaerae were prized for their artistic and intellectual as well as sexual prowess, and wandered where they liked, from the theatre to the symposium. At the end of a banquet, when wives were sent off to bed like children, hetaerae stayed on to enjoy revelry and debate.

The flip side of the history of the wife and mother, the status of whore might allow a woman to move through spaces that were off-limits to wives and virtuous maidens, selling herself yet remaining autonomous. If a woman's place was under wedlock, whoring could be the key to the world outside and, occasionally, to wealth, power and political influence.

Yet we rarely hear of the children these women must have borne, and less about how they raised them, what constellations of care they constructed in the absence of respectable family. Because these women were seen as whores above all, we recall them through a lens that leaves their mothering in obscurity.

In 2011, archaeologist Jill Eyers was trying to answer a question that had been around since Yewden Villa, a Roman archaeological site in Hampshire, had been unearthed a century earlier: what the hell happened here?

Alongside the remains of what appears to have been a large living complex, the site also contained the bones of ninety-seven newborn babies. 'The only explanation you keep coming back to is that it's got to be a brothel,' Eyers told the BBC. 'Roman prostitutes forced to kill their own children,' crowed the *Daily Mail*, above an article smacking its lips over the 'Invaders' hidden culture of death and debauchery'.

But – the only explanation? Other archaeologists argued the site could have been anything from an obstetrics hospital to a temple of ritual sacrifice. There was nothing about the ruins, they pointed out, that suggested a brothel – unless dead babies themselves scream *whorehouse*.

Eyers's explanation assumes prostitutes would have had to get rid of their children one way or another. But there are less drastic ways to deal with a kid you can't look after. Like professional women in any other field, sex workers have often paid other women to look after their babies. Or, like other unwed mothers, they have given them up to be adopted by respectable families.

In the nineteenth century, a fallen women could make her case to a foundling hospital. If she was deemed worthy of redemption, they could take her secret child and allow her to return to good society for a second chance at a respectable life. But if you were a prostitute whose life had anyway fallen far beyond the bounds of respectability, perhaps you might have liked to keep your illegitimate baby?

Eyers isn't the only one to have linked the archaeological remains of dead children with the sex trade. And it is true that illegitimate children have often been murdered – by mothers, fathers and other members of shame-fearing families. But while infanticide leaves bones to dig up, the bonds of families that didn't involve marriage or fathers often went undocumented even by contemporary legal records. Histories of whores who mothered, the private lives of these public women, are mostly lost.

One exception is Barbara Minchinton's *The Women of Little Lon*, which illuminates the teeming domestic life of Victorian Melbourne's red-light district, where women owned and ran brothels that evaded male ownership and control.

Contemporary media reports dwelt on the women of Little Lon's 'riotous conduct' and 'disorderly behaviour'. They were 'loose women' and 'great talkers and loud laughers' who were 'independent to the point of insolence'. But, Minchinton writes, they could also be found 'helping each other, looking after children and dancing together in the streets'. They attended to one another in labour, shared the care of elderly relatives and took the stand for one another in court – defending criminal charges, but also in divorce proceedings.

When Sarah Saqui – something of a local celebrity, known for her elegance, musical talents and her ties to the Duke of Edinburgh – confirmed that she and her friend Mrs Fagan lived together at one of Little Lon's fancier brothels, a judge finally granted Mrs Fagan the divorce her husband had refused.

Such gems aside, court transcripts and newspaper reports leave the historian to reconstruct Little Lon's life stories around incidents of violence, theft and public disorder. Yet even these dramas offer glimpses of women who were both fierce fighters and fierce mothers – such as the case Richard Day brought against Hannah Moses for unpaid wages.

Day worked as a domestic in the 'boarding house' where Hannah let rooms to half a dozen women who 'seemed unusually active at night'. But the household also accommodated a number of their children. The dispute erupted after one of the kids flicked tea into Day's eye and he 'boxed the child's ears'. Hannah and her lady 'lodgers' ran him out of the house – but not before beating him so badly he feared they would 'break his head' if he ever darkened their door again.

Through much of Little Lon's heyday, the law of coverture meant a married woman could not own property, execute a will or have any financial dealings in her own name. The only woman who existed as a legal individual was a *femme sole* – divorced, widowed or unwed – and some of these women became very rich, doing business in and beyond the sex trade, owning whole streets where brothels merged and interspersed with family homes of varying respectability.

But if being single gave them their legal rights, community allowed them to thrive. Tenancy records hint at life-long bonds between women who cohabited consistently, or lived together on and off for decades. Without husbands, they must have given one another the comfort and companionship of marriage; unlike marriage, these bonds could extend across different households and be dissolved and reconstituted at will.

'Flash brothel'-keeper Madame Brussels adopted a daughter whom she raised alongside her own illegitimate children. But there must have been many less formal arrangements.

Emma Westcott and her brother 'spent their childhood in and around the back lanes' of Little Lon, while their mother, Emily, worked at a brothel run by Sarah Fraser, one of the community's most successful businesswomen. When Emily fell ill, Sarah kept paying her wages, ensuring she was cared for until the end of her life. Emma was twelve and there are no records of how she spent the rest of her childhood. But if Sarah's care extended to her employee's children, then Emma must have learned a few tricks of the trade from her benefactor – because she went on to run several upmarket brothels of her own, while raising her four fatherless children.

Yet Emma's success did not last.

Her story reverses the trajectory of those who arrived in Little Lon looking for a living compatible with single mothering after their marriages failed: in her forties, Emma quit the sex trade, found a husband and moved away – but only after the law put her out of business.

In Victorian Melbourne, as in most societies around the world before and since, selling sex was not a legal offence. Rather, women could be prosecuted under vagrancy laws for soliciting, behaving 'in a riotous or indecent manner' being 'idle and disorderly' or 'having no visible lawful means of support'.

The 1907 Police Offences Act – part of a moralistic drive

that 'put respectable women behind hedges and lawns in the suburbs, and thrust streetwalkers into the path of bullies and pimps' – expanded definitions of soliciting and banned brothels. Women like Emma, with the resources to start over, were the lucky few.

Those turned out onto the streets when establishments like hers closed continued to work – but without the solidarity and security of a common roof over their heads, vulnerable to violence, extortion and police harassment.

Vagrancy legislation dates back to fourteenth century England, where feudal lords struggled for enough hands to work their lands after the Black Death. Unemployment was effectively outlawed: anyone found loitering unproductively could be compelled to pick up a hoe or thrown into prison or the workhouse.

Subsequent vagrancy legislation across the Western world continued to criminalise beggars, hawkers, drifters, whores and refuseniks, who didn't have to commit a specific offence to be convicted of living a vagabond life: roaming beyond the proper structures of work and home, embodying restlessness, otherness and nonconformity.

Soliciting was defined in language such as 'loitering' or 'wandering in a place of public resort' and didn't just target sex workers but made a crime of begging or giving charity to those who should be the workhouse if they couldn't earn a wage. But as laws against charity were lifted, women continued to be criminalised for using sex to fund lives beyond the patriarchal home.

From the start, laws against sex work weren't just about

controlling what women did with their bodies, but how they spent their time and claimed public space.

Centuries after plague devastated the workforce in rural Europe, the United Sates revived vagrancy legislation in response to a different labour crisis – brought about by the abolition of slavery. Millions of African Americans were now free to refuse work they didn't want to do. And this didn't just leave plantations short of muscle, it also precipitated the 'servant problem'.

There were plenty of opportunities in domestic service for young Black women heading north to cities like New York, Chicago and Philadelphia. But as Saidiya Hartman explores in *Wayward Women, Beautiful Experiments*, they didn't strike out from the South just to be mammies or maids. They were seeking work, but more, they were seeking freedom. Autonomy. New ways to live and love.

Some built fairly conventional families with cohabiting male partners but were too poor to marry. Some partnered up with other women. Others raised children alone, or in households of extended kin and as-kin. Some sold sex. Many didn't. But none were respectable, so all were whores.

Hartman writes,

Vagrancy statutes were implemented and expanded to conscript young coloured women to domestic work and regulate them in proper households – most often white homes, or male-headed households, with a proper he, not someone pretending to be a husband or merely outfitted like a man, not lovers passing for sisters or a pretend Mrs shacking up with a boarder, not households comprised of three women and a child. For state authorities, black homes were disorderly houses ... The domestic was the locus for prostitution and criminality. Is this man your husband? Where is the father of your child? Why is your child unattended? These questions, if not properly answered, might land you in the workhouse or reformatory.

A young Black woman could be arrested and confined for being 'in danger of becoming morally depraved'. If she had 'children outside of wedlock or mixed-race children, her conviction was nearly guaranteed'. And reformatories were worse than prison, because sentences were indefinite and the only way out was usually into the domestic service.

To return to society, a wayward woman had to renounce her own children, her motherhood, whatever bonds she called family, and apply herself to the care of a respectable white household.

To be an unwed mother, lesbian or sex worker was much the same in the eyes of the law. Like single mothers and queers, whores are ostensibly condemned for the kind of sex they have. But such virulent persecution is never provoked just by who you sleep with.

As a slur, *whore* might mean any woman who has too much, or the wrong kind of, sex. Sex with the wrong people, or in the wrong places. From a woman's perspective, having sex to *get* what she needs might be completely different from having sex because sex *is* what she needs. But those throwing the word *whore* around have rarely given a fuck how women feel about the sex we have.

Hartman's extraordinary history deftly conjures what sex might have felt like for these wayward women, savouring a taste of the freedom that abolition promised but did not deliver. But it wasn't just their free love that was criminalised. What reformers, state institutions and respectable white society feared and condemned had less to do with sex than domesticity: their defiant claim on 'idleness as their only luxury' and refusal to 'care for others who didn't care for you'.

The real threat was the company and homes they kept, those they refused, and how the rhythms of their lives challenged racial, gender and economic norms.

In patriarchal societies that refuse to see women as fully sexual beings, we've always been expected to have sex as a means to some other end: love, money, motherhood, security. Heterosexuality itself becomes transactional. What patriarchy condemns, is women using our sexuality for ourselves – as an end in itself, or a means to our own ends, trading our bodies not for the security of the married home, but to fund nonconforming lives, loves and families.

There has always been an affinity between queerness and prostitution: queer people, falling foul of normative gender roles, may sell sex for much the same reasons single mothers do. But the role of mothering in queer and wayward spaces is often forgotten because we tend to see motherhood itself as conformity.

One of patriarchy's biggest victories has been to deny that women birthing or raising children outside the hetero-monogamous norm are mothers at all.

In 2011, the year after the Cameron government came to power, young people took to the streets in what were called the 'London riots'. The spark was the police killing of a Black man suspected of gang-related crime. But the public disorder it ignited targeted retailers of brand-name trainers. A generation whose worth was too often defined by consumer culture grabbed things they wanted but couldn't afford to buy.

In the media and political discourse that followed, the rioters were called the feral children of fatherless families – of promiscuous, irresponsible mothers whose dependence on state benefits taught their children to claim what they had neither worked for nor earned. The discontent that drove them to smash and grab wasn't the result of structural problems but bad mothering – a narrative to justify public spending cuts that would leave a third of British children living in poverty.

When the state slashes benefits and public services, women suffer more than men, children suffer more than adults, and mothers suffer more than those without children. And single-mother families are acutely vulnerable, both to poverty and to attacks on our social legitimacy.

Because single mothers are the public face of the welfare state, and have been for least as long as anything like a welfare state has actually existed.

In the United States, the Progressive Era at the turn of the twentieth century was a period of intense social reform. And social welfare activists who wanted to uplift the poor spearheaded their campaigns with the cause of lone mothers.

Who, after all, could be more in need than women and children without husbands and fathers to protect and provide for them?

Yet this was not a socialist project. Single mothers were a worthy cause because they were at acute risk of destitution. They needed money. But also, they were a prime target for the bigger progressive project of social improvement. At the core of the progressive movement were first-wave feminists, and first-wave feminism was prone to entanglement with eugenics – the kind of eugenics that made mothers the 'bearers of the race' and held how women birthed and raised their children to be essential to a morally healthy society.

So they wanted mothers – even single ones – to be able to stay at home and focus on raising the next generation. But also, they wanted to make sure they did it right. And so charitable donations – and then the public funds they successfully lobbied the state to distribute – came with close scrutiny of recipients' lives.

Single mothers had to open their homes to monthly inspections and give detailed account of how they spent their time and meagre handouts. If their homes were not clean enough, if they were found to be drinking, engaging in disorderly or immoral behaviour, working outside the home or consorting with men, their money was cut off.

What happened within the male-headed household was private business. Even, until recently, if that included violence that would be a criminal matter anywhere else. But when the state stepped in to provide for families without a man in charge, it also took on the role of patriarchal authority over these women's homes and bodies.

If a woman's domestic labours didn't directly serve a man then they became accountable to public institutions – and so the lives and labours of welfare moms, like whores, were public property.

Initially, US reformers only bothered with single mums with some potential for respectability. Charitable initiatives were keen to 'Americanise' Italian and Irish single-mother families but ignored women of colour. And the first state support – Mothers' Pensions – was for white widows only.

In 1935, Aid to Dependent Children (later Aid to Families with Dependent Children, or ADFC) extended welfare to divorced, separated and unwed moms, with racial barriers lifted in most states. But policing of their private lives persisted. And it wasn't just their homes that were open to intrusion. Some state authorities went straight for single mothers' bodies – particularly if they were Black or Brown bodies. Through the middle years of the twentieth century, a eugenic drive to stamp out state dependency saw welfare moms coerced into sterilisation under threat of losing their benefits.

In 1972 Johnnie Tillmon, a Black single mother of six and chair of the National Welfare Rights Organization (NWRO), likened the welfare state to an abusive husband:

The truth is that AFDC is like a supersexist marriage. You trade in a man for the man. But you can't divorce him if he treats you bad. He can divorce you, of course, cut you off anytime he wants. But in that case, he keeps the kids, not you. The man runs everything. In ordinary marriage, sex is supposed to be for your husband. On AFDC, you're not supposed to have any sex at all. You give up control

of your own body. It's a condition of aid. You may even
have to agree to get your tubes tied so you can never have
more children just to avoid being off welfare. The man,
the welfare system, controls your money. He tells you what
to buy, what not to buy, where to buy it, and how much
things cost.

The British welfare state was established in the aftermath of
the Second World War, and one of its driving forces was MP
and veteran suffragette Eleanor Rathbone.

In 1924 Rathbone published *The Disinherited Family*,
making a detailed case for the contribution of women's unpaid
labour to economy. Like her counterparts in the States, she
saw mothering as vital work that women did for society as a
whole. But Rathbone didn't want to bring mothering under
state control, so much as to free it from dependence on men.
She wanted all mothers to receive an independent income
that would establish them as equals within the family home –
and so empower them to resist marital rape and free them to
leave abusive husbands.

Rathbone just lived to see the Family Allowances Act
passed in 1945, but it fell well short of her ambitions. Child
benefit was extended to single mums who, before the war, had
been excluded from welfare on moral grounds. And it was
paid directly to mothers: this was the first time many wives
had money in their pockets that didn't come by way of their
husbands. But benefits targeted directly at women weren't
enough to live on, so much as a top-up to the male wage.

The British welfare state was built on the basic unit of
the male-headed household. Council housing, which was

supposed to ensure every family had a roof over their heads, also defined family in nuclear, heteronormative terms. Even war widows and their children were left out in the cold.

Through the latter half of the twentieth century, feminists demanded the right to work – to earn their autonomy the same way men did. But as women became ever more active outside the home, breaking into new realms of professional and public life, parallel campaigns continued to fight for the economic autonomy of women who didn't go out to work.

In the States, Black women like Tillmon were the driving force behind the welfare rights movement of the 1960s and 1970s, calling for state support in the form of a Guaranteed Adequate Income that anticipated today's universal basic income (UBI) proposals.

Asserting the value of their work in the home, these wel-fare warriors talked about 'mother power'. But they stressed that there was more to caring labours than bringing up kids. NWRO vice-chair Beulah Sanders rejected the notion that waged work was empowering for women whose time and talents were better spent getting 'out into the community, mixing with the people, finding out what their problems are and trying to help solve those problems'.

And in Europe, Wages for Housework framed funding for care not just as payment due for the work women did to support the productive economy, but as a challenge to capi-talism itself.

Using 'housework' as an umbrella term for all the unpaid, feminised labours that prop up the profit-making economy – from birthing workers to sexual services to emotional labour performed not just at home but in the workplace – they rejected notions of care and domesticity as natural embodiments of female nature. But more, in framing these services as work, they also asserted women's right to withdraw their labour – and instead practise love and care in ways that didn't serve individual men, patriarchy or capitalism at all.

In this spirit, from 1975, Wages for Housework campaigns including the ECP collaborated from the Kings Cross Women's Centre. Working on principles of collective self-help, they supported one another to access benefits, resisted police harassment of sex workers walking their kids to school through the King's Cross red-light district and campaigned for reparations for slavery and neo-colonialism.

Kay, a single mother of two and Wages for Housework activist since the 1980s, says Income Support, which was available to anyone out of work and came with a lone-parent premium for single mothers, was part of what made their work possible.

'It wasn't much,' she says, 'but it made a huge amount of difference.' Along with Housing Benefit, help from her own mum and a network of single mothers who exchanged babysitting and second-hand kids' clothes, 'it meant I could be involved in campaigning and organising at the Centre'.

Within second-wave feminism's great flowering of movements, fighting patriarchy on so many fronts, there were tensions between middle-class white women escaping the confines of domestic life and women of colour fighting to stay at home and raise their kids. Just as women who wanted to eradicate commodification of the female body clashed with women for whom selling sex was a better option than the miserable pay of other feminised forms of employment.

Feminists fighting for the same rights as men didn't always see eye-to-eye with those more concerned with empowering motherhood. Yet like Rathbone, many who came after her saw these struggles as two sides of the same coin. Only equal rights at the ballot box could bring women equal rights in the bedroom.

There was no reason these aims should be in conflict – until capitalism made peace with one at the expense of the other.

Neoliberalism, which arrived as British economic policy with the country's first female prime minister, didn't mind expanding the workforce to include women, particularly if they were forced to accept lower wages than men. Equal rights were OK, so long as gendered responsibilities kept women's freedom to exercise those rights in check.

Attacks on 'irresponsible' single mums were a hallmark of Thatcherite nastiness, and it was Peter Lilley, who served under Thatcher and then Major, who promised to 'root out ... young ladies who get pregnant just to jump the housing queue' along with the rest of 'the something-for-nothing society'. Yet the biggest attacks on public welfare came later, from the centre-left Blair and Clinton governments.

Thatcher was no feminist and never pretended to be. But it was the Blair administration, who claimed bringing more women into government than ever before as a feminist victory, which confirmed how completely a feminism focused on liberating individual women had abandoned the struggle to liberate care.

One of first things New Labour did after eighteen years in

opposition was to abolish the lone-parent benefit for single mothers, a move that spurred Wages for Housework to help single mothers form a new autonomous campaign: Single Mothers' Self-Defence.

Kay says,

*It was Tony Blair's women – Harriet Harman was the head of welfare – they were the ones who came in and rubber-stamped the cut to mothers' money. They forced us out into waged work whether or not we wanted a second job – and they knew very well that women's wages were crap. They knew very well they were putting us in a situation where we were desperate. We had to put food on the table and keep a home for our children. And so we'd have to take any job, with any conditions, with whatever the employer was trying to do to us. For a lot of us, it was three or four jobs.*

Income Support didn't necessarily lift single mothers out of poverty. But Nina Lopez of the ECP says it was based on 'implicit acknowledgement that as a single mother you were raising children and so you were entitled to societal support'.

Successive neoliberal reforms have attacked this assumption, making the *raison d'être* of the welfare state not to support those out of paid work, but to force them into it. And the UK's most recent overhaul of welfare continues this work. According to the single-parent-family charity Gingerbread, Universal Credit has 'increased expectations for single parents to move into work' and forced them to justify themselves to 'hostile' advisors.

Society says mothers must always put their children first,

but the welfare state insists they prioritise getting back into paid work above all else. Welfare mums are told the hours they spend looking after their kids have no value, yet childcare costs more than they earn going out to work. Before they're through the first year a gainfully employed mother would expect to take as maternity leave, single mothers on welfare are compelled to attend 'work-focused interviews' and show they're striving to free themselves from dependence on the state.

Half a century after Tillmon compared welfare to an abusive marriage, a report by Legal Action for Women likened these demands to a husband asking his wife 'what did you do all day?' as if raising children wasn't real work.

Tony Blair described single mothers as 'workless', Lopez recalls. 'We knew very well he meant worthless.'

Women demanded lives and identities defined by more than just motherhood. Neoliberals have twisted this demand to frame forcing single mums into work as a kind of female empowerment: only by learning to stand on our own two feet can we achieve autonomy and self-respect.

But autonomy is not the same as independence, and the idea that you cannot be autonomous if you depend on others is an odd one. We all depend on other people. Workers depend on employers, bosses depend on employees, and the entire profit-making economy depends on the reproductive labours that birth, raise, feed and care for workers and consumers. Human beings only exist as individuals in relation to one another – and what is society, if not a vast web of interdependence?

But neoliberals don't believe in society. Society, as we are told Thatcher famously said, does not exist. What she actually said was:

> Who is society? There is no such thing! There are individual men and women and there are families and no government can do anything except through people and people must look after themselves first.

Neoliberalism demands people look after themselves, eschewing dependence on others, and look after themselves *first*, eschewing responsibility for others. And yet, there is one social unit neoliberalism does believe in.

There are individuals, and there are *families*.

And the same regimes that shame mums for dependence on the state are more than happy for us to sacrifice our autonomy to individual men.

In 1996, Bill Clinton's massive overhaul of the welfare system forced those out of work to take any job they could. But more, it aggressively promoted the nuclear family, giving states financial incentives to reduce births outside marriage. And it launched a new offensive against the privacy of the single-mother family by diverting public funds to support single mothers into tracking down absent fathers and forcing them to pay up instead.

Still today single mothers are denied benefits unless they cooperate with efforts to force their Kindesvaters to pay maintenance. Investigating the effect of these policies on single-mother families for ProPublica, journalist Eli Hager writes:

The moms described it as humiliating and sometimes terrifying to be questioned about their sexual histories by agents of the state, in small interview rooms, just to obtain a basic form of government help. Some were required to submit their children to genetic testing in order to receive aid.

Others fear domestic violence or emotional abuse if they name fathers to the authorities. Caseworkers from multiple states shared instances of mothers saying that dads had threatened to retaliate by killing or kidnapping the mom or her child.

Policymakers say forcing fathers to take responsibility encourages them to play an active role in their children's lives. Mothers Hager spoke to didn't quite see it this way, fearing 'that an absent dad forced to pay support would spitefully seek custody or greater involvement in medical and educational decisions about the child'.

But if hoping that state-enforced financial ties will evolves into bonds of love seems far-fetched, nor does the effort of tracking down these men save the state much money, because most are themselves struggling financially. The whole point is to enforce the dynamics of private responsibility and dependence encapsulated in the nuclear family, and making women dependent on men inevitably gives men power over women.

Neoliberals don't celebrate motherhood like the Victorians did. With few families able to survive on a single male wage, there is no romanticisation of domesticity. But in their commitment to the nuclear family, they still depend on feminised selflessness and compassion.

The more collective responsibility is disdained, public spending slashed and services privatised, the greater the burden on family to support children, the elderly, sick, unemployed, overworked, underpaid and undervalued.

And this is why the welfare queen is the target of so much hatred.

Not because single mums weigh particularly heavily on the public purse, but because the welfare mum upends a fundamental principle on which the whole system is built: mothers aren't supposed to depend on the welfare state, we're supposed to negate the need for one.

And like the Victorians, neoliberals don't just make women responsible for physical labours of care. For all their crazed individualism, they don't think individuals are solely responsible for their own choices and circumstances.

Individuals' mums are responsible, too.

Neoliberals don't think social inequality is to blame when deprived youth riot in the street: it's a problem mothers must solve – mainly by raising them in family units that embody values of personal responsibility and unpaid care. They don't think the LA riots were the fault of state violence, or an economy that built its wealth on Black labour and then denied Black communities a share in it. They were the fault of women who raise children without fathers.

For decades, single mums with the temerity to ask for something back – from a society that doesn't exist yet seems abjectly dependent on how we run our personal lives – have been told to get off our arses and take responsibility. After the first wave of neoliberal reforms, many did so by turning to the free market to trade the same labours mums have always fallen back on. Women selling sex in King's Cross, whose numbers exploded in the 1980s, called themselves 'Thatcher's girls'.

Sex work can be a choice, and there are women – like Meghan, whose role as a dominatrix is a rewarding mix of theatre and therapy – who find it empowering. But as ever, women's choices, and particularly the choices of single mothers, are dictated by circumstance. And the ECP insists that most women who sell sex do so only because their choices are so impoverished.

Because, as Kay says, women's wages are crap.

Sex work can mean favourable hourly rates and flexibility around single mothering – without having to account to officials for how you spend your time and money. And yet boundaries between public and private are still blurred.

When Sutcliffe killed, society saw violent crime as a professional risk prostitutes took when they chose to engage in transactional sex on the streets, on common grounds and in rented rooms. In a society that excepts – or at least expects – 'partner violence' there is nowhere the public woman is safe from private abuse.

These days, the internet offers ways to make sex work safer, as well as more compatible with mothering. Webcamming means you can work from home once the kids are in bed without shelling out for a babysitter. Sex workers can advertise and book clients online, networking to share information about those who might be dangerous. But legal regimes around the world are cracking down on these online spaces, apparently doing everything in their power to force prostitutes back out on the street.

Vagrancy laws have now been almost entirely scrapped. In 2022, the British government launched a consultation to repeal a two-hundred-year-old vagrancy act that still criminalises rough sleeping. But laws against soliciting still echo medieval statutes against vagabond life.

Still, in the UK and elsewhere, soliciting or working out of a brothel is illegal – meaning that just two women sharing a flat, where they can see clients while keeping an eye out for one another, are at risk of arrest and prosecution.

As if in recognition that so much hetero sex is transactional, a man and woman alone, exchanging money for sex, is a private matter, not a criminal one. It's when things get more organised, when women band together and create spaces of mutual protection, that the law steps in.

Stella Winter, a single mum, ECP member and former nurse, had been surviving on cleaning jobs – 'exhausting, hard physical work and badly paid' – until a friend introduced her to work at a massage parlour. 'I raised two children on the proceeds of prostitution. The money was an escape from what would have been the unbearable drudgery and occasional terror of poverty.'

But mums doing sex work 'are terrified that social services will be on our back trying to take our children away', she writes.

In the States, more than two hundred thousand children go into the public care system each year; in England, around thirty thousand. And every year, several thousand British children are adopted. Less than four per cent of these adoptions happen with the birth mother's consent.

The story of each woman whose children are taken from her by the state is inevitably complex. But almost every one will have tried and failed to prove herself a fit mother. And if social workers know she sells sex, this is an uphill battle.

'Social services' starting point is that mothers who are doing sex work are bad mothers or suspicious or irresponsible,' Niki Adams of the ECP told openDemocracy. 'They are deeply disrespectful and dismissive of the bond between mother and child.'

The most common reason social services impose a child protection plan is not abuse but neglect – a charge that conjures images of children unloved and uncared for. In fact, neglect can mean leaving a twelve-year-old to babysit a four-year-old while you go to work. It can mean not being able to keep the fridge stocked or not living up to a social worker's idea of what a family home should look like.

Child protection services are not supposed to break up families only because they are poor. But once a teacher, social worker, neighbour – or, often, a Kindesvater – has raised concerns over a woman's mothering, things like occasional drug use, getting drunk in front of a child, being repeatedly late for school or failing to provide an adequate breakfast every day can be enough to charge a mother with neglect.

It's an open secret that poor, disabled, Black and ethnic minority mothers are losing their children because of things middle-class parents do without raising an eyebrow. As lawyers representing mothers in family courts in the Bronx told the *New Yorker*: child protection has become for Black women what the criminal justice system is for Black men.

Social services are part of the public infrastructure of care envisioned by Progressive Era reformers. But society's most vulnerable carers see them as the enemy: ask for help and you risk losing your family altogether. Even reporting domestic abuse can be acutely dangerous, because a mother who fails to shield her children from violence she herself suffers can be accused of neglect.

And in the UK, the number of children going into care has soared as child protection services have been privatised. The profit motive has not worked well for a sector that separates children from their mothers, unless you measure success by the number of families torn apart.

In 2000, the Wages for Housework campaign, now based at the Crossroads Women's Centre in north London, launched Global Women's Strike: a nexus of autonomous organisations including the English Collective of Prostitutes, Single Mothers' Self-Defence and WinVisible – 'a multi-racial community group of women with visible and invisible disabilities'. Wages Due Lesbians has become Queer Strike, and Black Women for Wages for Housework is now better known as Women of Colour in the GWS.

Nina Lopez is one of the coordinators of Support Not Separation, which defends mothers of all these intersecting identities against the growing threat of having their children taken from them. The premise of Support Not Separation's campaigns is that if the state spent as much money supporting single mothers as it does investigating them – as it spends on fostering arrangements and adoption services – many more children could stay with the mothers who love and care for them.

'The relationship between mother and child has never been valued to the point where society should financially pay for it. And that is really at the heart of it,' Lopez says.

At the heart of all of Global Women's Strike's campaigns is the demand for society to value women's work – and support it, with unconditional payments that aren't designed to keep mothers at home, or to force them out of it, that don't dictate that they must, or must not, have a man about the house.

But Wages for Housework has always stressed that while *sex work is work* and *all mothers are working mothers*, it shouldn't have to be this way. Work is alienated labour. It's what capitalism tells us we must do to earn a living – and a sense of self-worth. Threatening strike is a statement about how dependent society is on those of us so easily shamed for our dependence. But it's also a call to transform care, to reclaim love, sexuality and mothering for ourselves.

And in concrete terms, Global Women's Strike is now calling for a 'Care Income' – a form of unconditional guaranteed income that 'would prioritise and support the work of all those, of every gender, who care for people, for the urban and rural environment, and for the natural world.'

Conservatives say family is the bedrock of society. And they are right. Families don't just reproduce human life, creating more bodies, more workers and consumers to drive the economy. They reproduce cultural and social norms, dynamics of oppression and power. Which is why those who hold power have always feared and persecuted wayward motherhoods.

Calling single mothers whores, patriarchy erases motherhoods that challenge its hegemony. Criminalising whoring, it denies women the economic means they have always used to support experiments in love and domesticity – the liquidity that keeps loose women moving freely, shifting into new constellations of care and sending ripples through society as a whole.

The work of scholars like Saidiya Hartman and Barbara Minchinton sheds much-needed light on these suppressed histories of riotously, disorderly and publicly queer mothering. Re-examining the past to elicit narratives beyond brutality and oppression – beyond the fallen woman, the ultimate victim and outcast – they also hint at possible futures. They invite imaginative exploration of vagabond motherhood as a site of social power.

A Care Income would make these experiments more than just imaginative.

Since the pandemic, care has become an issue 'feminists can't avoid anymore,' Kay says, 'but they don't acknowledge that Wages for Housework has been campaigning for fifty years on this.'

These conversations are the latest incarnation of arguments Selma James – who founded Wages for Housework, internationalised the movement and is still an activist in her nineties – welfare warriors on both sides of the Atlantic and theorists like Silvia Federici have been making since the 1970s, and Eleanor Rathbone before them.

But now, increasingly, we're not just talking about the exploitation of female labour, we're connecting feminist struggles with ecological ones. Human health to planetary health. It's not just mums who are driven to exhaustion and hysteria. Our soils are drained and our weather systems whipped into a frenzy.

It has never been clearer that we need to shift the entire economy away from work that turns resources into profit and waste, towards labours that revive, regenerate and sustain. And while better-funded feminist and environmental organisations try to tweak the system, the women challenging its fundamental logic are doing so from the grassroots up.

Progressive Era reformers believed mothering was essential to a healthy society and so they wanted to fund reproductive labour. But mostly, these women didn't have children of their own because they saw mothering as incompatible with political work. They crossed the gendered divide between care and power. And from their elevated position, they tried to engineer society by controlling how those at the bottom of the social heap conducted their personal lives.

But if the split between work and care is gendered then the ecological crisis is a feminist issue – and the women whose feminism is ambitious enough to fight for the change we need aren't running for political office, they're up to their necks in the minutiae of individual women's struggles against Child Protection and the police.

GWS activists prepare detailed reports, compiling case studies and expert briefings, lobbying for welfare and legislative change. But mostly, their day-to-day work is on the front lines of battles to keep families together, sharing legal resources, informing women of their rights and petitioning and picketing courts.

If care was economically autonomous, perhaps more of us would be fighting alongside them.

A Care Income would empower single mothers to resist coercion and control – and to do so collectively. Society dumps vast responsibilities on mothers. A Care Income would give us the means to *take* responsibility, and take it beyond our own homes – reversing the dynamic of public institutions interfering in our private lives and unleashing the wild solidarity of vagabond mothering as a force for social change.

# Chapter 7

## Activists and Othermothers

When I became a single mum, I wanted to know: why, when we talk of reproductive rights, do we talk only of the right not to have children? What becomes of our rights when we decide to keep a pregnancy?

Have we sacrificed our right, then, to autonomy?

On some level, I'd believed I had. When I was pregnant my choice looked clear and binary: termination, or caring for a man as well as a child.

Having made my choice, a feminism of rights and choices quickly unravelled.

The gendered expectations and responsibilities. The precarity of the mother-self. The impossibility of doing it all. The time, at a party to commemorate my friend who died of cancer while I was pregnant, when men I'd known for years patted my boyfriend on the back, topped up his drink and scolded me for having my baby out so late.

Why, I demanded, does *reproductive rights* treat reproduction as something that begins and ends in the body, ignoring the labours that come after?

Of course, this question is answered – as a Black woman writer pointed out when I ranted in the pub – by the reproductive justice movement, led by women of colour, which elevates the right to have children alongside the right not to, as well as 'the right to parent the children we have in safe and sustainable communities'. And reproductive justice is about more than just rights, demanding the material means to exercise those rights.

To understand my identity as a single mother, I needed a feminism that didn't carry an underlying suspicion – or even outright rejection – of motherhood. Motherhood made feminism acutely relevant to me; I needed a feminism that made motherhood relevant. A feminism for the journey that began when I walked away from the abortion clinic still pregnant.

The kind of feminism I was raised on was all about claiming the freedoms of men. But while white feminists were busy escaping motherhood, feminists of colour have expanded it. Because for women who have been forcibly sterilised, had their children taken from them, reproduction is not capitulation to oppression – it's an act of resistance.

In *We Live for the We: The Political Power of Black Motherhood*, Dani McClain quotes 'Mama-activist' Trina Greene Brown: 'We are raising children who were never meant to survive . . . People who are raising kids who *were* meant to survive have a lot to learn from us.'

If about a quarter of children in Western countries are being raised in lone-parent households, we cannot be dismissed as a motley collection of aberrations and personal failures. Our sheer numbers show the heteronormative nuclear family isn't working, our numbers are rising, and our homes are myriad experiments in another way to mother.

And yet, if white mothers like me are working off-script, the same can't easily be said of mothers of colour.

In the United States, nineteen per cent of white children live in single-parent families compared to twenty-nine per cent of Hispanic children and just over half of Black children. If for white American families, single mothering is the most popular alternative to the dominant family model, for Black households, it *is* the dominant model.

Single moms of colour have family traditions to fall back on.

When I asked Lisa how she'd dodged the myth of happy-ever-after married bliss, she scoffed, 'The girls in those movies never looked like me.'

*I still remember this one girl in high school who had an active dad – like, she was the exception. There was all these different variations of family, but only one or two with Mom and Dad both at home, and they were white.*

*My mom's all, 'I did it by myself.' But she's a goddamn liar because she had a huge network. Like, I didn't even know my mom was my mom, really, because she was so young we were kind of raised like sisters. I call my grandfather 'Daddy' because he was, like, my only father figure. I also had my great grandmother in my life until I was in college – she died when I was in freshman year. So there was always someone to pick me up or drop me off. It was blood. It was family.*

*And, all right, it's a little bit different, but I guess I'm trying*

*to model the same type of thing here on this Berlin island,*
*where there's just so many hands that I don't miss anything.*

For white patriarchy, which has been tearing at the fabric
of Black families for centuries, this intergenerational reproduction of love and resilience is a hereditary disorder.

An unavoidable text in the modern history of single
motherhood, the infamous 'Moynihan Report' commissioned
by Lyndon B. Johnson's Great Society administration in 1965,
called the African American family a 'tangle of pathology'
characterised by 'divorce, separation, and desertion, female
family head, children in broken homes, and illegitimacy'.

Sociologist Daniel Patrick Moynihan argued that poverty
and low educational and professional achievement among
African Americans were rooted in Black American family
structure. Single Black mothers weren't giving their children
enough attention, and growing up in homes without strong
male role models was stunting Black boys.

Even in Black families with fathers around, 'matriarchal'
Black wives undermined male authority, emasculating
husbands and sons. Moynihan quoted stats on educational
achievement – thirty-nine per cent of white college graduates were female, compared to fifty-three per cent of
graduates of colour – not as a victory of Black gender equality but as evidence of a toxic imbalance in the Black family.

A man finds his worth in working to support his family,
Moynihan argued. Partnered to a Black woman who earns
more than he does, or father to children supported by welfare
channelled to mothers, the Black American father was hardly
a man at all.

*The Negro Family: The Case for National Action*, to grant the report its full title, angered Black feminists. But Moynihan's diagnosis resonated with many progressives, all the way up to Martin Luther King.

Moynihan praised the achievements of the Civil Rights movement. Now, he wanted national action to complete its project by fully assimilating Black culture into white. African Americans would only get their share in the American dream if Black families were truly American – and that meant patriarchal, in the original sense of the word.

But also, importantly, Moynihan identified slavery as the root of the Black American family's nonconformity.

Many cultural threads weave through the networks of care that support mothers of colour in the United States and Europe. In Black communities, these may include matri-focused African traditions – faint but persistent lines of social practice that survived even as Africans were kidnapped and cut from their roots.

But kinship bonds weren't just brutally severed by the journey west. They were severed again and again in slavery. Denying Black humanity, slavery assaulted the place where humanity is nurtured. These sustained attacks – and the resilience of that humanity in spite of them – are a part of what shapes Black American families today.

Feminists, particularly white feminists, have often equated marriage – which made a woman her husband's property, subsumed her individual identity and yoked her to unpaid labour – with slavery. Slavery and marriage were both a kind of ownership. An enslaved woman couldn't legally wed because she was already the property of her white master. Like wives, slaves took their master's name.

Yet the analogy between marriage and slavery falters into the vast gulf between the lives of white women granted the status of *wife* and *mother* and Black women who performed wifely and mothering labours on their behalf. Black women kept the white mistress's home, satisfied her husband's sexual demands, fed her white babies at their breasts. The care of an enslaved woman's own family was an extreme perversion of the 'working mother's' double burden – performing all these labours again, subversively, for her own family.

I could not begin to imagine what this kind of mothering felt like, without Toni Morrison's words:

What was left to hurt her now? News of Halle's death? No. She had been prepared for that better than she had been for his life. The last of her children, whom she barely glanced at when he was born because it wasn't worth the trouble to try and learn the features you would never see change into adulthood anyway. Seven times she had done that: held a little foot; examined the fat fingertips with her own – fingers she never saw become the male or female hands a mother would recognise anywhere. She didn't know to this day what their permanent teeth looked like; or how they held their heads when they walked. Did Patty lose her lisp? What colour did Famous' skin finally take? Was that a cleft in Johnny's chin or just a dimple that would disappear soon's his jawbone changed? Four girls, and the last time she saw them there was no hair under their arms. Does

Ardelia still love the burned bottom of bread? All seven were gone or dead. What would be the point of looking too hard at the youngest one?

Slavery stole Black motherhoods and it stole Black childhoods. And yet it failed to extinguish the humanity of enslaved people, who knew themselves and one another to be mothers, children, fathers and kin, and persisted in nurturing loved ones they couldn't protect.

Often, children born into slavery were fathered by white men who raped to increase their wealth. But while slavers wanted Black bodies to multiply only as capital, enslaved mothers continued to reproduce Black families, emotionally and culturally – as Barbara Omolade recounts in *The Rising Song of African American Women*:

In rejecting and ignoring the negative notions associated with Black single-motherhood, especially the separation of marriage from family, Black women assumed the role of family head. In the absence of spouses and mates, the Black single mother assumed that she and her children were a family. She protected, nurtured and fought for a new kind of family, one which emerged outside the patriarchy of her man, yet remained within the oppressive sphere of the racial patriarch. Her family developed within a slave community which provided sustenance, love and resistance from the horrors of slavery. The slave community also socialised, protected and reproduced human beings who were born into families and who expected to have families of their own.

When these women were emancipated, many 'became enraged at the thought of being owned and taken by any man even if he had black skin'.

Black women within the rural black community often defied the restrictions on their womanhood and sexuality by living alone (near family and kin) and working their own farms, running their own lives without men as mates and protectors, frequently sojourning for truth and God ... women often lived with women both as emotional and sexual companions. Women in urban black communities had several male lovers and companions and did not submit to them in traditional ways because they maintained an active life as community workers, political and social activists, and workers within the paid labour force.

Omolade's image of the sexually and economically autonomous, politically defiant Black woman, emancipated far beyond her white contemporaries, is as thrilling to me as a twenty-first-century single mother as it has been frightening to white patriarchy.

But because they were rebelling against the oppression of racial patriarchy, rather than oppression at the hands of their own menfolk, many Black women also felt profound responsibility to care for and uplift Black men. As they claimed the rights of free citizens, so they claimed their status as wives, their right to respectable families and to care for those families under respectable designations they had so long been denied. And so, equally, they wanted their men recognised as husbands and fathers.

In law, abolition made this possible. But in practice, attacks on the Black family did not end with slavery. The Fordist family wage, designed to allow white working men to keep a wife at home, wasn't extended to Black men, who were excluded from unions and forced into jobs that didn't pay enough to provide for their families. When Mothers' Pensions were introduced to support widows, mothers of colour were ineligible, and when they were replaced by Aid to Dependent Children, most southern states still excluded Black women on the grounds that they were 'employable mothers'.

The real enemy of the Black nuclear family was not the untameable Black woman who'd taken her liberation too far. It was a white-supremacist society that denied Black mothering economic support – from Black men or welfare – because it continued to demand Black women's labour in white homes, and didn't deem Black children worthy of the dedicated mothering white children needed.

It was a social and economic order that saw the reproduction and nurture of white children, white families and white culture as the only proper use of mothering.

Moynihan wanted to put things right by extending the family wage to Black men and reforming welfare to encourage Black families to stay together. But when these reforms were voted down, he got on board with measures to penalise mothers who dared go it alone. By making single motherhood even more financially wretched, the state gave Black women the burden of keeping the Black nuclear family together.

Predictably, this approach failed. And over subsequent

decades, the more it failed, the more it blamed and punished single mothers – from Reagan's attacks on the welfare queen to Clinton forcing mums to choose benefits and the privacy of their sex lives.

And yet Black women kept mothering on their own terms, reproducing resilient constellations of care that have bequeathed American culture a rich history of family beyond the patriarchal norm.

Taking poverty, crime and drug use as proof of their inadequacy, the Moynihan Report didn't bother to examine how Black women mothered against these social ills, how Black families managed without wage-earning men, how they organised, struggled, provided for and protected their children.

But as Clinton enacted his family-focused welfare reforms – by which time some seventy per cent of African American babies were being born to unmarried mothers – a team of ethnographers were following the family lives of Black mothers in Harlem, a neighbourhood that exemplified Moynihan's 'broken Negro family'.

*Stress and Resilience: The Social Context of Reproduction in Central Harlem* by Leith Mullings and Alaka Wali provides answers to questions Moynihan failed to ask.

Most of the households in the study were 'female-headed', but far from broken, their family ties were strong and extensive. Almost all the mothers said family was extremely important to them, but definitions of the word were elastic, from immediate blood-kin to far-reaching networks including 'people who are close to me even though they go their own way'.

Some spoke of 'church family' and one defined family as

'the people that are close to you and that you love and be with the rest of your life, and your dog.' One said, 'Sometimes siblings can be more than just a relative . . . and a friend is more family than siblings sometimes.'

Another, 'Sisterhood is real; I have friends who are as close as sisters.'

These mothers reported, on average, five or six people in their lives 'whom they could count on for everyday favours, rely on when they were sick, spend time with in social activities, ask to look after their children, talk to about personal matters, count on for a loan of several hundred dollars in an emergency, share happiness with, lean on, give help to, and share their most private feelings with.'

Most mothers had some contact with, and support from, their children's fathers. But the role of these men wasn't all or nothing and didn't replace other bonds of care. A father might attend the birth of his child but not support them financially. He might help out in an emergency but not day-to-day. His own mother might be involved be in his children's lives, even if he rarely saw them.

Mothers, grandmothers, siblings, fathers, aunties, uncles, cousins and friends allowed these mothers to work, organise, have nights off. To write and perform. Some women pregnant with their first child already had relatives at home who depended on them. One mother had eight sisters, each of whom played a special role in the life of one of her eight children. Some moms left their children with their own mothers or grandmothers, permanently or as a temporary arrangement in tough times.

Yet for all this richly networked support, they were stretched to their limits and stretched again by poverty and racism in the workplace, schools, welfare offices and a health-care system that refused to take Black women's health seriously.

Putting food on the table and keeping a clean home were an uphill battle in an underserved neighbourhood where landlords neglected their properties. Persistent leaks stained mopped floors, mildew crept across the walls. Bathrooms filled with washing up when kitchen plumbing failed. Nights were spent patrolling for cockroaches. One woman took in a cat she was allergic to, suffering a rash across her face rather than leaving her baby vulnerable to rats.

The ethnographers noted that no matter the effort it demanded, these mothers almost always kept spotless homes. But to do so, housekeeping extended beyond what we usually count among domestic duties.

It meant pursing landlords through an opaque and racist legal system that one mother described as 'mortifying theatre'. It meant forming tenants' associations, organising rent strikes, running committees, holding block parties to empower community ties, campaigning to have garbage removed from the streets. They joined environmental action groups to document pollution from Harlem's factories, sewage treatment plant and bus station, turned vacant lots into community gardens and rallied volunteers to renovate a derelict building so it could house the homeless.

Just as family embraced kin beyond blood, marriage and the four walls of a woman's own home, so keeping house meant caring for a whole community, its streets, its buildings, its very air.

*

Patricia Hill Collins traces a history of the 'othermothering' Mullings documented in Harlem back to African traditions of communal childcare, through the collective responsibility enslaved communities took for children separated from bloodmothers, and the community activism that has shaped African American cultures ever since.

Othermothers ease the pressures on bloodmothers, sharing the load. They ensure a child has more than one adult they can turn to, love and learn from, or pick up the pieces when a bloodmother cannot cope. When women othermother one another's children, they multiply a brood of siblings. They create family bonds not of law or blood, not sanctified by sex or money, but forged in mutual solidarity.

A child's bond with an othermother may be as important, or more so, than that with a father, a grandmother or even a bloodmother. But othermothering also stands for mothering as political work: activism as care, and care as political activism. Checking up on any kid you find loitering on your street corner. Defending every Black child threatened by oppression, marginalisation or violence.

And othermothering is the work of elders who develop mentoring relationships with younger women – 'mothering the mind' – to help them realise their identities as mothers, organisers, as women in and of themselves, and as upstanding members of the community.

When I began exploring histories of single motherhood, I knew it was a family form more common, and more accepted, in Black communities than white. I knew the welfare queen was a racialised stereotype, and that the politics of mothering were bound with the politics of race.

I didn't realise, though, just how comprehensively the feminism of women of colour answered so many of my most fundamental questions. Needing bigger ideas of family to survive, women of colour have let politics into the family and family into politics.

Omolade was active in Black nationalism, despite its often patriarchal ethos. Refusing to limit her role in the struggle to reproducing the patriarchal Black family, she followed in the footsteps of her mentor, civil rights pioneer Ella Baker, empowering networks of community activism and care – and worked with Black American Sisterhood of Single Mothers to resist both racist and patriarchal oppression.

Women like Omolade, like Loretta Ross – who was shamed as a teen mom and then robbed of her fertility by medical malpractice, before becoming one of the founders of the reproductive justice movement – and generations of single Black mothers whose care has shaped their communities, offer a venerable history of radical love and resistance.

They meet my experience of motherhood not as surrender, but a political awakening, and show that beyond the nuclear family, there are other, better, ways to raise children.

If I began this project comparing my motherhood to married motherhood – *my motherhood is just as valid!* – this turned out to be an easy win: the myth of the perfect nuclear family rapidly unravelled. But these activists, agitators and othermothers present much more challenging models to aspire to.

The rich web of care that supported Harlem mothers didn't

just catch them if they fell, it was exhausting in itself. Having six people you can rely on means you have six people you'll make room for in a life already at full capacity.

They talked about the comfort of having people in your life you can be completely honest with, people who understand. About the rewards of helping others and being depended on – not to mention the block parties: 'I'm telling you, you have never seen such a sense of community in your life,' one mother said of an event to celebrate the building they had collectively renovated.

But they also talked about the stresses of kinwork – of arguments and jealousies, of feeling under-appreciated by one person or not being able to do enough for another. And the wider you open your love, the more pain you're exposed to.

When we become mothers, there is a raw period beginning with birth when the bounds of our empathy are exploded. If love is the expansion of the self, in new motherhood the self is porous. Pain, anyone's pain, pain we might pass on the street, or see in humanitarian disasters on the news, intrusive thoughts of abandoned children or mothers unable to feed and protect their families, can be overwhelming.

Gradually, we put the boundaries back up. We cannot function swimming in a sea of raw empathy, exposed to universal pains. So we relearn detachment: the defensive skill of compartmentalising. There's a permanent shift of frontiers to include our children in our new, expanded selves. And perhaps those boundaries will always be a little more porous, particularly to the suffering of children. But those borders also reaffirm the otherness of those beyond them.

At least, this was my experience – maybe not one shared by all mothers.

McClain says she felt a 'wave of recognition' reading a description of the raw vulnerability of new motherhood by Alyssa Knickerbocker, a white mother who, in time, was able to regrow 'a barrier between oneself and the world'.

'I wonder whether we black parents inhabit a different reality,' McClain writes. 'For us, does this anxious vigilance, the fear for our own children and others that Knickerbocker describes as an "excess of empathy", eventually fade away? I don't want to be held hostage by fear, but I'm not sure how to avoid that.'

If a woman can never fully put those walls back up – or if she erects them differently, further out, encompassing more – her motherhood is forever raw at the edges. And this is not an abstract concern, but a persistent state of physical vulnerability to societal violence.

Studies show that discrimination against Black children manifests in mothers' bodies. Hyper-vigilance – worry, fear – mean lost sleep, high blood pressure and raised inflammatory markers.

At the height of the Covid pandemic, when a racist health-care system was, in the words of A. Rochaun Meadows-Fernandez, 'more likely to kill you' than the virus, the founder of the #FreeBlackMotherhood movement wrote of how trauma passed from generation to generation in Black families is compounded by daily news of Black men, women and children being killed by police: 'As Black mothers, grief is embedded in our being. It accumulates and manifests as body aches and pains.'

\*

Reproductive work doesn't begin and end in the body. But nor does it end in the care we do for our own families or in our own homes.

For a single mother like me, needing support and connection, othermothering is an exciting proposition. Networks of female solidarity can free us from dependence on individual men. The more women support one another and share our responsibilities, the more we are empowered to make single motherhood a positive choice – and even upend the dynamics of heterosexual relationships.

But the potential of othermothering is far greater than just giving individual women more freedom or making dating less awful. And the challenge it poses is to open our boundaries, to expand our care. To unfurl from the heart of humanity and understand how all family dynamics are in conversation with greater relations of power.

If white feminism has often focused on breaking into masculinised realms of power, this struggle has never been truly radical because fighting for equality within oppressive power structures is quite different from tearing them down altogether – or creating alternatives.

Women of colour, who have been oppressed by an entire white-supremacist social order, have had to think bigger. But what white feminists have often failed to grasp is that fighting patriarchy and fighting white supremacy aren't separate struggles.

Because patriarchy is always racial.

White patriarchy attacks Black mothering because it is the practice of raising *children who were never meant to survive* and of reproducing cultures it abhors. But equally, white women haven't just been kept at home to make babies – we've been kept at home to make *white* babies.

Patriarchy's fundamental claim on women is rooted in biological reproduction. Patriarchy says that when a man impregnates a woman, the child is *his*. And if our children belong to men, our mothering belongs to men too.

Patriarchy claims our babies, and so our bodies, our motherly labours and our selves.

Where women have reproductive rights – the right to abortion – men cannot claim new life still embedded in women's bodies. But as soon as a child is born things get messy. Raising the next generation is claimed as something we do for fathers, for society, the state, the nation, the race.

No society in historical memory has done more to reduce women to baby-making machines than Nazi Germany. But today, far-right regimes in Italy and Hungary explicitly link family values, 'traditional marriage' and raising the national fertility rate to immigration control, speaking the language of 'national extinction' and 'great replacement'. Neo-fascist prime minister Viktor Orbán calls migrants a 'poisonous' security risk or 'Muslim invaders' – and in the same breath brands his country 'family-friendly Hungary'.

'In all of Europe there are fewer and fewer children, and the answer of the West to this is migration,' he said in 2019. 'They want as many migrants to enter as there are missing kids, so the numbers will add up. We Hungarians have a different way of thinking. Instead of just numbers, we want Hungarian children. Migration for us is surrender.'

But in post-Brexit Britain, right-wing politicians eye

Orbán's policy and rhetoric with admiration and envy, weaving its logic into their own nationalism.

At the sinister National Conservatism conference in May 2023, Tory rising star Miriam Cates complained that no-fault divorce had undermined 'what is objectively the most successful institution for the raising of children' in a speech that also blamed the country's declining birthrate on too many women going to university and immigrants leaving too few homes for young people (native British ones, presumably) to start families in.

These patriarchal narratives imagine female reproduction as a passive process. It is the virile, masculine essence that seeds life in the fertile landscape of the female body. But also, motherly care, the reproductive labours that come after gestation, are reduced to passive reproduction of patriarchy itself.

Victorian ideals that still hang over us today understood mothering as hugely important to shaping society – but this wasn't considered work because a mother's influence was a matter of innate feminine nature. The perfect Victorian mother embodied purity, piety, domesticity and submissiveness in her essential being. The home she kept was an extension of her body, enveloping her husband and children in gentle, nurturing care.

When men like Orbán demand women dedicate themselves to motherhood, this is the kind of motherhood they're talking about. Biological reproduction of the race – and the passive reproduction of native, white-supremacist patriarchal culture.

Othermothering is radical because it challenges patriarchy's fundamental claim on life. If parental relationships are defined by practice – something you *do* rather than something you *are*, a matter of work not genetics – men have no claim on children they don't actively care for.

We don't own our children – they are not property; they are autonomous people in their own right. But children *belong* to those who love and care for them, in the sense of being part of something bigger than themselves.

During pregnancy, a baby belongs to their bloodmother in the most immediate sense: they are still a physical part of her. And very often, this intense connection keeps evolving in the mutual belonging of a mother to her child and a child to her mother. But to sustain this bond you have to keep mothering, in ways that become more complex as a child becomes ever-more themselves.

You have do the work – not just of providing for a child materially, but meeting their needs to learn and grow, to be seen and heard, as an autonomous individual who actively participates in the bonds that hold them. And if belonging is something we create by nurturing one another's autonomy, women and children are not the property of men; we don't belong to patriarchy, capitalism – the productivist economy – or any other authority that demands we *care for those who do not care for us*.

*Revolutionary Mothering: Love on the Front Lines*, a 2014 anthology inspired by the work of Black and queer feminists of the second-wave feminist era, imagines mothering as inherently radical. As 'a practice of creating, nurturing, affirming and supporting life', Alexis Pauline Gumbs writes, mothering embodies everything that the destructive forces of patriarchy, white supremacy, capitalism and homophobia are not:

The radical potential of the word 'mother' comes after the 'm'. It is the space that 'other' takes in our mouths when we say it. We are something else. We know it from how fearfully institutions wield social norms and try to shut us down. We know it from how we are transforming the planet with our every messy step toward making life possible. Mamas who unlearn domination by refusing to dominate their children, extended family and friends, community caregivers, radical childcare collectives, all of us breaking cycles of abuse by deciding what we want to replicate from our past and what we need urgently to transform, are m/othering ourselves.

Othermothering as a social practice affirms children's belonging not just to parents but to whole communities, making their care a collective responsibility. And so, binding these communities together, actively creating a collective sense of belonging, mothering is empowered not just to nurture children, but nurture the futures we want for our children.

Or as Gumbs puts it, revolutionary mothering, child care as resistance, is an intergenerational lifeforce with the power to transform the world.

Which makes just *coping* feel pretty inadequate.

If these are the narratives that make single mothering power-ful – not just the labours of the women in this chapter, but of Global Women's Strike activists, who, while I'm trying to get my head round the forces that oppress mothering, are out there fighting them – then the harder I look for validation, the more I feel like a *bad single mother.*

But maybe that's because I'm still untangling my motherhood from passive ideals we either embody with our entire being, or fail against. Mothering as social practice doesn't reduce us to *good mothers* and *bad mothers*. It's a current we can tap into, a wave of momentum that leads to places where we can expand our care. It's something we can all do – and always do more.

And it's a way of thinking about things we already do.

Like when Imogen takes F for the weekend so I can work, and I use my break to call a newly single mum I met last week – because she didn't seem OK, and I'm not sure anyone else is checking in on her.

When Ella, who lives next door with her two boys, spends two hours sitting on the front step shooting questions at me till I've nailed down an argument that wouldn't come together on the page, I know there must be plenty of other things she should be doing – but praise be, that a single mum moved into my block who is generous enough to *mother my mind*. And when I scrape out my overdraft so Ella can make her rent because her wages are late – it's an easy thing to do, but there's something satisfying about using the little slack any one of us might have as collective wiggle room.

When Maya's kid comes down with flu the night before Maya's first day in a new nursing job, she calls for help through our online group. At seven the next morning, our friend Lilot drops the feverish child with me, before driving Maya to work, her own kid to kindergarten, and finally getting herself to college.

When Maya returns ten hours later to pick up her little one and finds a hot meal waiting for her, the relish with which she wolfs it down is mine – because I know: nothing tastes better than a meal you didn't have to cook yourself.

And that's reason enough to do any of these things.

But if we reimagine these little moments of solidarity as resonating with practices of love and interdependence that are compelled towards hopeful futures – then the everyday kindnesses that make single mothering less lonely and less exhausting become acts of resistance against the forces that say single mothering must be lonely and exhausting.

Giving one another the care society says belongs to men is how we ease our dependence on those who do not care for us – and how we empower and affirm one another's autonomy. It's how we choose to belong to something bigger. It's company on the journey that begins when we choose to mother – whether that means walking away from the abortion clinic, or towards the fertility clinic, or in each moment we commit to making the best for ourselves and our kids of circumstances we would never have chosen.

# Chapter 8

## Matrixes of Love

I'd been staying with my parents when I found out I was pregnant, but when we left the hospital, my sister took me home with her. I couldn't make this huge decision with my mum and dad around.

Once the boyfriend had flown in from Berlin, we talked it over and over in my sister's spare room. I worked a bit. Didn't smoke. Couldn't see Emily because she had shingles, which might be dangerous to the baby if I decided to keep it.

Then one day, I got a cab to my parents' flat.

I remember chatting to the driver as I watched mid-morning London roll by. I don't remember what I was thinking or feeling. Maybe because I had managed to separate what I felt from what I was thinking, and what I was thinking from what I knew. Getting a cab all the way from Hackney to Muswell Hill is something I'd only do only in an emergency. An act of 'self care' in a moment of collapse, maybe. But my small talk with the cabbie was upbeat and unforced.

When I got there I sat my mother down and told her I was pregnant.

She burst into tears.

They were happy tears.

She says it wasn't just my news that surprised her; her reaction did too. She couldn't imagine herself a grandmother any more than I could imagine myself a mother. She didn't know she wanted a grandchild. And I didn't know I'd decided she would be having one. But when I saw her excitement I knew it was mine too. Of course it was.

Why would I have come except to share good news?

Well, there was one other thing. I hadn't done what I was supposed to do, and collected my life – my self – together before I became something . . . more? Less? What if this baby meant being stalled in this desultory state for ever?

My mum told me what I wanted to hear. She only made her first film once she had two children. 'Motherhood focuses you,' she said. 'I only got serious when every moment in front of the lightbox had to count.'

A baby's world is an opening web of human connection. It begins tightly knotted, one life embedded in another. Gradually, mimicking stages of mammalian evolution, from sea creature to cub, increasingly human in form, its interactions develop from chemicals swashing through a conjoined nervous system to the quickening of a body within a body.

At this stage of my pregnancy, the boyfriend pressed his palm against my belly in awe and envy, anxious for a faint tremor by which to know our child.

But if this is the most intense of all human connections – complete, physical, two beings in one – it was also a relationship that had yet to begin. When F appeared on the labour ward, when I examined her crumpled face for the first time, holding her tenacious instinct to my breast, she was as new to me as she was to her father.

I didn't get to hold my baby till after doctors had whisked her away, cleaned her off and passed her to her father. But a C-section and not doing 'skin-on-skin' didn't hinder our bonding.

I've heard fathers claim to be biologically incapable of the intense connection a woman has with a child they have carried for nine months. But not every mother falls instantly when she meets the baby she has been gestating – even if she was agonisingly conscious of every moment of the transition from foetus to newborn.

I was lucky that the things mothers are supposed to feel came as easily as they did. But my pleasure in meeting her for the first time was just the start. 'I love you even more than yesterday,' I would coo in wonder, because yesterday had already been the biggest love I'd ever felt.

Those feelings were charged with hormones. But hormones don't explain away love. If oxytocin rushed through my veins when I held her, it was a chemical expression of love as much as its cause. And if someone had tested her father's blood, they would have found oxytocin and prolactin there too. The feeling, the knowledge, of being responsible for a helpless infant stimulates a chemical response. Any human body that gets close to a baby, practising care and connection, produces these hormones.

The more you care, the more you love; the more you love, the more you care. A virtuous feedback loop of chemical, physical, emotional and social practice.

*

New babies want to be held. All the time. All people need connection. Still-becoming people need it intensely. F's world was pure sensation. Sounds were emotions. When she cried, consisting in herself as raw feeling, her cries were my distress. I, the body she was yet to distinguish from her own being, had to interpret her cries and adjust the world – the bigger reality she couldn't yet grapple with – to needs she couldn't articulate.

But it all changes so fast.

Our bond wasn't a passive fact of genetics or shared physical history. It was something we did together, all the time, through touch, taste, sound and smell, gazing into one another's eyes in fascinated search for the point where she and I were now not one but two.

After four weeks, F propped against my knees in a wash of morning light from the window above the bed, playing with this evolving sense of separate and togetherness, she smiled. I nudged her father awake. He said she probably had wind. But I knew her smile when I saw it. Felt it. The delight in each of us, in both of us, blooming across her face, my pleasure at her pleasure, her pleasure at mine, the complexities of our connection unfurling.

Soon, her father saw it too. She returned his smiles. And then our laughter.

This was something she needed as much as milk and warmth. To experience emotions that extended beyond herself. Reflected back, her feelings were finding form. She was finding form. In discovering a world bigger than she was, she was beginning to locate her self.

And the bigger world she was transfixed by was people.

For a time, any face that loomed into view provoked radiant delight. Her smiles were prolific, and almost irresistibly reciprocated.

I took her to a party when she was still a warm little larva – *good like bread* as the Italians say – and while I was engrossed in adult conversation I thought I'd forgotten how to do, she circulated the room, embrace to embrace, face to face, each new human a happy surprise. My gut suddenly flipped at the realisation I didn't know where she was. A moment later she was passed back, content as ever.

Babies need connection because they cannot survive without care. A lot of care. And they actively work at that connection, with anyone who happens be around. But we are not hungry bodies first, and then conscious minds, or thinking selves that happen to be located in feeling bodies. Just as hormones make love and love makes hormones, survival compels connection but connection is compelling in itself.

It's our reason to be.

In late-capitalist societies, children often don't get the chance to bond with very many people. Luckily, love is not a finite resource. And love is not work. Love is an experience of connection. But care, even when it's an expression of love, or when it engenders love, is work.

And to thrive, everyone needs love *and* care.

Not just babies.

As with so many late-capitalist families, it was the toddler years we couldn't get through in once piece. And, as in so many late-capitalist families, it was inside me, Mum, that the shatter began.

I lost my grip after I fucked up at work one day. The fuck-up itself, in retrospect, wasn't a huge deal. But I began to unravel. Called into my boss's office, I sobbed pathetically and she shooed me home for the weekend. As I walked away, I came together a little around the sense that something had happened. The humiliation at least felt tangible.

So I held on to that.

But when I woke the next morning, I couldn't pull myself together. F hopped and chirruped, trying to get me out of bed. I buried my face. I didn't want her to see me like this, which only accelerated the unravelling. At her insistence, I dragged myself to a kitchen chair. Where I sat. On a chair. In a kitchen. Piled with dirty dishes. My kitchen. My limp hands and dull head that didn't know what to hold. Which job to apply themselves to. My husband, shuffling and gaping.

I looked at him and pleaded: 'I don't know what to do.'

He made tentatively soothing noises but looked as blankly uncomfortable as my boss had the day before. And then F skipped in clutching a book. She tugged my arm, led me back to bed, snuggled in and placed the book in my lap.

It was Rudyard Kipling's *Just So Stories*. My mother read these stories to me when I was a child, over and over. And this particular copy, a vintage edition with a red cloth cover, had been a gift from Emily when she came to visit a few weeks after I gave birth.

I'd tried to read it to F many times, but she was too young and always shoved it away in favour of something with fewer words and brighter pictures. Now she waited with patient expectation. And so, chiming in with my own mother's voice across the decades, across the gulf of being cared for and caring, I read, 'for this befell and behappened and became and was, oh my Best Beloved ...' Soothed and soothing, holding and held.

My favourite *Just So* story, 'The Cat That Walked by Himself' casts Woman as the primal domesticator, who lures the Dog, the Horse and the Cow into servitude with her singing magic. And before, she domesticated Man himself:

> Of course the Man was wild too. He was dreadfully wild. He didn't even begin to be tame till he met the Woman, and she told him that she did not like living in his wild ways. She picked out a nice dry Cave, instead of a heap of wet leaves, to lie down in; and she strewed clean sand on the floor; and she lit a nice fire of wood at the back of the Cave; and she hung a dried wild-horse skin, tail-down, across the opening of the Cave; and she said, 'Wipe your feet, dear, when you come in, and now we'll keep house.'

Man goes out hunting with the Dog and Woman tends to their nicely appointed cave, roasting mutton with wild fenugreek and keeping the hearth warm and swept. The Cat insinuates himself into this privileged set-up in with the arrival of the Baby: 'new and pink and fat and small, and the Woman is very fond of him.'

But she's also so desperate for relief, the fickle feline outmanoeuvres her by amusing the Baby so she can get on with cavework.

Origin stories take the reality we perceive and trace back its threads. Kipling was writing at the tail end of the Victorian era, so of course it was the Woman, the sentimental heart of the home, who domesticated her wild lover.

But the family portrait his story sketches persisted through the twentieth century. Not just in children's stories but in evolutionary theory. What bound the primal pair together was a transactional exchange of protection and protein on one side, care and sex on the other. Men competed for the most fecund young women, and women for the fiercest hunters, whom they tamed with monogamous devotion.

Males needed female monogamy to ensure they were providing only for their own biological offspring (as per Darwin). Females needed something like marriage to ensure that, even if her man followed his evolutionary drive to reproduce prodigiously (science again), her offspring didn't have to share his protection and provision (economics).

Cave whores, single mothers and their children don't get a mention: we can assume they were left out in the cold (I think that's called morality).

And from that day to this, so it was, oh Best Beloved.

It's not just incels who still insist on the myth of the meat–sex deal as proof that female subservience and domesticity, male aggression and promiscuity, are a biological reality. More enlightened notions – about things like gender equality – often assume it's *progress* that has freed women from our innate dependence. Civilisation, technology to lighten the load of domestic work and modern assertions like *people have rights* and *women are people too*.

Yet these days, the plot holes in the nuclear cave family story have become hard to ignore. And one is a problem even

Kipling noticed: Woman's long hours alone with a mewling infant.

Attachment theory explains the process of becoming that F and I were so busy with. It says that a new person's sense of self forms in the bilateral mother–child bond, and that this connection becomes the model for all their other, and future, relationships. The work of mothering, so the theory goes, is not just to gestate and feed babies, but to socialise them into autonomous individuals.

The psychologists who developed this theory didn't just observe human mothers and babies – mainly white, middle-class ones – they also looked at other apes. And most apes are devoted mothers who care for one child at a time.

Chimp mums are so attached, they almost never put their babies down or let anyone else hold them. And they'll only get pregnant again once their kid is ready to fend for itself, which takes about four years. Most primates are like chimps. But women are primates who are very unlike chimps. We can bear more children, at closer intervals, than anyone can manage alone.

If the biological reality of human reproduction tells us anything about family, it's that caring for children isn't something women are supposed to do all by ourselves, no matter how well we might be provided for materially.

And *how* we're provided for materially is also much more complex and communal than men putting food on the table.

In 1989, US anthropologist Kristen Hawkes published a paper titled 'Hardworking Hadza grandmothers', which caused a stir by providing evidence for 'the grandmother hypothesis'.

The grandmother hypothesis, which had been around since the 1960s, wasn't actually an answer to questions about child-care, to which male scientists hadn't given much thought. Their question was: what is the point of old women?

Why, they wondered, do women outlive men, and not just their men – their own fertility? Why does women's reproduction suddenly shut down? And how come they get a whole phase of life after they've stopped being any use for making babies?

The grandmother hypothesis drew a new figure into the cave family portrait (it wasn't a cat). If a woman has her own mother around to help her care for them she can have more children, more quickly – an obvious evolutionary advantage.

The Hadza live in what is now Tanzania. Their culture, which used to stretch across vast swathes of the Rift Valley and beyond, is thought to be thousands of years old and to have changed little in all that time. The Hadza communities Hawkes followed still make their living foraging for wild fruit, tubers, honey and eggs, and hunting with poisoned arrows.

Only men hunt large game. But Hadza cuisine is largely vegetarian. Most days, hunters don't catch anything. When they do bring home the bacon – twice a month maybe, if they're lucky – it's an occasion for the whole community to feast together. But day-to-day, it's gatherers – mostly women – who put food on the table.

What Hawkes learned when she hung out with Hadza grandmothers was that they weren't just babysitters:

experienced older women were the most productive gatherers. The biggest contributors of calories to the collective pot.

If Hadza families are 'natural', then we have a new (or very old) archetypal breadwinner. Not the strapping man wielding his spear, but the wizened old lady with pockets full of baobab and digging-stick in hand.

For a long time, Europeans murdered people like the Hadza, robbed them of their land, tried to force them into farming or paraded them in zoos as a chapter in a story that began with apes and evolved into magnificence of Western industrialism. With the growing sense that something, somewhere along the way, went horribly wrong, Westerners now look to the few hunter-gatherer societies who haven't been colonised out of existence for clues to some pre-fall state.

If these cultures haven't changed since the Pleistocene era in which modern humans evolved then – so the thinking goes – their way of life must follow a blueprint written into our genes.

And none of these societies are structured around anything like the nuclear family. But also, they don't look much like each other. That mothers give infants immediate physical care, and that raising children is a collective responsibility, are pretty much universal. But who looks after kids and how is as culturally diverse is our biology is universal, as Sarah Blaffer Hrdy, the leading evolutionary anthropologist of collective child-rearing, explores in her book *Mothers and Others: The Evolutionary Origins of Mutual Understanding*.

Anthropologists call people who care for children but

are not their biological parents 'alloparents'. Grandmothers do a lot of alloparenting. But so do siblings and, in the various ways these terms might be applied, aunties, uncles and cousins.

And the role of fathers is particularly diverse. Most Hadza kids don't live in the same family group as their fathers. Yanomamo children in Brazil and Venezuela have only a one in three chance of living with both parents by the time they are ten. In various other hunter-gatherer societies around the world, women have multiple male partners to make sure their families are well supported.

We don't know how Pleistocene families organised things, but Hrdy says, 'the situation among our hunter-gather ancestors may not have been that different from what goes on in much of the world today. The needs of children outstrip what most fathers are able or willing to provide.'

There's no universal template for how we're supposed to manage family responsibilities. But the one model that's completely anomalous, that has only taken off under capitalism, is one where a child is solely dependent on one woman, who is in turn solely dependent on one man.

The nuclear family is what psychologists and anthropologists call WEIRD – peculiar to Western, educated, industrialised, rich, democratic societies. But you don't have to go as far back as the Pleistocene, or as far from the family homes of northern Europe as the Rift Valley, to know that it takes a village to raise a child, or that grannies are special.

The data is patchy, but studies suggest that having a

maternal grandmother around does far more for a child's chances of surviving their early, vulnerable years than the presence of a father.

In the UK, forty per cent of grandparents provide regular childcare, many of them supporting strained nuclear families. But grandmothers are particularly special in single-mother families.

In the dark days of Mother and Baby Homes, the fate of an unwed mother and child often turned on telling Mum: if she was accepting and supportive they had a good chance of avoiding institutional confinement and separation.

Historically, the children of young single mothers have often been raised as their siblings. Their true parentage might be kept hidden. Often it was an open secret. Now, as in Lisa's case, it's usually no secret all. Teen motherhood is roundly condemned in WEIRD societies. Policymakers and do-gooders shake their heads at tragic girls stunted by premature motherhood. But it wouldn't ruin their chances in life if WEIRD mothering wasn't such an isolated responsibility. And plenty of youthful grandmothers make sure that it doesn't.

Even those of us who rein in our fertility until a more socially acceptable stage of life can find our lives more intimately bound to our mothers in middle age than we've been since our own childhoods. Among my circle of single mum friends in Berlin, it's not those of us with new partners or co-parenting arrangements with exes whom the rest of us envy, so much as the locals who have their own mums close by.

Or even living in.

In the United States, twenty-two per cent of single moms live with at least one of their own parents, and most grandparents caring for their daughters' children are women. If grandmotherly care is more 'natural' than fatherly care, it seems grandmothers are reclaiming their rightful place when nuclear families fail. But how these families manage their responsibilities isn't as simple as slipping comfortably into biologically determined roles.

'She's been the one that I've yelled and screamed at on the phone and she's also lifted me up when I've been at rock bottom,' one single mother told researchers studying 'new family forms' in the UK.

'Grandmothers as Replacement Parents and Partners: The Role of Grandmotherhood in Single Parent Families' found that single mothers were hugely grateful for the support of their own mothers. And grandmothers talked about how rewarding it was to give. Particularly if they were retired, or if their partners had died, bonding closely to their grandchildren and being intimately involved in their daughters' lives – the feeling of being depended on – gave meaning to what might otherwise have been a lonely time of life.

Yet in white families in particular, single mothers experienced this dependence as a source of guilt and grandmothers were acutely aware of this, anxious not to step on their daughters' toes and undermine their sense of independence.

The study's authors frame these tensions in terms of 'confused roles'. Because the grandmothers weren't just babysitting but supporting their daughters emotionally – talking through worries about the kids – they were both replacement fathers to their grandchildren and replacement partners to their daughters.

'I think the things that I talk to my mom about are things

that I should be really talking to my kids' dad about,' one mother said. Another: 'My mum has become like a surrogate father to them and this is really good. Familiarity definitely breeds contempt and I can tell them not to do something until I am blue in the face.'

As if, in the proper way of things, a father was less familiar, some kind of neutral bystander to the mother–child relationship. And the authors see things this way too, if they understand sharing worries about children to be something fathers do to support their wives.

Black and ethnic minority families, though, didn't suffer from these comparisons with the nuclear family. They tended to see grandmothering as a natural extension of mothering. And white single mothers, the study implies, should really take a leaf out of the Black-single-mothering book:

> It seems important for mothers to feel that grandparenting is more than simply a new form of parenting and parental support. It is a relationship with equal importance and significance for all of the family members; it is a network for mutual support, which increases the well-being of all involved.

And though the white families in the study – and the paper's authors – seem to have forgotten their history, these relationships aren't a new phenomenon that's emerging because the nuclear family is in sudden decline.

In 1958, anthropologist Madeline Kerr published a vibrant study of a Liverpool slum community, whom she gave the pseudonym *The People of Ship Street*.

The people of Ship Street are Catholic, of Irish stock. The men are dockers, sailors, factory workers, builders, scalers, drivers, shop workers, fruit porters, unemployed or in prison. But we don't hear much from the men, who hand their wage packets over to their wives and are shooed out of the house with pocket money for the pub or betting shop.

'A similar classification of the women's jobs is not really possible,' Kerr notes. No. Quite. But jobs aren't the focus of life on Ship Street. Family is.

And families are huge.

Kerr bumps into Mrs G sitting on a wall and 'getting a bit of sun' with her youngest two, and asks where the rest of her family are. 'They're not a family, they're a gang,' Mrs G says grimly.

Contraception is taboo and abortion illegal. Mums admit to taking pills to induce miscarriage, without much success. Yet once they arrive, the infants of Ship Street are indulged and doted on, by older brothers and sisters as much as mums and grandmothers – who may be called 'Mother' by all generations, and are the keepers of rent books and the authorities everyone turns to in an emergency.

Ship Street girls mostly marry by the time they're twenty-five and move their husbands into their own maternal homes. A few men manage, briefly, to extract their wives from this matrix and set up new households. But as soon as wives become mothers, they move back in with Mum, telling their husbands they can come too, or do as they please.

'I couldn't get on without me mother. I could get on without my husband. I don't notice him,' says a thirty-nine-year-old mum of five. Kerr says this statement 'epitomises what the Mums in the area feel about the relative values of mothers and husbands'.

Ship Street is not a sexually liberated community, and yet single motherhood carries almost no social stigma – and makes no difference to how children are raised, which is, in any case, collectively.

Marian, a married woman of twenty-two with no children yet, watches enviously as her sister, Molly, gets ready for an evening out at the dance hall. Molly is twenty and has a baby but no husband. 'Well I didn't tell you to get married,' she quips at Marian, as – I picture her – she slips restless feet into dancing shoes and hands her baby over to an older child, careful not to let a goodnight kiss smudge her lipstick.

The girls of Ship Street are 'mad on dancing'. Boys go too, to pick up girls, strutting and preening their Teddy-boy quiffs. When Kerr's researchers ask these young men if they'd have a single mum for a wife, 'most of them say they would not refuse to marry a girl if they are in love with her, just because she has an illegitimate baby by another man'.

Kerr and her team spent several years visiting families at all hours, pulling up chairs around dinner tables, hanging out in the pub, dutifully recording Ship Street's routines and melodramas. It's hard to believe, as rich and funny and full of humanity as her study is, that Kerr didn't warm to the mums of Ship Street. But what she was trying to uncover in these investigations was the source of an immaturity she perceived in a community with a stubborn aversion to bettering themselves.

As Kerr was gathering her data, British slums were being

cleared. Already, some of Ship Street's tall, crumbling houses were being torn down and their big, fluid families reconfigured into new-build flats with indoor toilets and water that ran hot straight from the tap.

But the people of Ship Street staunchly resisted this move. For Kerr, this is because they are pathologically insular. And the root of their degeneracy is what she calls 'the Power of Mum'.

Kerr was writing before attachment theory went mainstream. But psychoanalysis had already made mothering hugely important to the development of the psyche, just as the Victorians had made it central to moral and social development.

Kerr continued the Victorian tradition of finding fault with how working-class women breastfed. Ship Street mums didn't do it enough, and just to keep bellies full rather than as a focus of emotional bonding. But 1950s mothers weren't supposed to spoil their children with too much love. Kerr notes with grave disapproval that Ship Street babies are fed and soothed on demand, cuddled incessantly. Most damning of all, they sleep through the night – and in their mothers' beds.

At the same time, Kerr insists the mums are spread too thin. Infants spend far too much time in the care of older children, and older children spend far too much time roaming the streets with one another.

The result of these mothers refusing to follow expert advice (doctors do tell them how they should be mothering but are ignored) is an infantilised community (Kerr proves this with Rorschach tests). Not just individual men and women but the whole subculture of Ship Street is arrested at an immature stage of development. Why else would these people bond so tightly round a motley bunch of ball-breaking housewives and old nannas?

'The daughter gives up the pleasures or gratification of a home of her own with her husband to return to her Mum and so lose responsibility,' Kerr writes. A home of her own, kitted out with the mod cons of post-war consumer capitalism was everything a 1950s woman was meant to desire.

But these new homes weren't just reshaping the urban landscape. They were reshaping family. They were the physical infrastructure of the male-headed household. Homes in which the Power of Mum would be subsumed by the duties of the wife. Homes a woman wouldn't be shooing her man out of but waiting alone all day in, watching the clock for her only adult company to return.

Through the night, the new, nuclear mum would be dragging herself out of the marital bed where she met her man's needs, to the baby's room to meet theirs, at the three-hour intervals dictated by experts, wife then mother, back and forth, till it was time to get hubby's breakfast on, painting over dark circles before he woke.

No longer a powerful nexus within a dynamic community but a lonely individual donning different masks.

Ship Street households expanded and contracted. Young women left home to marry, returned to have children, moved out again – never more than a street or two away – to make room for younger sisters, ever-poised to swoop back in if space opened up. Bonds within households formed a rich *network of mutual support*, but so did bonds between them, as constellations of care morphed to the rhythms of birth, childhood, mothering and old age.

The move to nuclear homes arrested this fluidity into a static structure, with defined capacity that defined identities. If there's any room for a grandmother, she's demoted from matriarch to burden. People start asking why old women exist at all.

And a mother without a husband is a problem. Her singleness is homelessness. Even if her parents, or a married sister, can squeeze them into their two-up-two-down – well, it's hard to imagine Molly swanning off to the dance hall so freely if she had to leave her baby with a couple already arguing over housework and childcare.

Ship Street was a minor front in the nuclear family's colonisation of European culture. Long before working-class neighbourhoods were remodelled into council flats, urbanisation itself broke up extended families.

Powered by fossil fuels, economic growth exploded. GDP only became the defining measure of economic success after the Second World War, to compare the success of competing capitalist and communist economies. But what GDP measures – production: the total the value of goods and services – soared with the Industrial Revolution.

What GDP doesn't measure is what this growth cost: community, care, reproductive labour. The fabric of working-class life was pulled apart as men and women left rural communities and settled into tenement slums.

Life was dominated by long, gruelling hours in factories. Home was where you collapsed, exhausted and spent – domestic spaces whose life-force was sucked into capitalist production. If you had any surplus wealth and energy, they were spaces to escape from, to better yourself out of, in the great capitalist endeavour of personal striving.

Historically, single mothers have fared better in rural communities, where families were big, flexible and connected enough to make room for them. They've also fared better – being allowed to keep their children and having family around to help raise them – in working-class communities than middle-class ones.

The higher up the socio-economic scale you go, the more resources you'd expect a family to be able to extend to an unwed daughter and her child. But in terms of social and emotional capacity, the reverse has tended to be true.

The people of Ship Street had no impulse for social climbing and loathed snobbery. Ties with family members who married up, moved away and adopted middle-class airs and graces were strained. To Kerr, this was a sign of their obstinate insularity and resistance to progress. But a more aspiring community probably wouldn't have been so accommodating of unwed motherhood, the shame of which was always felt more keenly by the middle classes.

If your identity is defined by your standing in an anonymous social hierarchy, having a loose woman and her illegitimate child about the house might be an intolerable disgrace on your family's good name. But if the people whose opinions you care about *know* Molly – *That Molly! She's always been too free, but my, isn't her baby bonny!* – a bit of gossip mightn't be enough to expel her from the bosom of her family.

\*

The Victorians made the housewife an aspirational identity. But while the urbanising working classes were crammed into tiny tenement units, the mother who embodied True Womanhood was the head of a collective operation. Her household might include widowed grandmothers and unmarried sisters, but also cooks, butlers, nurses, governesses – or at least a maid or two.

The redux housewife of Kerr's time was a much lonelier woman.

Mass production of the post-war economic boom broke labour down into individualised, repetitive tasks with little connection to the larger project a worker contributed to, or collaboration between colleagues. What gave work meaning was the wages it afforded a man to keep a family at home. And what gave meaning to his wife's labours was the mass-produced stuff those wages bought.

If for the Victorians domesticity was capitalism's spiritual counterweight – or moral dumping ground – in the 1950s it embodied the consumerism that is productivism's devoted other half. The 1950s housewife didn't have maids to scold or companions to talk to. She had white goods.

Mechanised help was supposed to bring joy to her lonely labours. But with every new time-saving device, expectations rose. Meals became more elaborate, homes had to sparkle ever brighter. Market competition drove industrial advancements, and the housewife did her bit by competing with her peers for the best-kept home, equipped with things other wives didn't have – yet.

Things instead of people.

And things to enhance the only significant adult relationship in her life. His meals had to be perfect, his shirts perfectly pressed, and she too had to be perfect. Fashion and beauty products exploded onto the market. The sexuality women had reclaimed a generation earlier – in the interwar years, when the strictures of Victorian morality loosened – was packaged and sold back to them as accoutrements to perfect wifedom: female sexuality wedded to consumer culture.

First-wave feminists of the Victorian era believed women had an essential role in play in public life, but they still held mothering and homemaking to be profoundly worthy occupations in their own right. It was only once the domestic space became the lonely, isolated nuclear home that second-wave feminists made escaping it an end in itself.

And we have escaped, to a point.

But in our hurry to break chains to the kitchen sink and smash through glass ceilings, we've broken bonds forged by mothering itself. Too often, we've confused the bondage of constricted, isolated motherhood and domestic servitude with bonds of love and female solidarity. The fabric of female power.

Without the robust family matrix, we're left with a mother–child bond so intensely pressured it can be crushing. And the romantic pair bond: in a bid for independence, we've ended up more dependent on men than ever.

Western society is obsessed with progress. We're a culture of personal betterment, with a deeply embedded sense of the forward march of history. And these days, feminism is a core plotline in the story of how far we've come. Late capitalism may be plagued with all kinds of horrors and injustices, *but just look at women*. Look how free we are, now that enlightened society has civilised itself.

The mums of Ship Street, bound to domestic and maternal duties, bodies exhausted from ten pregnancies in a lifetime, are a case study of precisely the kind of lives feminism has sought to free us from. But a feminism focused on individual freedoms, on allowing women to live like men, has left desperately little room for mothering, which is, by nature, collective, communal work.

*Progress* also has a distinctly colonialist whiff about it. It's synonymous with technological development, and a story that begins with 'primitive' tribal societies, then settled agrarian ones, developing into ever-more hierarchal communities and city-states. Until we arrive at the magnificence of Western Civilisation, which the 'developing' world must be made to emulate.

In this spirit, the patriarchal family has been brutally imposed on colonised communities around the world, breaking up Indigenous systems of kinship and instilling Western notions of gender. And yet WEIRD ideas about progress don't just assume our foremothers were less sophisticated and more oppressed than we are, they see white, Western feminism as the pinnacle of women's liberation.

In *Black Feminist Thought*, Patricia Hill Collins unpicks how white feminists have dismissed Black maternal politics as 'politically immature' – echoing Kerr's slurs on Ship Street as a community that never grew up and cut the apron strings. The community activism of women of colour who assert the power of mothering isn't feminism at all, these progressive white women have insisted, because their struggles don't centre women's individual rights.

But most women still have children, and individualism is crap for mums.

The whole Western idea of the free individual was, from the start, conceived in opposition to the connectedness of mothering. But if the Enlightenment understood mothering – and so women – as part of nature, and therefore excluded from rights and norms that govern society, science soon made mothering exceptional even within nature.

The nuclear cave family confirmed the norms of patriarchy. In its gendered dualism, it is a very Victorian myth. But it's also a very Darwinian myth.

The Darwinian story of evolution, the creation myth that underpins Western notions of progress, is one of competitive struggle. The drive for life, to feed and reproduce, pits plants and animals against one other. Those with sharper claws to kill, swifter hooves to escape, fiercer antlers to fend off sexual rivals, are more likely to survive and reproduce.

There was little room in Darwin's narrative for cooperation and connectedness. When Darwinian scientists talk of cooperation at all, they fuss about it being a perplexing paradox or problematise it as 'altruism' – an awkward exception to the rule.

And motherhood is the paradigm case for altruism.

Organisms aren't supposed to do things for one another. Unless, of course, they're helping their own offspring and therefore ensuring the ongoing reproduction of their own genes.

When a mother feeds her children, or exhausts herself caring for them, she's just prioritising the imperative to reproduce over the imperative to survive; her genes over her self. When mothers say they would die for their children, Darwinian theory says this is all proper and natural, the expression of 'selfish' unconscious drives.

Fathers also provide for their children for the same reason mothers do. But they won't make the same sacrifices a mother will because they're less invested in any individual child. A mother who carries a baby for nine months makes a big investment; a father can always make *more of me*.

When a vampire bat feeds an unrelated member of its colony, when painted wolves slow down for an injured member of the pack, things get more complicated. Darwinian scientists struggle with care that isn't motherly. But, still, they insist, these apparently altruistic acts can be explained away by the statistical chance of each individual who makes a sacrifice benefitting from the same one day.

And so, Darwinism imposes a kind of social contract on the natural world.

But Darwinian struggle is only one side of the story. Other perspectives have described the natural world as an expansive flowering of interdependent systems. When Russian naturalist and political theorist Peter Kropotkin coined the term 'mutual aid' he was arguing that cooperation, not competition, was the driving force of evolution: the model that natural selection favoured above all.

As we understand more and more about the intricate complexity of ecosystems, new pictures of the patterns on which life proliferates are coming into focus. Ones that resonate with Kropotkin and make *nature red in tooth and claw* sound a bit melodramatic.

In the 1960s, microbiologist Lynn Margulis made one of evolutionary biology's most important breakthroughs when she described how eukaryotic cells evolved through *symbiogenesis* – literally, 'becoming by living together'.

Chloroplasts, sub-cellular organelles – responsible for photosynthesis, the fundamental transfer of energy that powers life on Earth – were once free-roaming organisms in their own right. It was only when they became engulfed in larger eukaryotic cells that life evolved beyond microscopic unicellular organisms.

In other words, the vast complexity of multicellular ecology began with cells opening their boundaries, merging and becoming more than the sum of their parts; with porousness, connection and the expansion, merging and dissolution of distinct entities. Long before any creature got pregnant, it was a body within a body, a life within a life, not quite one thing, not quite two, that got everything rolling.

From the minutiae of cellular life, Margulis zoomed right out. With James Lovelock she developed the Gaia hypothesis, which describes the entire planet as a unified, self-regulating system.

All life is connected through symbiotic relationships between species – bees need flowering plants, flowering plants need bees – and more complex webs.

The famous images of Alaskan bears guzzling on the annual salmon run look like a massacre. But catching more fish than they can eat, bears fertilise soils along riverbanks with their leftovers, nourishing the surrounding forest, whose shade and debris provide just the right conditions for salmon to breed. Bears wouldn't survive winter hibernation without their feast of fish; salmon fry wouldn't emerge in spring without their grizzly aggressors.

The Gaia hypothesis describes how all these intimate, localised relationships between organic life are also interdependent on a global scale. They interact with one another, with the atmosphere, water cycles and soils, in a vast complexity of virtuous feedback loops that tend towards balance – keeping the composition of gases in the atmosphere *just so* – and so, tend towards life.

The more we understand about the world, the harder it becomes to tease out individual interests. The harder it becomes, in fact, to pick out the individual from the network.

The more we know about the microbiome – a vast ecosystem of bacteria, protozoa and fungi that live in, and on, our bodies and are essential to our immune systems, digestion and even mental health – the more the human body looks less like a thing in itself than a community that's evolved in symbiosis.

Most of the DNA in our bodies isn't human at all, it's bacterial. And our rational, thinking minds, it turns out, aren't just influenced by hormones but by the non-human life we host in our bellies.

A world-view based on breaking complex systems into ever-smaller, more manageable components to be objectively studied has been incredibly powerful for understanding how things function mechanically, bringing many boons of science and technology, not least in medicine.

But we lose sight of the bigger picture. We sometimes forget that the only sense in which atoms, cells, genes, bodies, families, species, *selves* exist independently is metaphorical.

Darwinians are right that cooperation serves individuals. But if you come at it the other way, starting from symbiosis and cooperation as the norm, and take individualism and competition as the exception, you don't need concepts like altruism, which make anomalies of collectivism and care.

And making an anomaly of care makes an anomaly of mothering.

It pretends that mothers, and females more generally, are special. That our base drives are fundamentally different from those of male animals. It makes half the species an exceptional case.

Individual genes aren't selves and they don't have interests. Pretending they do is no less – I'd say far more – anthropomorphic than using the human metaphor of love.

All life is all rooted in connection. And how we experience connection, at its most intense, is love. We don't know what an alpha wolf is feeling when she paces around a member of her pack with a fractured leg, scanning the horizon, turning back to nuzzle her charge, holding up the whole tribe's progress.

But I feel like I can relate.

Hrdy says collective child-rearing was key to human evolution. It was within this intensely cooperative work – which demands so many hands, so much love – that empathy emerged.

Whether or not other animals experience something we might call love, human empathy – the capacity to see things from other another's perspective – is unique. *I see you*, but also, *I see that you see me* – and so I understand myself to be an individual, just like you. Empathy is how we connect to one another, but it's also how we recognise ourselves: you can't do one without the other.

Being able to see things from one another's perspectives, to comprehend that the world is not just as one perceives it but also as others perceive it, is the basis of abstract thought. I see things like this, you see them like that, and together we paint a richer, more interesting picture of the world.

This is culture. The human ability to create, to endlessly understand the world anew. For better or worse, art, politics, religion and science are all cooperative activities that we do because we have this extraordinary capacity – this *compulsion* – rooted in compassion.

If this is how people evolved, and all evolution is cooperative, then you can explain away the apparent individualism of animals that selfishly trample over one another's needs as a failure of empathy.

What appear to be anomalies, what looks like competition, are just casualties of a system that tends towards transcendent harmony without consciously attending to the needs of each individual within the whole.

Which is definitely no sillier than making an anomaly of love and care, calling genes selfish, or insisting that female nature is at odds with the fundamental principles of evolution.

But it is more demanding. It puts huge responsibility on humanity – the one species who do recognise the individual within the collective. The unique aspect of nature that has a visceral and reflective understanding of distinct selves with individual needs.

Forces of nature don't care when a baby antelope is torn apart by predators, when a storm demolishes a mangrove ecosystem, a bomb hits a city or a child dies. But we do. We might struggle to fully *feel* the enormity of genocide, or of a whole ecosystem being wiped out. But we can experience the loss of one individual like it's the end of the world.

Human beings are capable of terrible things. Even our motherly devotion falls short of an orangutan's. But like it or not, we are Gaia's conscience. The rational, intentional force of the biosphere and the sentimental heart of the planetary home.

All of us. Not. Just. Mothers.


Darwinism inspired Social Darwinism, which says progress and prosperity can only be achieved by pitting individuals against one another. And it inspired eugenics, which says you can engineer the kind of society you want by controlling whether, or how, individuals reproduce.

Symbiosis, cooperative evolution, mutual aid and collective child-rearing suggest different ways of living. Kinder, more hopeful and connected assumptions by which to shape families, societies, economies.

But Hrdy says there is also a dark side to collective child-rearing.

There are plenty of alloparents in nature, among wolves and elephants, meerkats and countless bird species. But besides humans, the only primates who rear their young collectively are callitrichids: marmosets and tamarins.

Whole tribes of marmosets hunt for insects to feed an alpha female's babies. Geoffroy's tamarins are polyandrous: females mate with as many males as possible, who share the care of her offspring between them, following her doggedly as she goes about her day, bothering her to stay still long enough when their babies need feeding.

Pulling together, callitrichids multiply quickly and share resources even among adults. But along with humans, these endearing, squirrel-sized monkeys are, Hrdy says, 'virtually the only primates where mothers have been observed to deliberately harm their own babies or leave newborns to die.' If a cotton-top tamarin gives birth without enough support around to ensure her offspring's survival, she'll walk away without a second glance – scientists have observed tamarin colonies where half of babies end their brief lives this way.

Humans and callitrichids are unique on our branch of the evolutionary family tree for our 'pronounced ambivalence toward newborns and their extremely contingent maternal commitment', Hrdy says.

And this might suggest a factor in postnatal depression, which soared during pandemic lockdowns in 2020.

The instant flowering of love I felt for my baby – would it have been so easy and uncomplicated if her father, grandparents, aunt and uncle hadn't crowded around the bed, as delighted with her as I was? If friends hadn't visited, nurses hadn't checked in, fussing over her latch, reassuring me over how long my milk was taking to come in and whether her head was the right shape? If I didn't know a welfare state would provide me with a full year of maternity leave to focus on this dazzling new relationship?

Or might I have been consumed by a raging mix of conflicting emotions, instincts, hormones, social expectations, love, fear, loneliness and, somewhere among it all, an ancient biological resistance to bilateral bonding with an infant who could not, in our evolutionary past, have survived without being enmeshed into a greater web of care?

Like many mums, I spent F's first weeks constantly checking she was alive. It wasn't just her helpless vulnerability; the fact of her was so marvellous I feared this new self, having appeared so suddenly, might vanish again. Each time I confirmed she was just soundly asleep, cold panic turned to a warm flood of gratitude that F *was*.

And with her living proof of my ability to care for a child, I assumed that if I had another one I'd be less fretful. I didn't have another one, so I don't know. But this wasn't the case for Ella.

Ella had her first child with a partner but was single when she had her second. With two children to look after, hundreds of miles from anyone she could call family, cot death-terror didn't just come in fleeting moments. It was a persistent state of anxiety that drifted into dark fantasy. She would picture a tiny coffin. Feel the weight of grief. But also, imagine visiting the baby's grave with her older child to lay flowers: a sad scene, yet one that had a certain rightness to it. When the inevitable came to pass, it would just be the two of them again. As it should be.

As she tells this story, we watch her little boy, eighteen months old now, stout legs powering across the park after a dog, shouting loud and bright as life itself. 'He's definitely with us now,' she smiles, as if savouring the relief that eluded her when she'd placed her palm against his gently heaving chest in those early months.

But historically, many single mothers never made it so far. If Ella felt guilty for suspecting her child wasn't fully of this world, lone mothers before us were explicitly told their babies should never have been born.

Mothers aren't perpetual motion machines or eternal springs of care. Motherly love is a gathering intensity that connects a new person into the world, one generation to the next. But the current must have something to draw down on and somewhere to flow.

When a child dies, we've all failed. When a mother, live pressure point in the network, mourns the death of her child she is the raw embodiment of a collective loss. And when a lone mother – knowing they will be cut off and cast out – abandons her baby, she's the perpetrator of a crime of which her whole community are guilty.

Making mothering exceptional can make it intensely lonely. Definitely hard work. Sometimes even deadly. But there is also pleasure to be had in the exceptional. When F was beginning to grasp a sense of herself in the connection between us, mothering certainly felt like a very special kind of magic.

Yet psychologist Heidi Keller, drawing on research from around the world, disputes the notion that babies need the undivided attention of one adult – as well as various Western, middle-class ideas that flow from it: babies become stressed with too many people around, you have to angle the pram so your baby is looking at you instead of out into the world, and so on.

Attachment theory organises familial relationships into a hierarchy. The primary relationship a child will model all future ones on is an intense, one-on-one bond. Fathers, and other hands-on carers, play secondary, supportive roles.

Other children, weirdly, are virtually irrelevant.

But mothers, Keller says, aren't that special. Babies don't innately prioritise one relationship over others. Big sisters and brothers in particular can be at least as important to social and emotional development as mums.

Attachment theory, as conceived in white, middle-class terms, doesn't just burden mothers with untenable responsibility, it informs toxic prejudices that run through Western educational systems, social services and family courts. Immigrant and ethnic minority mothers are found to be dangerously inattentive and disengaged.

Childcare provided by siblings is called *neglect*.

Reading Hrdy feels like scientific proof that perfect wedded bliss, the balance of the bigendered family, is a scam. The nuclear family isn't natural, it's a function of capitalism. And the mums of Ship Street flip the story of female reproduction as biological weakness, making mothering the social power at the heart of a community in which men were marginal hangers-on.

All these histories affirm my singleness, in that they confirm fatherhood's ambiguous, inconsistent, contingent relationship to mothering.

But they don't exactly make a case for lone motherhood.

In an introduction to Keller's book, psychologist Nandita Chaudhary writes of how the nuclear family is entwined with the logic of market capitalism, and says many Asians see small Western families and the over-attentiveness of Western mothers as a recipe for 'socially awkward, brattish and diffi-cult individuals'.

And the nuclear family is 'brittle'. And what happens when it breaks, Choudhury argues, calls into question the WEIRD primacy of the mother–child dyad. The misguided belief that 'the infant needs only a mother . . . could soon be challenged, because outcomes of single parenting have not been favour-able, to say the least.'

Ouch.

Choudhury doesn't specify the unfavourable outcomes of my kind of motherhood (enough people have). But Keller does expand on how WEIRD mothering more generally is to blame for raising *difficult individuals*: our focus on nurturing independence and 'psychological autonomy' tends towards individualism from the moment they're born.

I hadn't read up on attachment theory when I was bond-ing with my own baby. But I'd definitely absorbed the idea that lots of physical contact and face-to-face interaction was hugely important. F's becoming, which I felt so intimately involved in – was it really happening as I experienced it?

Was I doing it wrong? In some unnatural way?

And what does it mean that I've centred my life around a dyadic relationship so unnatural we might be hard-wired against this bond – to reject it even at unspeakable costs?

If this book is an effort to assert my motherhood as valid, to prove that, as much as my partnered friends, I can claim the supreme feminine identity of a *good mother*, is the whole project unravelling?

Giving up on the soulmate, have I burdened F with being

all the family I need, relying on puffed-up notions of the importance of mothering to give my life meaning?

In an interview, Kate Moss was asked how motherhood changed her. The honesty of her answer moved me: 'I was never lonely again'.

This feels almost transgressive. We're supposed to talk about how motherhood has taught us what's important in life. Refined our priorities. How mothering has made us less selfish. More invested in the future. We're not supposed to talk about what our children have given us. Or not like that.

We're not supposed to *need* them. Not like *that*.

Are F and I too close?

When F was two, and she expressed that innate human empathy – subtle enough to sense the healing power of a book that meant nothing to her – and collected together her unravelling mother, was I beginning to depend on her in some unhealthy way?

Imagine making a whole new person who had no choice but to love you unconditionally. Who gave you a reason to be, and had no autonomous power to refuse this relationship. Imagine this bond was so powerful you gave up on ever falling in love with a romantic partner and it didn't even feel like a loss.

According to an investigation in 2019, unease about the intimacy of the single-mother–child dyad drove social services to forcibly remove dozens of German children from single mothers – and three from grandmothers who were their primary carers – not because there was any suspicion of abuse or neglect, but because these relationships were judged to be *too close*.

*Jugendamt* officials condemned them as 'symbiotic'.

F and I are symbiotic. We need each other. But more, you could say we're in a state of symbiogenesis.

Capitalism puts impossible pressure on nuclear families and nuclear families put impossible pressure on mothers. But when my nuclear family broke, I was free – more, I was driven by necessity – to seek out the kinds of connection that cohabiting coupledom failed at, and a child doesn't provide.

The mother–child bond is a person's primal connection into the world. From there, from the moment of birth, she extends outwards, becoming more herself in every new connection. And since I've been single, it's something F and I are both doing – together, and in own separate ways.

The intensity of our bond, that huge love, is what gets me through. It centres me, giving my life stability I never had as a younger, childless woman. But just as F unfurls out from that core connection, so must I, building my own supple – imperfect, demanding, sometimes fragile – networks of mutual support.

Pick up any book on child psychology and, if you're a mother, you'll quickly learn that you're doing it all wrong. So, like the Ship Street mums, I've tended to give expert opinions a wide berth.

I've never read a parenting book in my life but I know enough from secondary reading that their prescriptions change with the times. So I won't panic about F becoming a sociopath because I've given her too much exclusive attention, because I've given her no siblings, or because I strapped her to my chest like a yummy mummy and not to my back like Senegalese mom.

If there was a formula, a universal template for how people should be, and a hack to raise them so they turned out that way, we'd have hit on it by now and the human condition would be solved. But also, I have a certain faith in our symbiogenesis.

Our *becoming by living together* has an expansive drive.

That I must rely on the generosity of friends to manage single mothering means F spends plenty of time in the company of other adults and other children. She has friends in whose family homes she is perfectly herself, but not the quite the self she is in ours. She has other contexts in which to see herself reflected back, other people to build shared ideas about the world with.

We go on family holidays with other single mothers and their children, making up a nuclear foursome of love and convenience that comes together and apart at will, or expands to encompass more mothers and more children. We descend on campsites, an extended family, a tribe of loose women and our disorderly offspring.

And nuclear families accommodate us, too. The people I think of as family in Berlin are friends who looked aghast when I announced my pregnancy, and then announced their own a few weeks later. Our children, O and F, are growing up together.

When the pandemic hit, we defied lockdown regulations that said F and I could only have indoor contact with her father, and bubbled up with our friends. Because public transport was off limits, and the half-hour bike ride between our homes exhausting for six-year-old legs, F would stay with them for a couple of days at a time, and then O with us. In this new intimacy, their relationship developed, their easy enthusiasm for one another broken by the kind of fights I used to have with my little sister.

Good, I thought.

These friends are a nuclear family under pressure. They fight over domestic duties, struggle financially. They have, since I began this book, lost a member of their extended family and suffered a terrible health crisis within their nuclear one. And yet they give me the support – constant, and last-ditch – that, yes, sometimes makes me smart with how much I depend on them.

F hasn't had the blessing of a grandmother who lives nearby. But the long conversations I have with my mother over the phone are a part of raising her that we do together, even at a distance. I've never questioned who I *should* be having these conversations with. But I wonder if, with a live-in Kindesvater, I would solicit so many opinions, from so many friends, when the responsibility is too much to bear alone.

These relationships have made possible the indulgence of reading, thinking and writing through the questions that becoming a single mother has raised for me. And, in the last push, with my (extended) deadline looming and answers to my questions still buried in thousands of pages of notes and trains of thought, my mum kept her promise that I'd find focus on creative work by flying over and moving in with us for a month to cook and clean and hang out with F.

\*

Single mothering may be an anomaly of late-capitalist social atomisation. But myriad family forms reproduced through countless generations in countless cultures prove, Hrdy says, that flexibility is 'the hallmark of the human family'.

If we are flexible enough to allow mothers to be both single and supported, autonomous and connected, then single mums might be the social body's free radicals, the charged molecules whose drive for balance and connection disrupts stable systems and is essential to metabolic processes.

Connection is the core of life. But sometimes you have to tear things apart to create the most vital bonds.

If attachment theory gave us a model of motherhood informed by observing chimps, the work of scientist Suzanne Simard suggests one I find much more compelling, revealed by unearthing the live roots of diverse ecosystems.

In *Finding the Mother Tree*, Simard describes how trees and other plants cooperate and nurture one another. Her research has transformed our understanding of what a forest is: not a collection of discrete plants and animals in competition, but an intricately networked community alive with mutual aid.

Through a web of fungi lacing the soil, trees and other plants share nutrients and water. They even communicate with one another through connections that Simard describes as functioning exactly like synapses in the brain. When they need help – an infusion of carbon, or enzymes to fight disease – they *ask* for it.

Mother trees are vital 'nodes' within this network. They pass on the fungi saplings need to join the 'wood-wide web' and, through this connective tissue, feed and nurture them. Mother trees support their young but this isn't a bilateral relationship and care doesn't all flow one way. A mother tree is a hub that nourishes its whole community. It holds water to see the ecosystem through drought. And it draws what it needs back from the collective – not just a family of biological kin but a complex interdependence of different species.

A mother tree isn't a half of anything; it's a powerful nexus, a living concentration of connections, reproducing and nurturing bonds, supporting and supported by a community whose resilience lies in diversity.

With so little written on the history of single motherhood itself, to understand the identity I fell into, I've turned instead to narratives of Black feminism, welfare warriors and sex workers. And one reason *single mother* has rarely been asserted as an affirming identity in its own right is precisely that it is so intensely intersectional.

Single motherhood is a point where these different identities' struggles – and their triumphs – intersect. A node of love and need that compels women to forge bonds within their specific communities, but also a commonality that invites empathic reflection between them. And we're far from alone in experiencing the nuclear family a jagged fragment that cuts in on itself.

Connecting with one another, with gay men and trans women who want children, with child-free adults who model alternative life paths for our kids, finding common ground between our own experiences and those of partnered mums and with family forms across cultures, classes and generations, single mothering is a perspective that might join in creatively reimagining the world.

Patriarchy has corralled and constricted love, calling heterosexuality and mothering its only 'natural' expressions. But cooperative evolution shows that all love is natural: sexuality doesn't have to further biological reproduction and motherly love is contiguous with the rest of human connection.

Same-sex parents model better-balanced nuclear families, whose private negotiations around childcare and domestic labour are much more sensible. And single mothers who shack up together echo their experiences, even if they keep their sexual and domestic lives separate.

But queer chosen families offer even more exciting practices for future families, as well as echoing those of the ancient past. Families bound not by normative gender roles, shared genetics or legal contracts, but active bonds of solidarity, love, sexuality, friendship and domesticity that defy rigid definition. Like othermothers, trans mothers who support their peers through transition, and house mothers in the drag community, extend the scope of mothering beyond raising children, to caring adult relationships and the work of building, sustaining and defending whole communities.

Queer families may encompass motherly, fatherly, sisterly and brotherly relationships. But if queer experiences show that families don't need children, children definitely need families. And with so many constellations possible, single mothering doesn't have to be the bitter end of social disintegration. It can be a new beginning.

# Chapter 9

## The Post-Capitalist Family

> To answer death with utopian futurity, to rival the social reproduction of capital on a global scale with a forward-dreaming diasporic accountability is a queer thing to do. A strange thing to do. A thing that changes family and the future forever.
>
> – ALEXIS PAULINE GUMBS

Eight weeks after her birthday, six weeks after mine, Imogen and I are finally enjoying a treat we've been promising each other.

We stretch out tired muscles in a pool of artificially salinated water. Through the steam, I'm rattling on at her about Hadza grandmothers. But Imogen knows all this. She's done ethnographic research for NGOs all over Africa, including for European social enterprises bringing the wonders of renewable power to remote, off-grid communities – and tearing apart their social fabric in the process.

As an environment journalist, I'm familiar with these initiatives' claims of liberating African women from the burden of collecting firewood. But, Imogen says, collecting wood is when women get together away from their menfolk and organise. Gathering is a site of female power. 'They love having an African woman collect the data,' she says, 'but they aren't interested in my analysis.'

And Imogen knows the power of extended family because as a single mother in her younger years, grandparents, other kin and as-kin made possible her work as a trade union leader in the anti-apartheid struggle.

'I've always thought this. Mothers aren't supposed to look after children. If we're fit enough to make babies, we're fit enough to be out working, gathering firewood, organising strikes – it's the oldies who should be stuck home with the kids.' It's the single mothering she's doing in northern Europe, confined, cut off from *real* life, in constant conflict with her Kindesvater, battling the job centre's paper abuse, that Imogen finds shocking.

'When I was a mother the first time, the struggle was political. There was an incredible sense of community – but also of hope. I was bringing my son into a world we believed we were making anew,' Jocelyn says. 'Mothering in capitalism is shit.'

Enveloped in the heat of fossil fuels gouged from the earth and burned conveniently out of sight, I gaze at a mute wooden Buddha overlooking the pool. Made by Indonesian hands, transported across the globe in hydrocarbon-powered ships, so we can pretend that incinerating the planet's future is spiritually enriching.

As I write, my phone goes off and I reach to silence it, but seeing Ginevra's number, I pick up. She asks if she can put me down as her daughter's next of kin. I'm touched, because I love her daughter, T. Her wise little face. How gravely she holds my gaze when she nestles in for a cuddle.

But I also regret she doesn't have a stronger bond with anyone but her mother.

*Next of kin* means *in an emergency*. I wish I could claim the honorific of *othermother*. But we hardly see each other. Sunday afternoons, sometimes. A glorious, wet camping trip last summer. Breathing spaces when the rush of life stills for a moment.

Months can pass with only intermittent WhatsApp messages, trying to fit each other in between work, school, therapists' appointments, playdates with school friends, schedules with Kindesvaters.

Next week? Next month?

Conversations run parallel on my phone. Sometimes, they loop and intersect. More connections should strengthen a network. But add another mother, and a date we can all keep only becomes more elusive: our threads through cyberspace a cobweb in the wind.

Imogen, Ginevra and I first connected over the dream of a different kind of family.

When I first split from the Kindesvater, Mariam and I wanted to move in together. We looked for a flat, but without a full-time work contract between us there was nothing on offer. Then, a couple of years later, Imogen reached out through the single mums Facebook group with a kind of manifesto.

She was moving from Cape Town to Berlin with her

nine-year-old daughter and a mission to set up a single mothers' co-living project. The first time we met was a few days after she arrived, at a community centre with a couple of dozen other women and children, scribbling dreams of home and family on rolls of packing paper.

We wanted to make co-living a site of collective care. Mothering shared, siblings multiplied. Spaces to work and play. And when they left, we'd still have each other, a disorderly collective for that special, female phase of life. More to draw our fledglings back to the nest than poor old Mum, more bets on grandmothering than the life choices of each of our daughters.

Now, I'm swotting up on the history (and prehistory) behind our dreams of motherly solidarity. But it's become an intellectual project, not an embodied one.

If my dream of a perfectly balanced two-parent home failed because *mother* and *father* turned out to be more different, less compatible, than I'd imagined, I believe living with other mothers would work because we speak a shared language from shared experiences. Our responsibilities are clear, mutually understood and articulated: not a matter of silently ingrained assumptions.

But I won't get to test my conviction because we're each struggling just the same. Separate lives, locked into identically overburdened routines. Identically exhausted. Running parallel, we yearn to converge. So we can othermother one another and one another's children.

Or just so we don't each have to cook our own dinners every damn day.

But we're too busy to make any of this happen. We're each

too focused on our own needs, the needs of our own children. And time is ticking: not our own biological clocks but those of our children, who are growing up and running out of use for our fantasy family.

Still, *the human family is nothing if not flexible.* Our household, mine and F's, might be the weirdest in human history. It might be exhausting. But it's a happy one.

It's a space where we spend a lot of time together, just the two of us. But we experience this time differently. If a year is a quarter of your whole life, then a day, a minute, feels very different from your middle-aged mum's days and minutes. The future is a distant, unlikely place. Events that came and went months ago are the misty past.

F's time comes in huge swathes that threaten to swallow her up. Boredom lurks in her every empty minute, while I long for a still moment of the present. Because with age, time contracts. The pull of the future becomes violent.

I try to be conscious of how, in all we do together, we're connecting across these alien temporal plains. To remember what it was like for time to be so big. But I rarely manage to snap out of the rush of my own vanishing moments to pause and fully empathise.

Until, suddenly, grown-up time, capitalist-busy time, stopped.

Coronatime ballooned.

Real life turned outside in.

The domestic was everything.

We didn't know how long coronatime would be, or what would come after. And I felt the future ease its grip. The dissonance of our timescapes collapsed. Venturing out like explorers in the ruins of a lost civilisation, birdsong, the growl of an occasional car, had a sudden wholeness.

At first, I thought we'd have to portion up coronatime: break it down into manageable pieces with a structured routine. Instead, we found chopping vegetables, threading beads, planting seeds, walking by the canal, with no thought to *when* or *what next*, left no space for boredom. Almost as if it had never been time F was afraid of at all, but rattling around in it all by herself.

It this acute present, something quickened in the collective body. And when we latched back on to the tug of history, some of us dared imagine it might have shifted course. So I arranged a video call with Margarita Mediavilla, a physicist who works with economists and engineers to model how human economies interact with energy and the environment.

The rush had stopped. We'd shut down production. Chinese greenhouse gas emissions, soaring year-on-year, fell by twenty-five per cent in weeks. Work that pushed people to the brink stopped. It stopped mattering. Suddenly, we had to decide which jobs were actually important. Most were horribly paid, or not paid at all.

Capitalism's warped logic had flipped.

Governments that had been ruthlessly slashing public spending were injecting cash directly into homes. Everyone was talking about connection, community. The power of touch. And in tackling a global crisis, it was clear the solutions were collective and caring, from networks of mutual aid springing up in the most individualistic societies, to wearing a mask to protect others.

Mediavilla noted all this but was not optimistic.

The problem, she said, is that we don't love nature.

It's not often you hear physicists talk about love. But she wasn't appealing to esoteric forces or saying we don't *value* nature. What she meant was, in love you extend the boundaries of the self. You encompass the object of your love into your own identity. If we *loved* nature, we wouldn't just admire it or account for its utility, we'd have an embodied experience of belonging to something bigger.

We'd be as committed to all life on Earth as we are to our own.

Economics, Mediavilla explains, is just a metaphor for the metabolism of society: the flow of energy and matter through the collective body of a nation – or a global network of trade, politics and exploitation.

Each cell of life on Earth has its own metabolism: biochemical processes that maintain its individual integrity. Cells interact, regulating flows of energy and matter through an organism, which is itself part of a self-regulating eco-system with other plants and animals and, in turn, the planetary whole.

For a while, as human lives and labours detached from the land, from the seasons, it was possible to imagine humanity as somehow distinct from all this. But the more we've drawn away, the more complexly our interactions with the rest of nature are mediated, the more tangible it becomes that all human activity is embedded in bigger cycles of life.

The faster capitalism gets, the wilder the weather.

And the metabolisms of our atomised domestic spaces

work at a furious rate. The smaller the household, the more it costs to run: in motherly labour, rent, fuel, groceries, the replicated collections of stuff each of our homes contains.

People say the climate crisis is hard to grasp emotionally. You cannot relate to a disaster on this scale until a tidal wave washes away your village or your family goes hungry. But I feel ecological collapse in my muscles. The speed at which money slips through my fingers. The constant struggle to keep pace.

We're living in a machine spinning out of control, a growth-based economy that's failing if it doesn't *literally* double in size every two or three decades. It's exhausting the planet, but it's exhausting people too.

I feel it when I pay someone on a fossil-fuelled scooter to bring an expensive, high-energy processed meal wrapped in indestructible polymer foam to my door. When I wonder how long the man on the scooter must work to pay for his own dinner. I feel it when I can only get a grip on my domestic space by tossing out waste biological cycles can't cope with. I'm dissipating my own exhaustion into global social, economic, ecological and atmospheric systems.

*Here, you decide what to do with this shit.*

If Ginevra, Imogen and I did merge our three little families we could quantify the little difference this would make to the planet as a whole using a carbon footprint calculator. Go online, tap in the kind of home you live in, what you buy and eat, how you travel. Out comes a number that represents your own personal share of responsibility for a global economy run on fossil fuels.

And then, if you're an ecologically responsible citizen of the world, you can chip away at that number. Give up meat, ride a bike, have your holidays at home.

These calculators were dreamed up by Big Oil. Not to help us design gentler, more communal futures but to shift responsibility for the climate crisis from systems onto individuals. Or from BP onto mothers.

Because when responsibility is personalised, it's also feminised. Cooking from scratch with local produce, persuading your kids to go vegan, sorting trash, doing the school run on foot, changing energy supplier, hand-washing laundry – all these are domestic duties.

Women's work.

Reducing the challenge of reshaping capitalism's interaction with the rest of the biosphere to a matter of personal lifestyle choice is a supremely neoliberal illusion. But shifting responsibility from industry to the domestic goes right back to the Victorians. It's the same story that blamed infant mortality in toxic slums on mums not breastfeeding properly.

Now, we're told if we just kept house better, a vast capitalist-industrial system of extraction and production wouldn't have to keep trashing the planet. It's not BP's fault. Women made them do it. Because we're lazy and we love shopping.

And because we have babies.

In 2017, a study came out comparing the impact of various 'individual lifestyle choices' on carbon footprints. It made headlines with the news that the biggest thing you can do, as an individual, is to have one less child. But none of the articles I saw under these headlines pointed out how stupid a statement this is.

All else being equal, the carbon footprint of two people is bigger than the carbon footprint of one person. Obviously. But then we're not taking about *personal* carbon footprints anymore.

As ever, the notion of the free individual with personal rights and responsibilities unravels with motherhood. As ever, the boundaries of the female self are blurred. And as ever, everything is our fault. As if, because humans are doing bad things to the planet, it's women's fault for making all these bad humans. The crisis doesn't just originate in the home, but in the female body. Eve is still responsible for the sins of humanity.

Of course, F did not ask to be born into an economy run on coal, gas, oil and neocolonialist industrial agriculture – a system that has exploitation programmed into its drive for expansion – but nor did I.

The problem isn't reproduction, it's production. Production has been the problem ever since we began pretending it was a linear process independent of complete metabolic cycles.

As ecofeminists have been saying for decades, pollution – from poisoned water supplies to nuclear waste to carbon emissions – is a problem created by men raised to expect some woman to come along and clean up the messes they make.

When F was six, she asked me to help her fill in a form to join the local library. After her name, age and address, she came to a question about gender. Multiple choice: *male, female, other.* She asked what this last category meant.

'Like, you don't identify as either a girl or a boy?'

She frowned at me doubtfully.

'Or – no,' I corrected myself, grasping for something she could relate to, 'not neither, both.'

'Oh yeah, that's me,' she said, inscribing a neat little cross in the box and moving swiftly on to the next question. And I thanked the Fates – not so much that there was a box she fitted into, but that diligently filling in a library form was much more important to her than anything little boxes might say about who she is.

F is growing up in a world where her biology doesn't have to define her gender and her gender doesn't have to define what kind of work she does, how she lives or who she loves.

Gender identities are proliferating, a blossoming of intricate, living narratives about connection, expression, love, sex, community. Voices and perspectives that reimagine *female* and *male*, giving creative momentum to categories that used to be stiflingly rigid.

When I think of F's future, I'm not too worried her staunch sense of self will be undermined by categories like *male*, *female* or *other*.

But sometimes, I wonder what it will mean to be *human*.

In 2017, when F was still at kindergarten, far-right politics was ascending in response to the 'migrant crisis' and Europe was fortifying its borders, I went to report on a conference on statelessness.

All day, activists and human rights lawyers from across Europe discussed the fine legalities of protecting migrants from detention and deportation. None of the organisations they belonged to were environmental ones, but when we shifted to the pub at the end of the day, conversation quickly turned to the climate crisis.

An Italian activist said grimly, 'If now, with just a few hundred thousand people arriving in dire need, we're having actual political debates about whether to rescue people from the Med or let children drown, when things really heat up, we'll be shooting them on sight.'

How do you mother a child for such a future? Even if she's on the right side of the Med – even if the world's wealthiest can protect ourselves at others' expense for a few more decades – what will become of our humanity?

Evolving gender perspectives can change how we think about work, family and much else. But the biggest gender problems we face today are about much more than just individual identities.

Women can step across the gendered divide between private and public life. Move from states of dependence into arenas of power. But these realms are still gendered, and still profoundly unequal. The schism between work and care is deeper than ever. Individual women can escape the home, but mothering hasn't.

Mediavilla describes the regenerative human and ecological resources that support all human societies as our 'nourishing base'. Neglecting this base doesn't just make single mum's lives horribly hard. Work–life balance isn't just a women's issue. The rupture between man and nature, production and reproduction, now threatens our humanity and the rest of life on Earth.

And there's another dangerous fault line running through the system. Capitalism doesn't care. But also, capitalism doesn't take responsibility. Because when we cleaved work from care, mind from body – power and responsibility also became dangerously detached.

Our choices – but also, rights, democracy – are embedded in the supreme Western value of *freedom*. Free speech, freedom of thought, the freedom to define our own identities. Women must be free to choose what we do with our bodies. Markets must be free. Companies are free to pollute, consumers are free to take our business elsewhere if we don't like it.

But a few hundred years back, Europeans basically thought freedom was a bad thing. People were bound to duties defined by their place in a rigid hierarchy: if everyone was free to do as they pleased, society would collapse.

The Enlightenment changed all this. But as David Graeber and David Wengrow argue in *The Dawn of Everything: A New History of Humanity*, its core ideas weren't just an organic development from shifts in European economics and social fabric; it was no coincidence that Rousseau was writing at a time when Europeans looking for new markets and resources to exploit met cultures that were far less hierarchical.

When they encountered Indigenous American societies that valued personal freedoms, Europeans were initially horrified – not least by how little control American men had over their women. Indigenous Americans, for their part, found Europeans' servility laughable.

And yet, as Graeber and Wengrow tell the story, intellectuals from these different cultures debated intensely. And Americans began to win the argument. The problem is, when Europeans embraced freedom, a few things got lost in translation.

When Indigenous Americans talked about freedom, they meant autonomy. People were free to make autonomous decisions about their own lives. They didn't have to submit to the arbitrary diktats of authority figures. But their autonomy was rooted in interdependence.

You were free to do as you liked, so long as you didn't piss off the people you depend on, or let down the people who depend on you – because then you end up pretty lonely, and no one can do much all by themselves.

But when Europeans got hold of freedom as a guiding principle, they romanticised it around the idea of the lone, heroic individual. To be free was to be independent. To make choices governed by nothing but your own free will. And the only way you can make decisions with no regard for their impact on others is if the people you depend on are not free.

Women weren't individuals in their own right because we are too close to nature, because our relationships are rooted in our bodies rather than rational choice. But also because the whole Enlightenment notion of the free, independent individual wouldn't have worked if it applied to everyone.

Women were not free, because they depended on men. Men were free because the people they depended on most weren't free, or even proper people. So men could play at being independent.

Freedom, then – the supreme value of Western Civilisation – was, from the start, based on exploitation. Which, given how things played out in the Americas alone, must be about the most egregious case of cultural appropriation in human history.

But also, it's based on pretty odd notions of dependence. Not just because independence is an illusion – we all depend on other people – but because the flip side of dependence isn't independence.

It's responsibility.

European, masculinised notions of freedom assume that if someone depends on you, you have power over them. And the more people depend on you, the more powerful you are, and so the freer you are to do what you like.

The way Americans saw it, the more people depend on you, the greater your responsibilities. Indigenous American societies, as diverse as they were in values and social structure, tended to organise themselves to ensure wealth and power weren't all concentrated in the same hands, and everyone had a keen sense of their dependencies and responsibilities.

Amassing power could even limit your freedom because your autonomous choices had to be governed by the needs of so many. And in this sense, American ideas of freedom, autonomy and dependence were kind of – *motherly*.

There are lots of things I can't do because I'm a mum. I can't stay out all night whenever I want. I can't take a job that'll consume all my time and energy. I can't take risks that might leave F motherless. I can't up sticks and take her away from the people and places that define her, however sick I might get of living in Berlin. Mostly, I can't even join colleagues for a drink after work.

So motherhood has drastically reduced my freedom. But it

hasn't reduced my autonomy. As a single mum, I make autonomous decisions about my life bound by my responsibilities.

Children's dependence on adults gives us a lot of power over them, but we rarely think of it as power, because it doesn't make us freer – it's a huge responsibility.

Women fought for equal rights, and won them. But having the same legal rights as men hasn't made us truly equal because we have so many responsibilities.

When women depend on men – for our daily bread, to support us through motherhood, to use their social capital to give us a leg-up in the workplace – this gives them power over us. But when men depend on women – to create and sustain their fatherhood and much else – we don't call it male dependence or female power. It's just another responsibility that limits women's freedom.

And when single mums depend on society, the state assumes the power to interfere in our personal lives – that's what we get for being so irresponsible.

When women talk about carrying the mental load, we're talking about responsibility. When fathers help out, when mothers delegate to their husbands, this isn't enough because the responsibility for ensuring things get done can be more exhausting than doing them.

When we talk about emotional labour – that's often about responsibility too. When women are expected to smooth over tensions in the workplace, the problem isn't just the work this involves, but the assumption that women are responsible for making everyone feel OK.

When minorities are expected to explain concepts around identity politics – to correct mistakes, and to do so nicely – it's not just the time and effort these things take. The outrage is that it should be a queer Black woman's responsibility to make sense of the gap between a straight white man's experiences and reality.

Growing up, Ella was the 'responsible one' in a family that included an abusive, alcoholic father. As a responsible young woman, she was a high achiever. And she went on to work in high-level roles at international development organisations. But she's also been let down by not one but two Kindesvaters.

Now a single mum of two boys, her professional aspirations are eclipsed by the responsibilities of mothering. 'All I care about is raising good men,' she says. 'If can bring up my kids to be different from the men in my life, nothing else matters.'

Clarity of purpose is great. But Ella doesn't sound resolute. She sounds kinda desperate. She hasn't decided motherhood is so fulfilling that her career isn't important anymore. She just knows she wouldn't be the first good woman to raise difficult men.

Ella knows her boys' characters, their ideas about the world, their life paths and how they'll handle future relationships are shaped by much that's beyond her control. But knowing her powers are limited doesn't spread the weight of this responsibility she carries alone.

Women are responsible for our children's social and emotional development, for the formation of their psyches. We're responsible for raising good men, and caring for bad ones. We're responsible for sex, and the consequences of sex. We're responsible for rape. Child malnutrition. Inflation. Atmospheric carbon concentrations.

The sins of humanity. And the sins of Big Oil.

Oil company execs are only responsible for increasing shareholder profits.

If Ella's responsibilities keep her awake at night, you have to wonder how much sleep Lee Raymond gets. Ella is responsible for two lovely boys who can be a bit hyperactive sometimes. As CEO of ExxonMobil, Raymond was responsible for one of most lethally extractive and polluting entities the planet has ever seen. And he used his power to bury important scientific data on climate change and pump money into climate-denial propaganda.

We tend to assume that people like Raymond are driven by greed. But I think there's more to it than that. Companies don't have responsibilities; they just have an inbuilt imperative to keep expanding. A company's greed is – like capitalism's greed, its drive for growth – infinite. But Raymond is, presumably, a person. And I don't think he was acting in his own interests so much as in the interests of the company, something greater than himself.

Lee Raymond looks like the most irresponsible man on a planet awash with irresponsible men. But maybe he's just a person who took his responsibilities so seriously he was ready to sacrifice the future of the biosphere – let alone his own humanity – to uphold them.

The freedom of free market capitalism is freedom from responsibility. Freedom to exploit. And so someone else must take responsibility for the fallout.

We vilify consumerism among the worst of late capitalism's great ills. But the insane levels of production we have today aren't a response to insatiable consumer desire. Consumer desire was, and continues to be, manufactured to keep economies expanding.

When mass production first exploded, women – housewives – were the ultimate consumers. Consumerism was productivism's goodly wife. And if there's any doubt whether these two halves of the capitalist machine are still gendered – why does no one expect production to stop making *more of me?*

Why does consumption have to restrain herself? Take responsibility. Go on a diet. Exercise that most Victorian, motherly impulse: self-sacrifice.

Tamsin, a journalist I used to work with who is also a single mother of five, set her family the challenge of living plastic-free for a month. She asked harried servers to use the reusable containers she brought shopping and travelled across Berlin to get her dry goods from a scoop-and-weigh. She gave up the pleasure of getting away from the screen to read the *Times Literary Supplement*, because the print edition was delivered in polythene. She got her kids making their own toothpaste from coconut oil and baking soda.

Tamsin's family didn't miss plastic. In fact, living without it felt so good her kids demanded she keep up all this extra work (except the toothpaste, which was revolting).

But if we just banned single-use plastics and made scoop-and-weigh the only legal way to sell dry goods, whole systems would have to change. They'd have to think of another way to sell toothpaste. And if that sounds like too radical an undertaking there's no point pretending that millions of Tamsins running ourselves ragged will change these systems with consumer power.

We are bombarded with the message that ecological salvation is about sacrifice. Giving up cars, flights, meat, cheap clothes, processed foods, treats for kids. Sauna days. The consumer consolations of living in a productivist economy.

And it's true, we do have to wean ourselves off these things. Consumerism is terrible for the planet and terrible for our mental health.

But people at their exhausted, hollowed-out, beyond-care limits are being asked to make personal sacrifices for the greater good, without any tangible sense of what the greater good might look like. And what it might look like, actually, is precisely what so many of us are craving – to slow the fuck down.

So let's stop talking about ecological action in terms of sacrifice.

Psychologists say addiction is a response to unmet need. Enjoying a glass of wine turns into alcoholism because it's compensating for something. And giving up the one thing that alleviates loneliness and anxiety is horribly hard. So let's leave our shopping habits aside for a moment and focus on restoring connection and meaning to our lives.

If we were serious about tackling climate change, resource depletion and biodiversity loss, we'd start from the other direction. We wouldn't tell people to stop buying things. We'd just stop producing them.

And if we're producing less, consuming less, then we should also be working less. And working less leaves more time for what's important.

*

Life on Earth hangs in the balance between work and care. So we need to pick up the unfinished work of Eleanor Rathbone, the suffragettes, Wages for Housework and the welfare rights movement – and free care from dependence on capitalism.

But we have to be a bit more ambitious than Rathbone was.

First-wave feminists fighting for care's autonomy from waged work were trying to free women to raise people fit for good society. Now that the whole biosphere is being whipped into fatal hysteria, we need to nurture into being a society fit for humanity.

So taking mothers out of the productive economy isn't enough. We'd be still be the exceptional case, our responsibilities out of all proportion with our powers. And anyway, none of the mums I know actually want to spend all our children's dependent years as full-time carers, exiled from where the action is.

We need a lot of care. Not just the kind that props up the growth machine, but the kind that undermines its power over everything else. So we need all hands on deck, not just those that are already full.

UBI, done right, has tantalising potential to give everyone the opportunity to opt out of capitalist production and do something more useful with their time. And UBI is having a moment, being trialled around the world, advocated from diverse perspectives. It has traction.

But those pushing for UBI aren't all trying to feminise the economy. It's also popular with free market libertarians who envision a society of hyper-independent entrepreneurs. Global Women's Strike's demand for a Care Income is better because it explicitly frames the same basic idea as a move to rebalance the economy away from such dystopias.

A Care Income would give us all real freedom to choose the kind of community activism Beulah Sanders of the National Welfare Rights Organization wanted women to be free to do, mixing and solving problems – or urban farming, food sharing, setting up a non-profit repair shop – over jobs that are horrible for people and horrible for the planet. We could divest our labour from companies that refuse to take responsibility for their ecological impact.

But if we're going to shrink production, we may as well start with more traditional labour demands: cutting working hours.

The forty-hour week isn't some essential magic number, even if our goal were to keep expanding the economy indefinitely. In 1930, Keynes published *Economic Possibilities for Our Grandchildren*, predicting that automation would shrink the working week to fifteen hours. But capitalism didn't use increased efficiency to give people more time off, it used it to expand production – because that's what it does. The working week only dropped from fifty or sixty hours to forty because governments intervened to reduce unemployment during the Great Depression.

Capitalism would have us all working the sixteen-hour days of a nineteenth-century cotton mill. Forty-odd hours a week is just the maximum we'll put up with. A little more in the United States and UK where neoliberalism all but crushed trade unions, a little less in France where people start setting fire to things if you impinge on workers' rights.

But in any case, these hours are based on the norm of a male worker, in his prime, with a wife to cook, clean, organise his social life, give him the joys of fatherhood, suck his dick and absorb the blows of frustration from spending most of his waking hours in meaningless, demeaning labour.

A worker who, thankfully, barely exists these days.

For everything's sake, it's about time we were a lot less tolerant of giving so much of ourselves to capitalism. So let's take a leaf out of the French book. Let's set fire to things. But more, let's make the normative worker someone who does exist.

Me, for example.

Someone who's really fucking busy and won't have anyone to care for me unless I care for them too. Or better still, someone who, ditto, but also has a frail relative to care for. Or a disabled child. Or five kids who have declared the house a plastic-free zone.

Or all of the above.

Because right now, we're being told to give stuff up so that things can carry on just as they are. Or not get *too* much worse: the climate heating up by two degrees instead of four. Hundreds of thousands of human lives lost or displaced instead of billions. But the survival of our biosphere in any recognisable form is incompatible with things carrying on as they are. The scale of transformation we need demands radical new visions of the future.

Getting over any self-destructive addiction is going to smart. But let's see how wedded we really are to productivism – if we love our disposal devices and ready meals more than breathable air and fertile soils – when ecological action means knocking off for the weekend on Wednesday.

Why not just assume everyone is responsible for care? Make it a social expectation – *surely, as a responsible human, you must have stuff you need to take care of* – and set working hours accordingly.

Because that's the thing about responsibility. People – from Ella to Lee Raymond – take it really seriously. Mostly, people step up when we know what's expected of us. Single mums hate being told *I could never do what you do!* because we're not special. You do what you gotta do. Because you know what your responsibilities are.

If we want autonomy from the capitalist growth machine then it's up to us to nurture alternatives. And if we empowered care with money and time, and understood the labour pains of birthing a sustainable future as something we all have do to survive, we might just surprise ourselves with how responsible we can be.

Care is work, so care needs pay. But responsibility needs power. And individual, personalised responsibility – the kind we're supposed to exercise with our atomised consumer choice – is weak. But in a society where we all felt responsible for one another, our collective power could be formidable.

What exactly that might look like is all to play for. A flowering of beautiful experiments of the kind whores, queers, othermothers and welfare queens have been doing for as long as patriarchy has condemned our love and domesticity.

Because BP are right. Sort of. The domestic is the locus of real environmental action. It's just that the eco-revolution we need isn't about tweaking consumer habits or working longer and harder to minimise our individual impact.

*Patriarchy*, in its original sense, referred to male rule over the family. From this core site of power it has become a globalised system of exploitation. So to create radical networks of mutual care outside its dominion, a transformation that unfurls from our most intense sites of connection – the microcosm where patriarchy first staked its claim on life – seems like a pretty good place to start.

The nuclear family splits productive and reproductive labours along gendered lines. It assumes female dependence on men, male power over women. And insularity: it makes care a private responsibility and assumes all the meaningful relationships a person needs are contained in the family home.

In a hyper-individualist society, the dependence of motherhood is a female vulnerability. But if we stop thinking of dependence as the opposite of freedom and celebrate interdependence as the fabric of any resilient social system, mothering becomes powerful and the domestic space a nexus of the connection that binds communities together.

If the nuclear family is the building block of capitalist society, the post-capitalist family won't be packaged into a stifling little brick stacked against other stifling little bricks, it'll be a buzzing hub in the network. Kitchens, workshops, community gardens and collective spaces of direct action could be bustling intersections that ease our dependence on the market economy.

Work and home might merge.

Before we split work from care, childhood was no more a cosseted, protected state than womanhood was. With no clear distinction between mothering and the rest of life, kids were their parents' apprentices. Their innate fascination with the tools and motions of their parents' labours was put to use as early as possible. Laws against child labour only arrived with the Industrial Revolution, when work in mines and factories was so dangerous and unpleasant that subjecting children to it was an abuse too far.

Beyond capitalism, we might conceive of all working spaces as humane enough for children, whose labours we expect to enrich, not deplete. Sites where work and play could overlap and we might all move a little closer to the embodied present of childhood.

Dani McClain says, 'white parents in particular need help with seeing the family as a site of political education.' In post-capitalist families, our children might learn the politics of collective responsibility by actively participating in communal labours of interdependence and belonging.

And kids – like most people – love being given a bit of responsibility.

The first-wave feminists who tried to uplift mothering believed men and women to be fundamentally different. Even their demand for female participation in public life was rooted in the idea that women's higher moral sensibilities meant they had a unique role to play in balancing the rigour and vigour of economics with care and compassion.

But getting more women into positions of power hasn't done much to make capitalism kinder. People are great at compartmentalising their responsibilities, and mums more practised at this than most.

So we need to empower feminised labour, not just women.

We need to shift the balance from masculinised labours to feminised ones.

But ultimately, we need to heal the divide.

Firestone's post-gender world is worth navigating towards. But the utopia we must measure our efforts against is a non-binary economy that values all care as work and expects all work to be caring. Where the domestic reclaims productive power, and all production is regenerative.

A society that understands responsibility and power as one and same.

Around the world – and particularly in places that haven't had their heart and soul completely colonised by Western dualism – there are myriad sites of connection where economics, science, politics and grassroots action are proving that the means of radical independence are already at our fingertips.

Global Women's Strike campaigns with natural farmers and land- and human-rights defenders in India, Thailand and Peru opposing corporate takeovers and industrial farming. Because from these grassroots perspectives, the unity of their struggles is clear.

We know the kind of agriculture that doesn't leave the earth barren is just how most of humanity fed itself until very recently, and how many still do. And if you're nurturing bio-diversity because you need it for a resilient food supply, loving nature is easy because there's no pay-off of interests. Economics is tangibly integrated into ecology and farming communities can see themselves as part of that natural diversity.

Grasping these dynamics in complex capitalist metabolisms is more complicated. And it doesn't help that neoclassical macroeconomic models showing the dynamics of capital, interest rates and inflation – the ones I'd been studying in that big book in my bubble of mothertime – have no inputs and no outputs.

The technocrats and politicians whose decisions shape our lives are working off descriptions of the social metabolism that don't show the flow of energy and matter. No resources in, no waste out. And no time – no account of working hours. Just money, whizzing around, unimpeded by biophysical reality. No wonder they start making wild claims about welfare mums being responsible for inflation.

But degrowth economists are coming up with new models that embed abstract flows of money back into human and ecological processes, accounting for reproductive labour as well as productive, the costs of growth as well as its profit, the time we spend as well as the money.

And whether or not they see it this way – some definitely do – this is feminist work. Recalibrating our collective metabolism, not to endlessly expand – and inevitably, cyclically, crash – but tend towards stability, is *a queer thing to do*. Doing so safely – before the bubble bursts in a humanitarian horror show of sudden collapse – *changes family and the future for ever*.

We also have new legal models to empower the responsibility of social institutions.

Over recent decades, various countries have granted nature legal rights, backing Indigenous traditions of respect for life with Western legal constructs so they can be upheld in colonial courts of law.

New Zealand has recognised the Te Awa Tupua ecosystem as 'an indivisible and living whole, comprising the Whanganui

River from the mountains to the sea, incorporating all its physical and metaphysical elements'. Iwi Māori people had been fighting for access to the land for more than a century, since colonials decided that preserving nature meant fencing it off from people. Now, they are free to take active responsibility for its wellbeing.

Elsewhere, experiments in participatory democracy are showing that when citizens' assemblies are given comprehensive data on environmental issues – and, crucially, are tasked with the explicit *responsibility* of making decisions in the *collective* good – they unanimously agree on measures drastically more radical than anything elected governments have been ready to pass.

Science underpins such hopeful experiments in doing things differently – harnessing the tension between the individual and collective as a source of momentum change – in clearer, more nuanced visions of nature.

Descriptions of the world like Lynn Margulis's work on symbiogenesis and Suzanne Simard's on forest ecosystems can help us reimagine humanity's place in nature. We don't have to be a cancer on the biosphere, condemned to wipe ourselves out through selfish greed. We can self-identify as the aspect of nature that isn't only engaged in her physical and biological processes, but another level of dynamism – conscious, creative and empathic – with the power to actively proliferate the patterns of transformation we need to survive.

All these things give me hope. They are rational principles, models and practices. And it is rational – axiomatic, even – to believe people *can* live in harmony with the rest of nature. But to believe we *will* is not rational.

My hope is not rational.

Cool evaluation of emissions figures, the tipping points we've passed, those on the near horizon, the scale and power of the capitalist machine, the depth of the divisions we have to heal, lead, I fear, to only one conclusion.

We're fucked.

And this is why we need love. Because love isn't rational. And because if our only hope is to connect everything back up, then love is what connection feels like when you do it for its own sake. Even when things are fucked.

In *The Millstone*, Drabble's protagonist calls her motherly love 'a bad investment'. Neoliberalism frames the choice to start a family as an investment in your personal future. Jane Mattes urges single mothers to ensure it's a rational investment. Darwinian evolutionary theory describes biological reproduction, altruism – everything we do, really – as an investment in genetic reproduction. Even psychological parenting theories treat love as a kind of investment: mothering becomes a results-driven exercise that can be optimised to produce a healthy, well-adjusted adult.

But these are the principles of production, not reproduction. Investments are about calculated risk. Love isn't like that. You don't love the people you love because they are, objectively, better than other people or more worthy of love.

And you keeping loving them even when they fall apart.

Mums try to care for our children in ways that instil certain values and help them lead happy, meaningful lives. But we're not marmosets. We can't write off our investment in the next generation if things head south.

Mothers even mother when the most basic responsibility of mothering – to keep our children safe – is impossible. Millions of people were born into slavery. The women who mothered them knew their children would be dehumanised as a resource, a capital investment. But they kept mothering anyway because love consists in itself.

We do not love strategically. And so, I understand loving nature as a rational proposition to reconnect, including – *especially* – with each other. But also, as a radical call to take joy in this work.

We need interdependence to save ourselves, but we must nurture the connective tissue of the society we want even if our odds of survival are dire. Because we might, in the process, at least reclaim parts of ourselves, heal things that have been broken. But also because we do things better when we do them for their own sake.

Verse composed to rouse the masses is dull and turgid. Fucking to get pregnant isn't sexy. Artistic and intellectual endeavours are most powerful when they're driven by the joy of seeing connections between things – the pieces falling into place – not because you've reverse-engineered the impact you want them to have.

The flow – when the gap between thought and feeling closes and the process itself is thrilling – is where the biggest leaps of creativity happen, setting in motion surprising patterns of transformation.

Simard's search for the mother tree didn't start out as scientific enquiry in the detached, objective sense. As a child, compelled by sheer wonder, she dug into the forest floor to reveal secret, subterranean worlds and engaged with all her senses. And she was drawn to birch trees because the earth she untangled from their roots and ate by the handful was so sweet.

Simard consumed the forest and let it consume her.

Later, as a forester, she watched as monocultural commercial plantations designed along Darwinian principles – weeding out the competition – withered and died under her care. And when she went on to empirically map the networks of interdependence she sensed intuitively, she revealed her sweet, beloved birch trees as vital points of connection other species depend on for their generous supply of sugars.

When Enlightenment thinkers first started taking the world apart and putting it back together in new ways, they didn't have the steam engine, keyhole surgery, climate change or regenerative reforestation in mind.

And when two cells merged and made photosynthesis possible, it would have been impossible to predict baobab trees, blue whales or the symbiotic relationship between salmon and grizzly bears – let alone a consciousness that might one day picture life beginning and fear its end.

Or a woman in the woods, a queer single mother thinking of her daughters, a scientist tasting a kindred spirit's kindness on her earthy fingertips, transforming our understanding of nature and the principles of forestry, all at the same time.

Tearing down structures that choke out life is one thing, but to proliferate life itself, the process of creation must be compelling in itself.

Our means of survival must also be our reason to survive.

*

If understanding my single motherhood is about resolving tensions between being *one, in and of myself* and belonging to something bigger – a supportive community, or an identity that connects me to other women mothering beyond the nuclear family – my struggle is that of living in a society that elevates individual freedom above all else, instead of understanding real autonomy as a consequence of connection.

And so having made my bid for freedom, there are moments when my responsibilities are overwhelming. My mind spins on unpaid bills, work deadlines, how F's doing at school, what would happen to her if anything happened to me, no money for emergencies, no time to do it all – and anyway, how can anyone possibly know how to raise a child into a world that's burning up? The daily grind and looming resources wars of a famished planet whip together in my spiralling anxiety. Poor F, this perfectly wonderful human whom the fates have given this one inadequate woman as a mother. How can I possibly be enough?

But this spiralling only happens when I'm alone.

And then, there she is. F. Waking up hungry, or coming home from school talking about pirates or weather systems or crows. She's not a job I'm inadequate to. In the abstract, my mothering can feel impossible. In the flesh, possible and impossible have nothing to do with it. It all just is. My mothering is, because F is.

With motherhood, I've learned that a moment as thoughtless and brief as conception can change everything. For me, the world with F in it is completely different from the world before and any world she wasn't part of would be a poorer one than this. She is both uniquely, entirely herself and inseparable from the brute reality of everything else to which she belongs, including the fraught relationship between her parents.

Love F, commit to her world.

And, at the same time, dare to dream of the world I want for her.


Trying to feel out the kind of love Mediavilla talks about, I measure my connectedness against motherly love because it's the biggest love I know. But I'm also wary to limits of this metaphor.

People say having children makes you less selfish, but I don't think this is true – if anything, it can make you more selfish. Every reasonable adult understands their own needs cannot always come first. But when your sense of self is expanded to include a child, your own child's needs risk trumping everything else.

When I tried to get F into a private school, I abandoned all inclinations to social responsibility to give her privileges other children are denied. And people say having children makes you more invested in the future, but again – *investment*. There are plenty of people trashing the planet so they can enough amass wealth to shield their kids from the consequences of a trashed planet.

If you're not careful, parental responsibility can go full Lee Raymond.

Mothering isn't to blame for the climate crisis. But it isn't enough to want to a safe and prosperous future for our own children.

We need to collapse divisions, explode the bounds of our

empathy. For those of us raising children – mothering in the narrowest sense – the mother–child bond might be a point of connection into something bigger, an experience of both radical acceptance and radical hope we can expand out from.

But it's just one possible point of connection, contiguous with every other practice of belonging and regeneration. And in this broader sense – as *a practice of creating, nurturing, affirming and supporting life – revolutionary* mothering is probably our only hope.

If Imogen, Ginevra and I couldn't get it together to build a family home together, all this rattling on about post-capitalist interdependence might sound like the ravings of a woman who spends too much time dreaming and not enough time doing.

I know.

But if mothering can be a radically creative practice, it's also a utopian practice.

As a mum, you get used to paradoxes. The tension between wanting to protect a child from the world and wanting them to embrace it with unbridled passion. Wanting to spare them any pain, and knowing a life without pain is as unimaginable as passively watching your child suffer. Looking at F and seeing the most marvellous human ever to walk the Earth, and knowing our world is home to two billion children, each as unique and astounding.

And though I understand autonomy and connection to be inextricably bound, in the logistics of my daily life, they remain in tension and that tension is something I have to live with.

So I think loving nature is also about being alive in the

tension between the possible and the utopia. Between the scale of transformation we need and the insignificance of any contribution I can make to nurturing it into being.

And if our embodied practice is as important – *more* important – than our utopias, there are billions of places to begin. Infinite sites of rupture we can work to heal in our own small ways.

It's easy to be cynical about coronatime now. After the first shock, governments quickly shifted the focus from helping people to bailing out airline companies and rebooting capitalism.

Briefly, the rapid progress of a microscopic pathogen from body to body had attuned us to a global connectedness. But by the time vaccines arrived, public outcry in the Global North was directed at delays of few weeks in local supply, even as private pharma companies were handed the patents for publicly funded research, prioritising profit over what was supposed to be a global solution to a global problem.

*It's terrible*, people shrugged, *but that's capitalism* . . .

We put the barriers back up so fast. We went back to believing there was no other way things might be. And, that those barriers will always insulate us against violence inflicted on those beyond them. How coronatime felt, that swell of breath in March 2020, has become as intangible a memory as the unbound time of childhood.

We went back to buying our bread in plastic wrappers and stopped wondering who'd risked their lives to stock our supermarket shelves. Before capitalism was even back up to full speed, romanticising this moment of pause had become a shameful sign of privilege. And looking back, it's not the stockpiling of toilet paper and hand sanitiser we satirise – not the shelf-emptying scramble to hoard bread – but our sourdough loaves.

But we can't afford to be too cynical.

When we entered the dissociated bubble of coronatime, people suddenly free to spend all day watching Netflix and ordering pizza found that domesticity offered more sustaining pleasures.

We didn't have to bake our own bread or survive on window-box tomatoes. But, like mutual aid networks, these quiet labours were a mark of our values in a moment of crisis. Tending to fermenting cultures, watching loaves rise and seedlings soar towards the light, grounded us when the world stopped making sense.

We discovered a latent instinct for care. And it felt good.

Coronatime also brought the private burdens on women into public focus. Conversations about care came to the fore, hit a nerve and haven't gone away.

We need to keep having these conversations. And I think we need to keep tending to our seedlings. If we were make-believing autonomy from capitalist superstructures that suddenly felt shaky, then committing to these little domestic pleasures might help us recall a moment when we did believe vaccine patents would be waived, and imagine a future in which autonomy is more than *just* play.

Just as for Tamsin and her family, their plastic-free month was, she writes, an 'adventure'; her kids 'embraced the whole experiment out of a fondness for the natural world'. After a couple of months, they couldn't keep up the work of living completely plastic-free, but the practice attuned them how they use resources, and they continue to do so more considerately – stitching unavoidable plastics into reusable fabric wraps, not because it'll shrink the Pacific Garbage Patch but because the *doing* of these things feels better than not doing them.

We have to fight the big fights on issues of global justice. To protest and demand legislative change: to regulate industry, ditch fossil fuel subsidies, fund care, slash working hours and reform democracy away from a social contract that grants power in *exchange* for a degree of responsibility, towards models that formulate them as one and the same.

But we also need localisation. – because it's not only an ecologically sound way of sharing resources, it can also mean working on a scale that feels embodied, tangibly experiencing the kind of connection we need on a global scale.

The English Collective of Prostitutes activists who resist police harassment are more attuned to the politics we need to mitigate the climate crisis than anyone heading a think-tank or NGO. And I don't imagine the Harlem othermothers woke up every morning asking themselves what they could do today to redefine family as a challenge to capitalist exploitation. Their creative responses to immediate responsibilities, their front-line intimacy with what wasn't working, made their labours powerful because they were more embodied than strategic.

Nurturing interdependence can mean checking in on neighbours, setting up a babysitting exchange, swapping used goods in the backyards of our apartment blocks, repairing things made to be thrown away, opening our homes to those

fleeing violence or hunger, cooperatising a local energy supplier, organising a rent strike, refusing to work late – things
worth doing for ourselves and each other even if their global
impact is negligible.

And yes. Buying less stuff. Giving up meat. Sorting my
trash. Not because BP says I must, but as a practice of devotion. A domestic ritual of connecting with my place in the
world – and the outrage that might push me to act bigger.

# Chapter 10

# Mother Ungendered

I ask the man in my bed one morning if he's sure he doesn't want kids. I'm not asking for me, this isn't a question of our future compatibility. In satiated intimacy, faces close enough to touch and too close to look at one another, we're deliberating what constitutes a life well-lived. On his Tinder profile he says he loves children but doesn't want any of his own.

We're the same age: forty. He's thoughtful, self-aware – feminist even. But I'm suspicious of the way he's stepping out of the scrum of biologically desperate women, as so many men his age do, enjoying their social and professional peak only later to surprise themselves by falling for a younger woman and finding they want do want families after all. (Some probably are genuinely surprised. No one else is.)

'Yeah,' he tells me, 'I just never felt that need to pass on my genes.'

His genes!

From where I'm standing – lying, our limbs laced so I can feel his smooth skin and hard muscle from every angle – he'd make excellent breeding stock. But that wasn't what I was talking about. What does my relationship with F have to do with genes?

There's a lengthy report in the *New York Times* that opens with the story of a Choice Mother of two who used the same privately arranged sperm donor twice. She wasn't the only one. This guy used multiple sperm banks and online networks to father, by his own admission, some two hundred and fifty children. Some of those investigating his activity think the real number could be anything up to a thousand.

I'm two-thirds down the page when my chest tightens at a phrase he's used to describe himself – 'a musical Viking' – recalls a conversation with Lisa and makes my chest tighten.

The article quotes mothers who are campaigning to have him stopped, but he hasn't broken any law. Two met by chance and saw an uncanny likeness between their children. The ethical worry is unwitting incest.

Does Lisa know? I don't think so. I hope she knows. I pick up my phone – but what will I say? *Are you sitting down??* – and find myself calling my friend Johanna instead.

Johanna doesn't know Lisa. But she doesn't think this is such a big deal: 'I assume she's been let down by men before, right?' Also: 'Most half-siblings share less than twenty per cent of their chromosomes' and 'at least he didn't rape anyone,' she offers, making a favourable comparison with Genghis Khan, who ravaged his way to fore-fathering millions 'and that seems to have worked out OK'.

Just a Viking then, not a Mongolian warlord?

Still, when I do get Lisa on the phone, I fumble for words

and she has to coax it out of me. She doubts this has anything to do with her. Until I read out his name.

Lisa lets out a long sound between a squeal and a moan, an extended vowel that doesn't quite resolve into the 'u' in *fuck* or the 'o' in *oh* or *god* or *no!*

But this is not the sound of someone who has just been dealt a life-altering blow. 'Fuck!' she finally manages. 'Jesus! *This* is why vasectomies—like, a woman just cannot make a hundred babies!' The audacity. 'Maybe I'll be upset later,' she wonders. Is it terrible for M to have hundreds of genetic siblings?

'You know what it really points to? That there is a need not being met. If reproductive services were properly funded you wouldn't have to make these dodgy private deals,' she concludes solidly.

I hadn't thought of it like that.

'Listen, if I went through all that expensive treatment, like people do, like some of these women in the article did, I would be pissed as hell. But I got it cheap off the internet, you know? Like, if you buy something on eBay, you take a risk. And I got my baby. She's perfect. I didn't get scammed. I didn't get an STD. I got my baby. And just this morning, I was looking at photos of M when she was tiny, cradled in her brother's arms, and I was thinking, this was the best intentional – you know, really *intentional* – decision I ever made.'

I feel a fool.

Lisa precisely gauged the whole operation so her family's wellbeing would be in no way dependent on the man who fathered her child. The mothers in the article feel cheated. Their children being part of some vast, shadowy constellation with one man at its centre is unnerving. But Lisa and I struggle to pin-point exactly what she should be wounded or raging over.

She oscillates between calling the Viking a jackass, a psycho, and sympathising with him having his name and picture splashed across the press. 'Bless his little heart,' she says. 'And bless his balls.'

Two hundred children. A thousand children. I know what Lisa means about vasectomies. Surely there should be some limit. Nature doesn't impose one, and culture, convention, law and social mores all failed in this case. It makes you want to reach for the scissors.

But what does it actually mean to father a hundred children? Obviously it meant *something* to this particular – narcissist? *More of me! More of me!* An undercover Genghis Khan conquering the human genome by stealth.

But really, as I realised on the phone to Lisa, it doesn't amount to much.

*Father* is a verb we rarely see outside of cold historical accounting: 'he fathered a dozen children by native women during his time in Rhodesia,' perhaps. To *mother* is far more intimate and involved. To father is a biological act over in seconds. To mother is, as Rachel Cusk says, *A Life's Work*.

Mother to rhyme with smother. A cloying, female thing, even when done by a male: to mother doesn't have to involve biology. In an excess of femininity, you might mother a boyfriend or a dog.

To father is a binary operation: you either fathered this child or you didn't. You can *be* a good or bad father but cannot *father* well or poorly. You can father too many or too few, but you cannot father too much or too little. Mothering is messier. To father is a bald act of creation. To mother is to spoil that which has been fathered.

I'm on a date, sort of. Stella and I are eating from big steaming bowls at a vegan Vietnamese round the corner from her building. Max is currently living with her and will be waiting when we come in from our meal. We'll all climb into her enormous bed together, for sex, or maybe we'll just watch the House of Cards season finale.

But dinner, as ever, is just us two.

Stella's son, X, is eleven and loves his school. If F and I moved into her building, she urges, our kids would go to there together, X can even take her in the mornings, one less job for me. We both regret that our children have no siblings, but this is the closest we're likely to get to doing much about it.

Stella says motherhood never felt natural to her. She never felt fully female, not properly made for such womanly work. If she went back, she says, and was told that she could only have X if first she went through five more pregnancies and births, she would do it, she would do anything, even toil to raise six kids, to make this person whom she loves so completely.

But if instead she were told X would still exist, she could still have him in her life, without having to bring him into the world herself, without being anyone's mother at all – she'd grab the chance.

'So, no more then,' I say.

'No more. I mean, I would love another child – I would do

it like a shot – if this time, I could be the father.' She fixes me with a pout and raised eyebrow.

'Don't even,' I laugh.

Now, I have a better idea: let's just abolish fatherhood altogether.

In 1979, *Kramer vs. Kramer* explored an emerging dilemma as gender roles and family responsibilities shifted. Meryl Streep plays a Smith graduate who gave up her job on a women's magazine to be a full-time mom. Her unmet ambitions drive her to walk out on her husband and their son, saying, 'He's better off without me.'

This happens at the start of the film and we don't hear from Streep again until its second half, by which time she's done enough therapy to stop thinking her need for an autonomous identity makes her an unfit mother. Meanwhile, we see her husband, Dustin Hoffman, transition from arsehole advertising exec who doesn't know which grade his son is in, to dedicated parent whose world revolves around his child.

Watching these scenes I thought, *this – this! – is what single motherhood is like!* The competing demands of work and child, the inevitable inadequacy to both, the suppressed anger at a child acting out against circumstances they cannot control. And, most of all, the warm companionship father and son settle into in their little household of two.

The court scenes don't come until the final half-hour, when Mr and Mrs Kramer are called to account less on their actual parenting than the gendered roles of mother and father, wife and husband. She is accused of failing in 'the most important relationship of her life' – not with her child but with her husband – and he is shamed for failing as bread-winner because his career has suffered under the pressures of single parenting.

Making her case for custody, Streep's character stumbles over rights and responsibilities once bound fast by rigid gender roles:

> I was his mommy for five and half years. And Ted took over that role for eighteen months. But I don't know how anyone can possibly believe that I have less of a stake in mothering that little boy than Mr Kramer does. I'm his mother. I'm his mother.

Slipping between *mother* the verb and *mother* the noun, she ultimately stakes her claim on the latter. Both parents have done the work of mothering, but *I'm his mother.*

It's Hoffman's character who describes the emotional labour of mothering:

> My wife always used to say to me, why can't a woman have the same ambitions as a man? I think she's right. Maybe I've learned that much. But by the same token, I'd like to know what law it is that says a woman is a better parent, simply by virtue of her sex. I think about what it means to be a good parent, it has to do with constancy, it has to do with patience, it has to do with listening to him, it has to do with pretending to listen to him when you can't even listen anymore. It has to do with love ... and I don't know where it's written that a woman has the corner on that

market, that a man has any less of those emotions than a woman does.

When the court rules that Streep's deserting mother should be allowed to break up the home Hoffman has made, this is presented as patently unjust, and *Kramer vs. Kramer* was a landmark for the fathers' rights movement. But the film's core narrative is not about the *rights* of fathers but the struggle to reconcile the *work* of mothering with the rest of life.

A famous woman writer is giving a talk in Berlin. The moderator, also a woman, asks: 'How did becoming a parent affect your work?'

The room spasms in collective cringe.

'Well, I wonder,' the famous woman writer says, 'would a man be asked that question?'

'Oh, you're so right!' the moderator exclaims. 'Be careful though! I said *parenting*, not motherhood.'

Maybe I'm the only one in the room who wouldn't have cringed at a question about motherhood. She doesn't write about it directly, but my favourite of her books resonates richly with the experience of single mothering. I would have liked to know, was this was just my reading? Could she have articulated such insights about domestic and working spaces, creative processes and female solidarity, without this experience?

We only have an hour to glean insights from an illustrious, decades-long career. So – even though I know there are other women gathered here who are mothers and writers, who struggle with the logistics of being both – it's not fair that the famous author should waste precious time talking about scheduling and housework.

But really, the injustice is not the minutes we might lose talking about how you balance nurturing new selves with 'creating new language' but the years we spend doing it. What's really not fair is not that men aren't asked how fatherhood has affected their intellectual work, but that we know the answer: mostly, it hasn't much.

And that word, *parenting*, erases all this – everything that might make the question worth asking. Did the moderator think that by erasing gender in her question she could erase the gender of the person she was asking?

You see the word 'parent' more and more, in places where it used to be spelled m-o-t-h-e-r. Single-parent families. Parenting classes. Expectant parents. Attachment parenting.

In 1985, Linda Gordon argued that what we take to be universal truths about children's needs are deeply rooted in the patriarchal power dynamics of nuclear family:

> One response to the recent feminist critique of men's lack of involvement in parenting has been to pretend that it is not true, to rewrite laws, parenting manuals, and psychological theories as if both men and women were equally active in child rearing. In fact, women continue to do most of the work and bear even more of the responsibility ... Psychological parenting theory is a theory about women's work, not about child raising in some gender-neutral way ... It is a prescription about how women with

children should spend their time, and one with roots in a nineteenth-century elite vision of family life.

When we talk about motherhood, we're talking about biological processes, feminised work and responsibilities, about notions of gender rooted in Enlightenment philosophy, the history of capitalism, theories of mind and race and class politics.

When we talk about parenting, we pretend none of these things matter. That motherhood isn't a feminist issue. But also, we're pretending the work women have done to break down gendered roles, the additional identities and labours women have taken on in public life, is automatically met from the other direction. That feminism, in fact, is responsible for levelling the playing field without men having to do anything much at all.

Which is why, four decades on, Gordon's words still ring true.

It's not fair that women who have achieved greatness in masculinised realms should have to answer questions about their babies. But these questions – about who does reproductive work and how – do have to be asked. Talk of parenting doesn't just leave them to be resolved behind closed doors, it erases them from our vocabulary.

When the courts of gender-progressive societies pretend to gender neutrality, they're exploiting this semantic fuzziness, this euphemistic erasure of the difference between the work of mothering and the status of being a father. Between the rights of fatherhood and the responsibilities of mothering: a mother's responsibilities are so great she can always be found wanting; a father's rights are clear and independent, his responsibilities an afterthought.

Properly, the only person who *might* be said to have free-standing rights in this constellation is the child. Each parent has the right to a fair hearing, but no one has inalienable rights to a relationship with another person. Relationships are something you actively *do*. Parental relationships take a lot of doing. They are hard work.

Mother is a verb. Mothering is a practice. It might have an origin story in our bodies, but C-sections, IVF and adoption do not make any less a mother. Mothering doesn't require a womb. Being able to lactate doesn't make you innately predisposed to self-sacrifice or multitasking. If we tend to be better at these things, it's because we have to be.

But if men can now nurture as well as we do, if they can take on the responsibilities of mothering – then let them apply for the role. Let them be mothers too. Let's ditch fatherhood, this amorphous identity based on dubious ideas about genetics, class, property and rights over other human beings.

A generation after *Kramer vs. Kramer*, the 2019 documentary *Seahorse* follows Freddy McConnell, a trans father, through the conception, pregnancy and birth of his child. Like *Kramer vs. Kramer*, which depicted single mothering better than much I've seen with a woman in the role, *Seahorse* intimately examines a process too trivial to warrant such rapt attention when women do it.

Freddy comes off testosterone – and from there goes

through the same process of selecting a sperm donor, the indignities of intrauterine insemination, as many a Single Mother by Choice. Pregnancy is a harrowing state of physical and psychic dysphoria: 'If men had to go through this all the time you'd just never hear the end of it,' Freddy says.

So much of this is familiar to mothers: the transformation of a body intensely pressured by societal expectations, the anxiety over how much of you will survive and how much will be changed for ever. But for a man whose gender some refuse to recognise, it's all intensified. While pregnant, Freddy says he wants to scream at cis mums, 'No, it's not the same, shut up!'

At the film's end, though, weeks after his son's birth, he says,

I think I can remember saying pregnancy was just a pragmatic choice and I just had to get through it and then I could just be a normal dad. But yeah, I'm less, like, clinging onto this notion of being – 'Oh, I'm just a normal dad'. That's not important. Like, I'm a dad, I'm a parent. I gave birth. All those things are true and – that's my experience.

He might scream at me to shut up, but I hear echoes of mothers whose pregnancy worries – about their bodies, having the right kind of birth, doing pregnancy well – evaporate once they hold their baby. That it-is-what-it-is, we-are-where-we-are feeling that everything has changed and how it changed no longer matters.

But more, I hear Freddy's change of attitude as the revelation that bringing a child into the world is something so profound it transcends gender.

How could it make him any less a man?

How could it make him *less* of anything?

The self isn't lost, it's expanded.

Childbirth is an experience so powerful Freddy is lost for words to describe it. But what comes after transcends everything we've witnessed him go through. 'It's a lot,' he says, gazing at the little person in his arms. 'They are an extension of you. And – I think anyone has the potential to feel that way.'

Despite grating questions from his mother's friends, who struggle to see the gravid belly stretching out his shirt as anything other than glaring evidence of motherhood, Freddy's identifying as a father is axiomatic. We have no concept of mothering that transcends gender. Freddy is a man and he is a parent: these two identities create the identity of father.

But this is not the identity Stella was referring to with her work-shy quip.

Men who gestate and give birth expand fatherhood in ways that might, in time, bring it closer to motherhood for society as a whole, shifting the focus from possession to practice, rights to responsibilities. Just as gay and single dads do.

But mostly, fatherhood only becomes equal to mothering in the absence of a mother. A growing minority of fathers in straight couples do share the work of mothering equally, or close to equally, with their partners. But this is still a choice. A private negotiation. Because parenting means mothering when applied to a woman and fatherhood when applied to a man.

And mothering is where the buck stops.

\*

In an episode of *This American Life* titled 'Unconditional Love', a US couple tell their story of adopting a seven-year-old boy from a Romanian orphanage. At first, the boy was very happy in his new family. But the more he felt part of it, the angrier he became.

Where the hell had his parents been all those years?

The boy quickly understood what it meant to have a mother, but not that there had been a time when he hadn't had one. A time when this woman who cared for him so completely hadn't even known he existed.

He became defiant and then violent, directing his rage at his mother. The couple hired a bodyguard to protect her. Fearing things would not end well, psychiatrists advised them to have the boy fostered out. His father was ready to give up. But for the boy's mother, this was unthinkable.

'He's my *son*,' she says.

Contained within her husband's determination to give this child love and a promising future was the potential for failure. But motherhood isn't something you get out of so easily. Just as her child could not comprehend a historic limit to her mothering, so for her there was no room for a future one.

Her responsibility was absolute. In this, at least, she and her son were of one mind.

Motherly love can be prompted by biological processes that precipitate emotional ones, and social ones that engender ideas like *mothers always put their children first, mothers love their children unconditionally* and *mothers feel more for their babies than fathers do.*

But equally, abstract ideas, social constructs like *mothers will give their lives for their children* or *he is my son* can be the starting point for embodied relationships that throb with the euphoric pity of oxytocin.

Statements about who we are become things we do.

We know men can open the boundaries of their selves. We all know men who put their children first, love them unconditionally and feel as much for their babies as any woman. But to bring the equality of same-sex relationships to all family constellations, we need language that closes the gap men like Freddy are narrowing.

Genderless identities to give everyone *who feels that way* or *has these emotions* their due – and to expand the possibilities of motherly responsibility.

In *What Gender is Motherhood?* sociologist Oyèrónkẹ́ Oyěwùmí recalls the chair at a Massachusetts conference asking participants to introduce themselves indicating their preferred pronouns. Oyewùmí says the idea amused her and she worried she might not keep up with the 'customised terms':

> What a pity, I thought. Learn to speak Yorùbá! North Americans would not have to reinvent the wheel if they adopted Yorùbá, one of the many African languages whose pronouns and personal names do not 'do gender'.

Even the Yoruba word for mother, *Ìyá*, is genderless, Oyěwùmí argues.

In Western tradition, it is man, in the image of the creator, who turns *woman* into *mother*. She is the channel for *his* child. But in the Ifá faith of Yoruba Nigeria, *Ìyá* is the source of all creation and 'the most fundamental social unit' is not the nuclear or extended family, not the male–female pair, but the Ìyà–child dyad.

This bond is formed in the spirit realm, independent of husbands or fathers. When an Ìyà gives birth to an already-existing soul – the moment of *ikúnlè* – two identities are created anew. But though these identities are born in an intensely bodily act, the role of Ìyá is primarily a spiritual one.

Ifa closes the Western split between body and spirit, vulnerability and power:

> Ìyá's relationship with their child is considered to be otherworldly, pre-earthly, preconception, pregestational, presocial, prenatal, lifelong, and posthumous. This relationship between Ìyá and child is timeless. The *ikúnlè* moment is both the moment in which Ìyá is at their most human because of the vulnerability attending childbirth, and it is also a moment in which Ìyá is transcendental.

Western science says F came into being in a grittily physical process that unfolded in my body. But the mysterious world within me seemed to hold much more than the division and multiplication of cells. I don't know much about the Ifa spirit world. But my bond with my child began in an unknowable realm that neither anatomical descriptions, nor my hopes and anxieties about becoming a mother, can fully grasp.

The belonging my body nurtured over nine months felt miraculous. But it preceded my identity as a mother, rather than defining it. I was only able to say *I am a mother* when F's becoming moved from this body-spirit-fleshy-imaginary state into my world – the one she was suddenly part of too – and we began our relationship as two earthly selves: one brand new, and one expanded by the new identity I took on in the *ikúnlẹ̀ moment.*

Coming from a Western mindset that splits the world along hard, gendered lines, it can take a bit of doing to get your head round the idea that this identity, so entangled with the corporal business of reproduction, can be anything other than *female* – hence the fits of floundering rage men like Freddy face: from fragile masculinity on one side and trans-exclusionary feminists on the other.

But *mother* as a genderless identity has the potential both to empower men's relationships with their children, and to free women who mother from feminised expectations of self-sacrifice, passivity, mental weakness. From wifedom.

If mothering were ungendered, if breastfeeding were ungendered, perhaps the court would have been in less of a hurry to stop Beth doing it. It couldn't be singled out as cheating if it was just one of many things this mother was doing for her child that no one else was doing. Held to equal, ungendered standards, the Kindesvater's mothering would be judged not on his anatomical capacity – to lactate or to ejaculate – but on what he was actively doing to nurture his child's belonging.

The sex-based rights brigade might froth at the idea that men can be mothers too. But by ungendering mothering, we might properly celebrate the 'female' biology they're so afraid will be disenfranchised, without shaming women who mother without gestating, who mother without being wives, who don't mother at all. If *mother* is an identity created anew in every mother–child bond, then it consists in itself rather than subsuming a woman's existing identity – and it isn't an ideal by which the womanhood of those who do not mother can be found wanting.

This shouldn't be hard to comprehend: the roles of high court judge, postman and emperor have been open almost exclusively to men. But not being an emperor or a postman doesn't mean a man hasn't fulfilled some Platonic masculine ideal. Few women get to be high court judges: we haven't had the power and resources society demands of the role. But there are now women who do the work of high court judging and there are men who, one way or another, do mothering.

We don't say *judgess*, poetess or lady policeman anymore. Remove the toxically masculine aspects of fatherhood, and what are we left with? Just as poetess sounds like a hobbled sort of poet, so father is just a lesser sort of mother.

Conversely, what are we left with if we banish the feminised powers my culture has imbued into mothering? The Victorian romanticisation of motherhood, the crucial importance of attachment mothering – at least these oppressive Western ideals give credit to how big motherhood feels.

I gave up my search for a soulmate when I realised nothing could match the expansion of the self that comes with motherhood. But coming away from a conversation with Imogen, who says 'mothering is shit' I wonder if I've swapped one phony ideal of a life well-lived – one insular and overburdened dyad – for another.

The curve of F's cheek, the stubborn set of her shoulders, her courage, give me such pleasure I fear it can't be right to love one person this much.

A *New Yorker* headline pops up on my phone one day: '"Parent" as a Verb: I Love You' and under it, the standfirst is a question: 'Is it possible to say "I love you" too much?'

I'm sure I say it too much. Far too much. And far too often, I accompany it with a look of abject admiration or gratuitous squeeze of those blessed shoulders. Where will we both be when she has no more use for my constancy and cuddles? I should read this article.

Algorithms seem to detect the headline's ambivalent hold on me because it appears in my feed again and again, setting off a twinge of guilt each time. Until reading Oyěwùmí gives me the courage to open the link.

According to the date at the top of the page, I've been putting it off for seventeen months. But this isn't the latest take on psychological parenting. It's a cartoon by Emily Flake, a mother wondering if words said so often lose their meaning. Flake says, *I love you, I love you, I love you,* 'as an article of faith, a futile attempt to transcend the dreadful impermanence of life. Isn't that what a prayer is for?'

From an Ifá perspective, perhaps it isn't even so futile. Oyěwùmí says she has often heard Yoruba people tell versions of the same story:

On the occasion of leaving home (for work, study or marriage) their Ìyá said, 'whenever you think of me just say amen because I am constantly praying for you.' This statement expresses very well the way in which many Yoruba think of Ìyá as their spiritual protector, greatest ally and cheerleader.

I think every mother knows the words of Ìyá's prayer. And anyway, as Flake ultimately asks, 'what I am gonna do, *not* say it?'

In Oyĕwùmí's reading of Ìyá, I've found the motherhood I've been looking for. Creative, embodied and transcendent, Ìyá is one, in and of themselves, not the wanting half of a bi-gendered whole. But empowering motherhood as an identity that is contingent on no man doesn't close the practice of mothering off from more complex constellations of care.

A Nigerian woman lamenting the hardships of raising a child alone in Berlin told me that single mothering was completely unremarkable in the community of her own childhood. She wasn't talking about genderless motherhood – she meant kids were raised by the community so no one much noticed or cared whether or not mums had husbands.

Around the world, allomothering is done by siblings, grannies, aunties, uncles and cousins as often as fathers. In the experiences and teachings of Black feminist motherhood, the allomother – or othermother – is a vital role independent of any genetic claim on a child.

To move beyond fatherhood means abandoning genetically determined rights and properly recognising these relationships consisting in active bonds of care, regardless of chromosomes, sex organs or gender.

Looking to motherhoods of cultures beyond my own, it's

unsettlingly clear that my motherhood – even as a 'divorced cis woman who has given up on heterosexuality' – is embedded in gendered constructs that are far from universal. The way I love F, the importance of motherhood to my identity, however natural or transcendent these things might feel, are conditioned on some pretty toxic cultural notions.

But that doesn't make my relationship with F any less powerful or embodied. It doesn't make my responsibilities any less real. My culture has made motherhood exceptional, and so only in motherhood could I experience the kind of love I have for F and the way this love grounds me.

Race is also a social construct, which has underpinned horrific abuses. In a utopian world, we might abolish race. But utopias aren't places you live in, they're ideals by which to deconstruct the world we do live in. Race is not a biological reality, but it is an unavoidable fact of life and pretending otherwise is toxically disingenuous.

We can recognise that race is at root a malignant idea dreamed up to divide and dehumanise people and, at the same time, we can celebrate racial identity, we can recognise Blackness as rich, powerful and unifying.

But celebrating Blackness, transwomanhood, say, or whoredom, isn't just about declaring *Black is beautiful, girl power, we are all female* or *sex work is work*. Because these social constructs engender social realities, and these social realities are where real power lies.

Oyěwùmí traces how colonialism subsumed Yoruba traditions of 'matripotency' to rigid gender hierarchies, and Westernised academia reinterpreted genderless Ifá deities, identities and practises as *male* or *female*. On home turf, these same patriarchal powers have shattered and shamed Europe's own matricentic traditions, from Ship Street to African diasporic communities.

As a middle-class white woman raised in a nuclear family, redefining my motherhood through practices like othermothering, empowered to survive and resist these oppressions, feels uncomfortable. And Torrey Peters makes the point in *Detransition, Baby* – no less weighty for the lightness and humour of her telling – that cis-het women must tread respectfully if we're going to use queer narratives to set our motherhood free.

But if we want to abolish the privileges of the nuclear family we need alternatives, and we will only find them in the practices of those who have learned to live without these privileges. Similarly, we can find alternatives to the selfish individualism of capitalism in the exceptional compassion and responsibility of mothering.

Better still, we could stop thinking of it as an exception, and call this love the universe's essential creative force.

As much as women might wish for the rights and freedoms of fatherhood, someone has to carry the responsibilities of mothering. And not just within families. What we need now, in an unequal world, in a biosphere ravaged by the excesses of capitalism, is not more fathers (sorry Stella) but more mothers, more othermothers, more people to attend to the neglected work of mothering society as a whole.

To assert ourselves as individuals, women have had to adopt male roles because the idea of an autonomous, rational, thinking member of society has been defined as male. And more and more of us have gained access to male privileges. But because we've divided human experience and labour into two distinct and unequal categories, these privileges have remained just that – privileges: something not everyone gets a share in.

Rather than opening the autonomous identity that used to be defined as male to include some people with wombs, while leaving its essential traits and privileges more or less intact, let's take the identity we call female as a starting point and expand it into something people of all biological configurations might want to inhabit. And where better to begin than family, and the most gendered identity of all? Mother.

# Bibliography

## 1: Conception

Stephanie Coontz, *Marriage, a History: How Love Conquered Marriage*, Penguin, 2006

Vanessa Heggie, '"Legitimate rape" – a medieval medical concept', *Guardian*, 20 August 2012

Margaret Drabble, *The Millstone*, Weidenfeld & Nicolson, 1965

## 2: I Love Men; I Just Don't Want One of My Own

Adrienne Rich, *Of Woman Born: Motherhood as Experience and Institution*, Bantam Books, 1976

Kristine Shields, 'The meaning of "virgin" morphed – we should reclaim the original intent', Medium, 13 March 2021

Monica Sjöö, Barbara Mor, *The Great Cosmic Mother: Rediscovering the Religion of the Earth*, Harper Collins, 1987

Helen Diner, *Mothers and Amazons: The First Feminine History of Culture*, The Julian Press, 1965 (First published 1930)

Marguerite Duras, *Practicalities*, Knopf, 2018 (first published in English 1990)

GQ Modern Lovers Survey, 2023

Wednesday Martin, 'The Bored Sex', *The Atlantic*, 14 February 2019

Maggie Nelson, *The Argonauts*, Melville House, 2016

Linda Gordon, *The Moral Property of Women: A History of Birth Control Politics in America*, University of Illinois Press, 2002

*Love Child*, BBC, 1996

April Gallwey, *Lone Motherhood in England, 1945–1990: Economy, Agency and Identity*, University of Warwick, 2011

Katherine Angel, *Tomorrow Sex Will Be Good Again: Women and Desire in the Age of Consent*, Verso, 2021

Shulamith Firestone, *The Dialectic of Sex: The Case for Feminist Revolution*, Bantam Books, 1972 (first published 1970)

Louis C.K., *Louis C.K. 2017*, Netflix, 2017

David Graeber and David Wengrow, *The Dawn of Everything: A New History of Humanity*, Macmillan, 2021

Torrey Peters, *Detransition, Baby*, Serpent's Tail, 2022 (first published 2021)

## 3: Half-lives of the Nuclear Family

Charlotte Proudman, 'I've seen abusers use family courts to control and torment victims – but change is coming', *Guardian*, 29 March 2023

Frances Raday, 'Gender equality and women's rights in the context of child custody and maintenance: An international and comparative analysis', UN Women, July 2019

Susan Beth Jacobs, 'The hidden gender bias behind "the best interest of the child" standard in custody decisions', *Georgia State Law Review*, 3 June 1997

Pat Thane and Tanya Evans, *Sinners? Scroungers? Saints? Unmarried Motherhood in Twentieth-Century England*, Oxford University Press, 2012

April Gallwey, *Lone Motherhood in England, 1945–1990: Economy, Agency and Identity*, University of Warwick, 2011

'A home of her own: Housing and women', Women's Budget Group, 8 July 2018

Jonathan Cribb et al., 'Pre-pandemic relative poverty rate for children of lone parents almost double that for children living with two parents', Institute for Fiscal Studies, 4 July 2022

'Report of the Special Rapporteur on extreme poverty and human rights on his visit to the United Kingdom of Great Britain and Northern Ireland', Human Rights Council of the UN General Assembly, 23 April 2019

Thomas Leopold, 'Gender differences in the consequences of divorce: A study of multiple outcomes,' *Demography*, 13 April 2018

Maya Oppenheim, 'Divorce enquiries to legal firms soar by 95% in pandemic with women driving surge in interest', *Independent*, 8 May 2021

Joanna Pepin et al., 'Marital status and mothers' time use: Childcare, housework, leisure, and sleep', *Demography*, 8 February 2018

Thomas Leopold, 'Gender differences in the consequences of divorce: A multiple outcome comparison of former spouses', German Socio-Economic Panel, June 2016

Amy Shearn, 'A 50/50 custody arrangement could save your marriage', *New York Times*, 8 October 2022

Belinda Fehlberg et al., 'Caring for children after parental separation: Would legislation for shared parenting time help children?', Oxford University Department of Social Policy and Intervention, May 2011

Linda Gordon, 'The perils of innocence, or what's wrong with putting children first', *The Journal of the History of Childhood and Youth*, January 2008

Adriana de Ruiter, '40 years of the Hague Convention on child abduction: Legal and societal changes in the rights of a child', European Parliament Directorate-General for Internal Policies, November 2020

'A good law, gone bad', Hague Mothers, 11 April 2022

'Stuck parent stories', GlobalARRK

Myrna Oliver, 'Richard Gardner, 72; Had theory on false claims of abuse against parents', *Los Angeles Times*, 12 June 2003

Richard Gardner, *True and False Accusations of Child Sex Abuse*, Creative Therapeutics, 1992

Joan S. Meier, et al., 'Child custody outcomes in cases involving parental alienation and abuse allegations', *GW Law Faculty Publications & Other Works*, 2019

Samantha Schmidt, '"A gendered trap": When mothers allege child abuse by fathers, the mothers often lose custody, study shows', *Washington Post*, 29 June 2019

Kirby Dick and Amy Ziering, *Allen v. Farrow*, HBO, 2021

William Bernet and Philip M. Koszyk, 'Treatment and prevention of parential alienation', *Psychiatric Times*, 12 March 2020

Suzanne Zaccour, 'Crazy women and hysterical mothers: The gendered use of mental-health labels in custody disputes', *Canadian Journal of Family Law*, 2018

Vassilis K. Fouskas, 'Shared parenting in Greece: three cheers for the Mitsotakis cabinet', openDemocracy, 29 June 2020

'Greece: Dangerous custody law to take effect', Human Rights Watch, 15 September 2021

Reem Alsalem, 'Custody, violence against women and violence against children: Report of the Special Rapporteur on violence against women and girls, its causes and consequences', Human Rights Council of the UN General Assembly, 13 April 2023

Helen Eriksson and Martin Kolk, 'Parental union dissolution and the gender revolution', *Stockholm Research Reports in Demography*, 21 June 2022

## 4: Capitalism Hates Mums

Silvia Federici, *Caliban and the Witch: Women, the Body and Primitive Accumulation*, Autonomedia, 2014 (first published 2004)

Adrienne Rich, *Of Woman Born: Motherhood as Experience and Institution*, Bantam Books, 1976

Mary Midgley, *Utopias, Dolphins and Computers: Problems in Philosophical Plumbing*, Routledge, 2000 (first published 1996)

Mila Kunis, *Jimmy Kimmel Live*, 10 June 2014

Stephanie Coontz, *Marriage, a History: How Love Conquered Marriage*, Penguin, 2006

Olympe de Gouges, *Declaration of the Rights of Woman and of the Female Citizen*, 1791

Mary Wollstonecraft, *A Vindication of the Rights of Woman with Strictures on Political and Moral Subjects*, Jonathan Bennett, 2017 (first published 1792)

Gabrielle Callaway, 'The disappearance of Mary Wollstonecraft', *Crimson Historical Review*, Spring 2019

*Olympe de Gouges: France's Forgotten Revolutionary Heroine*, BBC, 18 January 2021

Olympe de Gouges, *A Persecuted Patriotic Woman Addresses the National Convention*, 1793, translated by Clarissa Palmer, olympedegouges.eu

Anne Digby, 'Victorian values in public and private life', *Proceedings of the British Academy*, 1992

Sarah Knott, *Mother: An Unconventional History*, Penguin, 2019

Clíona Rattigan, *'What Else Could I Do?' Single Mothers and Infanticide, Ireland 1900–1950*, Irish Academic Press, 2012

James Kelly, '"An unnatural crime": Infanticide in early nineteenth-century Ireland', *Irish Economic and Social History*, 1 August 2019

Ellen Hauser, 'Single motherhood: Mythical madness and invisible "insanity"', *Motherhood and Single-Lone Parenting: A Twenty-first Century Perspective*, Demeter Press, 2016

Sumi Rabindrakumar, 'One in four: A profile of single parents in the UK', Gingerbread, February 2018

Sanah Ahsan, 'I'm a psychologist – and I believe we've been told devastating lies about mental health', *Guardian*, 6 September 2022

## 5: Choice and Circumstance

Aleks Krotoski, *Male Order*, BBC, 29 November 2021

Jane Mattes, *Single Mothers by Choice: A Guidebook for Single Women Who Are Considering or Have Chosen Motherhood*, Three Rivers Press, 1997 (first published 1994)

Melinda Cooper, *Family Values: Between Neoliberalism and the New Social Conservatism*, Princeton University Press, 2017

Jane D. Bock, 'Doing the right thing? Single mothers by choice and the struggle for legitimacy', *Gender and Society*, February 2000

Dwayne Avery, 'Every child needs a father', *Motherhood and Single-Lone Parenting: A Twenty-First Century Perspective*, Demeter Press, 2016

Sarah R. Hayford and Karen Benjamin Guzzo, 'The single mother by choice myth', *Contexts*, 7 December 2015

Naina Bajekal, 'Why so many women travel to Denmark for fertility treatments', *TIME*, 3 January 2019

Yasmin Nair, 'Gay marriage IS a conservative cause', 26 February 2013

## 6: Whores and Welfare Queens

Boris Johnson, 'The male sex is to blame for the appalling proliferation of single mothers', *Spectator*, 19 August 1995

*The Yorkshire Ripper Files: A Very British Crime Story*, BBC, 2019

Hallie Rubenhold, *The Five: The Untold Lives of the Women Killed by Jack the Ripper*, Doubleday, 2019

Sheila Quaid, 'Mothering in an age of austerity', *Austerity Policies – Bad Ideas in Practice*, Palgrave Macmillan, 2018

David Cameron, 'PM's speech on the fightback after the riots', UK Government, 15 August 2011

'Report of the Special Rapporteur on extreme poverty and human rights on his visit to the United Kingdom of Great

Britain and Northern Ireland', Human Rights Council of the UN General Assembly, 23 April 2019

Melinda Cooper, *Family Values: Between Neoliberalism and the New Social Conservatism*, Princeton University Press, 2017

Nickie Roberts, *Whores in History: Prostitution in Western Society*, Grafton, 1992

'Baby deaths link to Roman "brothel" in Buckinghamshire', BBC, 25 June 2010

Stephen Hull, 'Roman prostitutes were forced to kill their own children and bury them in mass graves at English "brothel"', Mail Online, 30 August 2011

Barbara Minchinton, *The Women of Little Lon: Sex Workers in Nineteenth-Century Melbourne*, La Trobe University Press, 2021

Saidiya Hartman, *Wayward Lives, Beautiful Experiments: Intimate Histories of Social Upheaval*, Serpent's Tail, 2021 (first published 2019)

Linda Gordon, *Pitied But Not Entitled: Single Mothers and the History of Welfare, 1890–1935*, Harvard University Press, 1995

Johnnie Tillmon, 'Welfare is a women's issue', *Ms.*, Spring 1972

Pat Thane and Tanya Evans, *Sinners? Scroungers? Saints? Unmarried Motherhood in Twentieth-Century England*, Oxford University Press, 2012

Eleanor Rathbone, *The Disinherited Family, With an Introductory Essay by Suzie Fleming*, Falling Wall Press, 1986

Sophie Lewis, *Abolish the Family: A Manifesto for Care and Liberation*, Verso, 2022

April Gallwey, *Lone Motherhood in England, 1945–1990: Economy, Agency and Identity*, University of Warwick, 2011

Amia Srinivasan, 'Does anyone have the right to sex?', *London Review of Books*, 22 March 2018

Wilson Sherwin and Frances Fox Piven, 'The radical feminist legacy of the National Welfare Rights Organization', *Women's Studies Quarterly*, Fall/Winter 2019

Silvia Federici, *Wages Against Housework*, Power of Women Collective and Falling Wall Press, 1975

Peter Lilley, 'I have a little list', Conservative Party Conference, 1992

'Submission of evidence to the Women's Budget Group Commission on a gender-equal economy', Gingerbread, March 2019

Anne Neale and Nina Lopez, 'Suffer the little children & their mothers: A dossier on the unjust separation of children from their mothers', Legal Action for Women, 2017

Margaret Thatcher, 'Interview for *Woman's Own* ("no such thing [as society]")', 23 Sep 1987', Margaret Thatcher Foundation

Nancy Fraser and Linda Gordon, 'A genealogy of dependency: Tracing a keyword of the U.S. welfare state', *Signs*, Winter 1994

Eli Hager and Adria Malcolm, 'These single moms are forced to choose: Reveal their sexual histories or forfeit welfare', ProPublica, 17 September 2021

Stella Winter, 'What it's like to be a mother and a sex worker', *i*, 15 September 2017

'Trends in foster care and adoption: FY 2012 – 2021', Children's Bureau, US Department of Health and Human Services, 1 November 2022

'Children's social care market study', UK Competition and Markets Authority, 10 March 2022

Claire Fenton-Glynn, 'Adoption without consent', EU Directorate General for Internal Affairs, Policy Department C: Citizens' Rights and Constitutional Affairs, 2015

Lauren Crosby Medlicott, 'Stop punishing sex worker mums by taking kids away, demand activists', openDemocracy, 25 July 2022

'Child neglect in England and Wales: Year ending March 2019',
UK Office for National Statistics
Andy Bilson, 'Children's social care: The way forward',
University of Central Lancashire, January 2022
Larissa MacFarquhar, 'When should a child be taken from his
parents?', *New Yorker*, 31 July 2017

## 7: Activists and Othermothers

Loretta Ross, 'Understanding reproductive justice: Transforming
the pro-choice movement', *Off Our Backs*, 2006
Dani McClain, *We Live for the We: The Political Power of Black
Motherhood*, Bold Type Books, 2019
Lydia R. Anderson, Paul F. Hemez and Rose M. Kreider, 'Living
arrangements of children: 2019', United States Census
Bureau, February 2022
Daniel Patrick Moynihan, 'The Negro family: The case for
national action', United States Government, 1965
Toni Morrison, *Beloved*, Vintage, 2007 (first published 1987)
Barbara Omolade, *The Rising Song of African American Women*,
Routledge, 1994
Leith Mullings and Alaka Wali, *Stress and Resilience: The Social
Context of Reproduction in Central Harlem*, Springer, 2001
Melinda Cooper, *Family Values: Between Neoliberalism and the
New Social Conservatism*, Princeton University Press, 2017
Patricia Hill Collins, *Black Feminist Thought: Knowledge,
Consciousness, and the Politics of Empowerment, Revised Tenth
Anniversary Edition*, Routledge, 2000
Barbara Omolade, *It's a Family Affair: The Real Lives of Black
Single Mothers*, Kitchen Table: Women of Color Press, 1986
A. Rochaun Meadows-Fernandez, 'The unbearable grief of Black
mothers', Vox, 28 May 2020
Shaun Walker, '"Baby machines": Eastern Europe's answer to
depopulation', *Guardian*, 4 March 2020

Miriam Cates, 'The conditions of growth', National
    Conservatism Conference, 27 May 2023
Alexis Pauline Gumbs, 'M/other ourselves: A Black queer feminist
    genealogy for radical mothering', in Alexis Pauline Gumbs,
    China Martens and Mai'a Williams (eds.), *Revolutionary
    Mothering: Love on the Front Lines*, PM Press, 2016


## 8: Matrixes of Love

Rudyard Kipling, *Just So Stories for Little Children*, Macmillan,
    1948 (first published 1902)
Rebecca Sear, 'The male breadwinner nuclear family is not the
    "traditional" human family, and promotion of this myth may
    have adverse health consequences', *Philosophical Transactions
    of the Royal Society*, 3 May 2021
Sarah Blaffer Hrdy, *Mothers and Others: The Evolutionary Origins
    of Mutual Understanding*, The Belknap Press, 2009
Kristen Hawkes et al., 'Hardworking Hadza grandmothers',
    *Comparative Socioecology: The Behavioral Ecology of Humans
    and Other Mammals*, Wiley-Blackwell, 1989
'5 million grandparents take on childcare responsibilities', Age
    UK, 29 September 2017
Pew Research Center, 'The changing profile of unmarried
    parents', 25 April 2018
Sue Sharpe, *Falling for Love: Teenage Mothers Talk*, Virago, 1987
Rebecca Sear, 'Beyond the nuclear family: A global perspective on
    families', Demography Today lecture series, 25 February 2019
Sarah Harper and Iva Ruicheva, 'Grandmothers as replacement
    parents and partners: The role of grandmotherhood in single
    parent families', *Journal of Intergenerational Relationships*, 2010
Sarah Knott, *Mother: An Unconventional History*, Penguin, 2019
Madeline Kerr, *The People of Ship Street*, Routledge & Began
    Paul, 1958
Pat Thane and Tanya Evans, *Sinners? Scroungers? Saints?*

*Unmarried Motherhood in Twentieth-Century England*, Oxford University Press, 2012

Stephanie Coontz, *Marriage, a History: How Love Conquered Marriage*, Penguin, 2006

*Nice Try!*, Curbed, *New York Magazine* and the Vox Media Podcast Network, November 2021

Patricia Hill Collins, *Black Feminist Thought: Knowledge, Consciousness, and the Politics of Empowerment, Revised Tenth Anniversary Edition*, Routledge, 2000

Peter Kropotkin, *Mutual Aid: A Factor of Evolution*, McClure Phillips & Co, 1902

Jonathan White, *Talking on the Water: Conversations about Nature and Creativity*, Trinity University Press, 2016

Nancy Baron, 'Salmon trees', Hakai Magazine, 22 April 2015

Anne Post, 'Why fish need trees and trees need fish', Alaska Fish & Wildlife News, Alaska Department of Fish and Game, November 2008

*The Evidence: Our Microbes and Our Health*, BBC World Service, 25 Mar 2023

*Dynasties: Painted Wolf*, BBC Natural History Unit, 2018

Sarah Myers and Emily H. Emmott, 'Communication across maternal social networks during England's first national lockdown and its association with postnatal depressive symptoms', *Frontiers in Psychology*, 11 May 2021

Heidi Keller, *The Myth of Attachment Theory: A Critical Understanding for Multicultural Societies*, Routledge, 2022

'Kate Moss talks to Megyn Kelly about modeling and motherhood', *Megyn Kelly Today*, 12 September 2018

Kaija Kutter, 'Ins Heim wegen zu viel Mutterliebe', *Die Tageszeitung*, 8 November 2019

Suzanne Simard, *Finding the Mother Tree: Discovering the Wisdom of the Forest*, Knopf, 2021

Sophie Lewis, *Abolish the Family: A Manifesto for Care and Liberation*, Verso, 2022

Ben Fergusson, *Tales from the Fatherland: Two Dads, One Adoption and the Meaning of Parenthood*, Little, Brown, 2022

## 9: The Post-Capitalist Family

Alexis Pauline Gumbs, 'M/other ourselves: A Black queer feminist genealogy for radical mothering', in Alexis Pauline Gumbs, China Martens and Mai'a Williams (eds), *Revolutionary Mothering: Love on the Front Lines*, PM Press, 2016

Ruby Russell, 'Coronavirus and climate change', Deutsche Welle, 5 March 2020

Mark Kaufman, 'The carbon footprint sham', *Mashable*

Margarita Mediavilla, 'Ecofeminism to escape collapse', *Resilience*, 17 June 2019

Seth Wynes and Kimberly A Nicholas, 'The climate mitigation gap: education and government recommendations miss the most effective individual actions', *Environmental Research Letters*, 12 July 2017

Meehan Crist, 'Is it OK to have a child?', *London Review of Books*, 5 March 2020

David Graeber and David Wengrow, *The Dawn of Everything: A New History of Humanity*, Macmillan, 2021

*The Power of Big Oil*, Frontline, 2022

Alice McCarthy, 'Exxon disputed climate findings for years. Its scientists knew better', *The Harvard Gazette*, 12 January 2023

Tamsin Walker, 'Plastic-free, but not so easy', Deutsche Welle, 11 October 2018

John Lanchester, 'Good new idea: John Lanchester makes the case for Universal Basic Income', *London Review of Books*, 18 July 2019

Ruby Russell, 'Working less to save the world?', Deutsche Welle, 19 June 2020

Philipp Frey, 'The ecological limits of work: On carbon emissions, carbon budgets and working time', Autonomy Research, 2019

John Maynard Keynes, 'Economic possibilities for our grandchildren', *Essays in Persuasion*, Harcourt Press, 1930

Ruth Beer et al., 'Vegetation history of the walnut forests in Kyrgyzstan (Central Asia)', *Quaternary Science Reviews*, March 2008

Fiona Marshall et al., 'Ancient herders enriched and restructured African grasslands', *Nature*, 29 August 2018

Ruby Russell, 'Could ditching growth save the planet?', Deutsche Welle, 1 October 2020

Ruby Russell, 'Rights of nature: Indigenous traditions become law', Deutsche Welle, 5 February 2020

Te Awa Tupua (Whanganui River Claims Settlement) Act 2017, New Zealand Ministry of Justice, 20 March 2017

Clive Spash, 'Science and uncommon thinking', plenary lecture at Degrowth Conference Budapest, 2016

Suzanne Simard, *Finding the Mother Tree: Discovering the Wisdom of the Forest*, Knopf, 2021

bell hooks, *All About Love: New Visions*, Harper, 2000

The Care Collective, *The Care Manifesto: The Politics of Interdependence*, Verso, 2020

## 10: Mother Ungendered

Adrienne Rich, *Of Woman Born: Motherhood as Experience and Institution*, Bantam Books, 1976

Linda Gordon, 'Child abuse, gender, and the myth of family independence: A historical critique', *Child Welfare*, 1985

Robert Benton (dir. and wr.), *Kramer vs. Kramer*, Columbia Pictures, 1979

Jeanie Finlay (dir. and wr.), *Seahorse: The Dad Who Gave Birth*, Glimmer Films, 2019

Sarah Knott, *Mother: An Unconventional History*, Penguin, 2019

Lucy Cooke, *Bitch: A Revolutionary Guide to Sex, Evolution and the Female Animal*, Doubleday, 2022

'Unconditional Love', *This American Life*, 15 September 2006

Sarah Blaffer Hrdy, *Mothers and Others: The Evolutionary Origins of Mutual Understanding*, The Belknap Press, 2009

Oyèrónkẹ́ Oyěwùmí, *What Gender is Motherhood? Changing Yoruba Ideals of Power, Procreation, and Identity in the Age of Modernity*, Palgrave Macmillan, 2016

Emily Flake, '"Parent" as a verb: I love you', *New Yorker*, 24 December 2019

Andrea Long Chu, *Females*, Verso, 2019

# Acknowledgements

I couldn't have written this book without countless conversations with single mums who have generously given me their stories and, in many cases, emotional, intellectual and logistical support. Big love and thanks to Jocelyn Muller, Kay Muwoki, Jacinta Nandi, Johanna Thompson, Michele Faguet, Adrienne Edmonds, Julieta Aranda, Verena Wirwohl and all the women whose experiences are in these pages.

I cannot thank Lucy Jones, Maree Hamilton and Clementine E. Burnley enough for years of inspiration, insight, criticism and kindness, for books, leads, essential tools and massive amounts of moral support. And I am deeply grateful to Susanna Forrest, Saskia Vogel, Louise Osborne, Katherine Hunt, Jennifer Collins and Jad Salfiti for invaluable feedback and advice.

Eternal thanks to Sofia Kounti and Vlasis Tritakis for all of the above – and for the to-the-bitter-end care that makes life possible.

Thanks to Erica Russell, for being my cheerleader and greatest ally, for conversations about mothering and the creative process that have made me feel less crazy, and for literally moving in to look after us. And to Adam Parker-Rhodes for conversations about evolution and much else, and for raising me on ideas that underpin this book.

I am indebted to Kay, Nina, Faith and Charlotte of Global Women's Strike, and to Margarita Mediavilla, for interviews that have been vital to my understanding of care.

Huge thanks also to Lorna Ather, Judith Schunk, Laura Hagen, Ashley Jones, Paula James, Michele James, Kody James-Aspinall, Siobhán Dowling, Michaela Stella Bagnoli, Kyna Gourley, Binta Durigo, Cheikh Sene, Elvira Durigo, Holly Young, Tamsin Walker, April Gallwey, Roz Osborne at GlobalARRK, Laura Macdougall, Musa Okwonga, Pip Day, Jen Pinkowski, Bronwen Parker-Rhodes, Harry Hardie, Max Leonard, Maxi Clausecker, Merlind, Rita, Rebecca and all the Totally Awesome Single Moms and Single Supermoms Berlin.

I am eternally grateful to my fantastic publisher and editor, Sharmaine Lovegrove, Adrian Noble and everyone at else at Dialogue, and at Seal – thanks especially to my editors Emily Taber and Emma Berry – and to David Bamford for copyediting.

Many thanks to the Society of Authors and the Authors' Foundation for a grant that helped me make time to write, and to The Reader Berlin for fantastic courses with Susanna and Saskia.

And thank you, F. Sorry I've been so busy with this stupid book.x

**Ruby Russell** is a single mom and environmental journalist. Originally from London, she currently lives in Berlin, Germany, with her kid and their cat.